Volunteering
& Giving Back

Chicken Soup for the Soul: Volunteering & Giving Back
101 Inspiring Stories of Purpose & Passion
Amy Newmark. Foreword by Carrie Morgridge.

Published by Chicken Soup for the Soul Publishing, LLC www.chickensoup.com
Copyright © 2015 by Chicken Soup for the Soul Publishing, LLC. All Rights Reserved.

The publisher gratefully acknowledges the many publishers and individuals who granted Chicken Soup for the Soul permission to reprint the cited material.

Front cover photo courtesy of iStockphoto.com/asiseeit (© Steve Debenport).
Back cover and interior photo courtesy of iStockphoto.com/Emrah_Oztas (© Emrah Oztas).
Photo of Amy Newmark courtesy of Susan Morrow at SwickPix.
Photo of Carrie Morgridge courtesy of William Thach.

Cover Design by Brian Taylor, Pneuma Books, LLC
Layout by Marie Killoran

Distributed to the booktrade by Simon & Schuster. SAN: 200-2442

Publisher's Cataloging-In-Publication Data
(Prepared by The Donohue Group, Inc.)

Chicken soup for the soul : volunteering & giving back : 101 inspiring
 stories of purpose & passion / [compiled by] Amy Newmark ; foreword by
 Carrie Morgridge.

  pages ; cm

 ISBN: 978-1-61159-951-0

  1. Voluntarism--Literary collections. 2. Voluntarism--Anecdotes. 3. Helping behavior--Literary collections. 4. Helping behavior--Anecdotes. 5. Anecdotes. I. Newmark, Amy. II. Morgridge, Carrie. III. Title: Volunteering & giving back IV. Title: Volunteering and giving back

HN49.V64 C45 2015

302/.14/02   2015942010

PRINTED IN THE UNITED STATES OF AMERICA

on acid∞free paper

25 24 23 22 21 20 19 18 17 16 15   01 02 03 04 05 06 07 08 09 10 11

Volunteering & Giving Back

101 Inspiring Stories of Purpose & Passion

Amy Newmark
Foreword by Carrie Morgridge

CSS

Chicken Soup for the Soul Publishing, LLC
Cos Cob, CT

For moments that become stories™

www.chickensoup.com

Contents

❶
~Who's Helping Whom?~

❷
~A Family Affair~

❸

~Lessons Learned~

❹

~The Spirit of Christmas~

❺

~Giving Back~

❻

~No Strangers Here~

❼

~A Calling~

❽

~With My Own Hands~

❾

~Filling a Need~

🔟
~Every Living Thing~

Foreword

Every day millions of people show up at non-profit organizations around the world and "report to work." They represent the army of caring, compassionate volunteers who are essential in making the lives of countless millions of people better because they give. They give of their time, and in some cases, of their treasure. One is not more important than the other.

In this book, *Chicken Soup for the Soul: Volunteering & Giving Back*, you will take many journeys around the world with people who have found their passion. You will understand firsthand how volunteering your time can transform causes that are important to you. If you feel that volunteering has become more of an obligation than a desire, maybe it is time to reevaluate how you share your time. This book may inspire you to hit the reset button and try giving to something completely new or find new ways to contribute to the same organization.

Giving is an integral part of our life. My husband John and I have actively contributed to our community since the day we got married. In some endeavors we gave of our time, for some we contributed treasure, and in many we gave both. As a couple, we have found that as much as we love spending time together, our favorite volunteer tasks are completely different. John loves to read books to children; it's in his DNA, and you can honestly see him light up. I, on the other hand, love construction. Interior Design was my major and I love making things with my own hands. Give me a nail gun or a jackhammer and I light up. One opportunity is not more important or better than the other; rather, it is what sings to our hearts and gives us the most fulfillment.

Corporate Social Responsibility is something that most of us are familiar with. In 1997 Cisco gave a large gift to establish the Cisco Foundation. The Foundation was established as a totally separate organization with its own board of directors. This was the beginning of what has become a significant presence of tech companies giving back in their communities. I am really proud to say that John P. Morgridge, my father-in-law, was a part of launching the movement. Today, the Foundation is still in place, focusing on many things, including access to education, health care, economic improvement and disaster relief. What's more touching is the employee matching program and volunteer program that Cisco has put in place; it is just part of their culture. It is in Cisco's DNA to make money, and it is embedded in their corporate culture to give back: both time and treasure. When you have a global workforce of more than 70,000 people, the impact one company can have is overwhelming!

Bank of America is another company dedicated to making a global impact by giving both time and treasure. They are on a mission to give back two billion dollars. This is their stated goal and it is in their mission — a global organization with a local touch. What really stands out is their employee volunteer time. They have reported more than two million volunteer hours given by Bank of America employees. According to *The NonProfit Times*, the time volunteered in 2013 was worth an estimated 163 billion dollars.

Amy Newmark and her husband Bill Rouhana have published more than 100 *Chicken Soup for the Soul* books since they purchased the company with an investor group in 2008. They made a decision to donate proceeds from every book to address the complex needs of our community, from hunger to our four-legged loved ones. Amy and Bill understand the power of helping others, and lead by producing epic books that are fresh and relevant for us to read, share and to be inspired by.

As you read through this book, identify the stories that you love the most. Compare them to your own volunteer activity or giving. You might be doing exactly what you want, and if so, share your successes, or better yet, invite friends to share their time with you. If you are looking for a new fit, these stories will inspire you to find what is out there and make a difference by connecting with an organization or cause that inspires you. Young or old, rich or poor, we all have something to share. It's a matter of finding your passion and then doing something that will not only have an impact on the recipient, but also on you.

~Carrie Morgridge
Author of *Every Gift Matters*
Vice President, The Morgridge Family Foundation

Introduction

There's a story in the original 1993 *Chicken Soup for the Soul* that everyone seems to remember. A tourist walking along a beach in Mexico sees a man bending down every so often to pick up a stranded starfish and throw it back into the sea. The tourist asks the man why he is bothering. He can't possibly save the thousands of starfish that have washed up on shore. How does he expect to make a difference given the immensity of the problem? The do-gooder bends down, picks up another starfish and tosses it into the water, saying, "Made a difference to that one."

That story may be apocryphal but it remains one of my favorites. It's a perfect way to start this collection of 101 stories from people who volunteer and give back, making a difference one person at a time. In fact, Carrie Morgridge, who wrote the foreword for this book and also helped us gather stories, cited yet another version of that same starfish story at the beginning of her recent bestseller, *Every Gift Matters*.

The subtitle of Carrie's book is "How Your Passion Can Change The World," and this book is filled with just that—passion. Every story is about people who are passionate about their volunteer work and their charitable giving, passionate about the new purpose they have found in their lives, and passionate about what volunteering has done for them. As you read the stories, you'll also find that these writers feel that the biggest beneficiaries of their altruistic endeavors are themselves!

That's why we start this volume with a chapter called "Who's Helping Whom?" You'll read about Ann Clark Van Hine, a 9/11 widow who finds healing and camaraderie in leading tours of the World Trade Center site and the 9/11 Tribute Center. Her volunteer work has led to many blessings for her, including two trips to Japan to share her story with survivors of the earthquake and tsunami there. Ann concludes her story by saying, "As I help others, my healing continues."

In Chapter 1, you'll also meet Toni Somers, who started playing guitar and leading sing-alongs at an assisted living facility twenty years ago because she needed something to do while visiting her sister there. Now, at eighty years old, Toni continues to volunteer at the facility, long after her sister's passing, because the sing-alongs have become part of her own social system and the residents have become her extended family.

Speaking of family, we read numerous stories about families volunteering together. It's a great way to create shared memories, bring teenagers out of their shells, and instill respect, compassion, and tolerance in kids starting at a young age. In Chapter 2, "A Family Affair," you'll meet Sumer Sorensen-Bain, whose young son Kylan set out to raise money for a birthday gift for his Ugandan pen pal, and ended up starting a youth network called the Difference Maker Movement. These kids and their parents are working together to make things happen all over the world.

Volunteering is a wonderful way for parents to connect with their children, particularly during those teenage years. You'll read about how Cathi LaMarche and her daughter bonded as they worked in a food pantry, and how her daughter, never a fan of getting up early, eagerly returned to do a morning shift after she learned about the extent of the hunger problem in their community.

It's not just our kids who learn valuable lessons from volunteering. We share some great ones in Chapter 3, which is called "Lessons Learned." I loved Nicole Webster's story about how tutoring a little boy for a whole school year made her realize that she had been ignoring the cute little boy in her own home — her brother. Nicole's volunteer work opened her eyes to the siblings she had been too "grown-up" to notice — and now she is best friends with her sister and brother.

You can't volunteer without learning how lucky you really are, and that's what Sharon Struth explains in her story about renovating a trailer home in Appalachia. When the woman living there complimented Sharon on her skin and her appearance, she realized how blessed she was, living a normal middle-class lifestyle, to have ready access to skin care products and regular haircuts, things that most of us take for granted.

Speaking of being grateful for what we have, that is really the basis for Chapter 4, "The Spirit of Christmas." I must warn you that we normally keep the magic alive for young readers in our books, but many of the stories in this chapter describe how our writers give Santa a little assist when it comes to distributing toys to all the good boys and girls out there.

Have you ever wondered where all the toys go after you donate them to Toys for Tots? Carrie Morgridge tells us how it works and also explains something I never knew — many of those "tots" are actually teenagers, and Toys for Tots would very much appreciate more donations of items for those older kids. Linda Lohman tells us about another way to assist Santa, a program called Christmas Promise, which has a team of volunteers dressed as Santa drop off backpacks filled with school supplies and stockings filled with personal care items for whole families, from babies to grandparents.

Some of the most giving people are the ones who went through hard times themselves. We share their stories in Chapter 5 — "Giving Back." And, not surprisingly, the dearth of personal care items for those in need is expressed again in Janice VanHorne-Lane's story about how she went from food-bank volunteer to food-bank client after her family fell on hard times. It was only when she was on the receiving end of the food bank's help, and receiving government assistance too, that she realized there was no way for her family to get soap, detergent, and personal hygiene items. When she got back on her feet again, Janice returned to volunteering at the food pantry and convinced them to start collecting soap, razors, detergent, facial tissues, and other non-food necessities. She says, "When I handed an elderly lady her bag she saw the bar of soap and the roll of toilet paper and she gasped, grabbed my hand, and cried, 'Thank you! Oh, thank you!' It was as if I had handed her a million dollars."

Thinking outside the box can lead to some great results, as Amanda Claire Yancey describes in her story. As a girl, Amanda used to see a woman picking up litter, carrying one of those trash claws and wearing a reflective vest. Amanda thought the woman was a bit crazy, but lo and behold, as a college student, she finds herself constantly picking up litter, to the point where her friends bought her a trash claw of her own. Amanda tells us that one day at the bus stop she started picking up litter. She was pleasantly surprised when all the strangers waiting for the bus with her starting picking up the litter, too.

There's nothing more heartwarming than when strangers spontaneously come together to help out, like a flash mob of giving! And that giving creates camaraderie and a sense of community. Chapter 6 is called "No Strangers Here" because it is filled with stories about these "instant communities." Take James Gemmell's story about how he and his paper-mill worker buddies set out to help farmers save their livestock by getting generators up and running during the ice storm crisis of 1998. James says, "I have to say that I have never worked so hard in my life. Certainly I have never been so cold, so dirty, and yet so happy…. I have an indelible memory of a big, gruff-looking farmer who, lost for words, took me in his arms and hugged me tightly when we managed to put his generator back into service. To him it meant the difference between life and death for his animals."

You can make a huge difference from the comfort of your own home, too. Alicia Rosen tells us about her mom, who devoted every evening, when she could have been relaxing, to calling five elderly people and chatting with them about their days. For many of those senior citizens, it was their only human contact all day.

A different kind of calling is covered in Chapter 7, "A Calling." Sometimes you just have to do something—you don't know why, but the impulse is there and you need to follow through. That's what happened to Jeremy Russell after a terrible auto accident that left him with a prosthetic leg and a traumatic brain injury. He discovered a talent for carving rock into amazing sculptures and is now working on a massive carving of a Bald Eagle inside a mountain in Colorado. The Cost of Freedom Eagle will have a 50-foot wingspan, and Jeremy has not only raised funds for carving it in honor of U.S. troops, but also has been able to help some local high school students with arts college scholarships.

Leslie Calderoni felt a calling, too, when she heard about two kids in Atlanta whose only Christmas wish was a new kidney for their grandmother. Even though Leslie lived in California, and this woman was a complete stranger, she picked up the phone and volunteered. Leslie ended up donating a kidney in a paired donation program. Her kidney went to someone in New Jersey while a kidney from someone else went to the grandmother in Atlanta.

Helping people deal with life and death situations seems to bring out the best in our writers, and many of them talked about helping strangers with their end-of-life needs. In Chapter 8, called "With My Own Hands," we meet Christine Cosse Gray, who provides massage and acupuncture services to hospice patients, "people who are near the end of their lives and don't get touched much anymore except for medical procedures." We have carpenters, seamstresses, church cleaners, knitters, musicians, and more in this chapter, people who use their talents to create joy for others. Even home gardeners, like John Farnam, who describes how he and his partner managed to grow 1,001 pounds of fresh vegetables in their personal garden to give away to twenty-four local families in Denver that needed food assistance.

Chapter 9 is about "Filling a Need," something our writers do as soon as they see an opportunity. John Farnam's partner Paul Heitzenrater describes how strongly he was affected one day when he saw a homeless teenager shivering on the street. Paul had just cleaned out his parents' house and happened to have a red wool blanket in his trunk. He stopped the car, jumped out, and gave the boy the blanket. And with that gesture the Red Blanket Project, which has provided hundreds of blankets and scarves to the needy in the Denver area, was born.

Filling a need can be as simple as weeding a cemetery plot on your daily walk, as Stuart Perkins does. He doesn't think it's a big deal, as he is walking through the cemetery anyway, but he does so much weeding in the cemetery on a regular basis that the family members who visit the graves always confuse him for staff. Stuart is just doing what his grandmother told him when she said, "If you see a need, fill it, and don't worry about who gets the credit."

In our last chapter, "Every Living Thing," we meet people who see a need and fill it, and get their appreciation in the form of slobbery kisses. At Chicken Soup for the Soul, we are big proponents of adopting dogs and cats from shelters, and we count numerous rescues among our own pets. So I was pleased to include a few stories about rescues in this book, including a wonderful one by Lisa Fowler about how volunteering at her local Humane Society shelter changed her life... and that of an adorable puppy named Hazel who now lives with her. B.J. Taylor tells us another animal story in the same chapter — she volunteers at a stable where she helps physically and mentally disabled kids and adults strengthen their bodies and their self-confidence through a therapeutic riding program. B.J. got over her own fear of horses by working at the stable... because after all, every one of these volunteering stories ends up with the writer talking about how he or she benefited too, right?

You may have received this book as a gift for volunteering. We know our volunteering books are often used to show appreciation. Or you may have picked up this book because you are looking for some ideas. You will undoubtedly be inspired to redouble your efforts wherever you are volunteering or to start up a new volunteering or charitable activity. I know that I was envious as I read the stories that were submitted for this book and edited the manuscript. I would love to pick up some more volunteer work, but right now, between my current volunteer commitment to my community and my work as author, editor-in-chief and publisher of Chicken Soup for the Soul, there just isn't any more time. I'm writing this introduction at 11 p.m. on a Sunday and I've been working all weekend!

But, like volunteering, this is work that I love. We work very hard at Chicken Soup for the Soul making these books and all of our other products, and while it's a business, it is also part of a much larger charitable effort. Chicken Soup for the Soul is a socially conscious company dedicated to improving the world around us. We give back a portion of all our revenues to causes ranging from animal adoption in the United States to fighting poverty in less developed parts of the world. All of our efforts support our mission to share happiness, inspiration, and wellness through everything we do, and that means putting a portion of our revenues to work doing good. Here are a few of the ways that we help:

Humpty Dumpty Institute: A portion of all Chicken Soup for the Soul sales goes to literacy, hunger and animal welfare programs that we work on with our charitable partner, the Humpty Dumpty Institute.

Pet Adoption Programs: We also donate Chicken Soup for the Soul pet food to rescue shelters and to new pet owners to encourage adoptions.

Giving Back with Books: The royalties from certain of our books go to specific charitable organizations, including the Alzheimer's Association, the American Humane Association, the Kennedy Krieger Institute, A World Fit For Kids, the Bob Woodruff Foundation, and Cancer Schmancer. The royalties from this book will go to The Morgridge Family Foundation, which makes investments that transform communities through education, conservation, the arts, and health and wellness.

Breakfast at School: A portion of sales from Chicken Soup for the Soul foods supports a Humpty Dumpty Institute program that provides kids a free breakfast at school every day.

We thank you for volunteering and giving back. I hope you will enjoy reading these stories and find them as inspiring as I have. Happy reading!

~Amy Newmark

Follow us on Twitter: @amynewmark @chickensoupsoul

Volunteering
& Giving Back

Who's Helping Whom?

Two Dollars' Worth of Trust

*Wherever there is a human in need, there is an opportunity for
kindness and to make a difference.*
~Kevin Heath

The game was over, the 49ers had beaten the Denver Broncos, and now Micheal and I were roaming the darkened streets of San Francisco in my little red Honda. We were lost, and Micheal was trying his best to keep calm.

This was 2000, before GPS was in every car — or at least every cell phone. Micheal, then ten years old, knew I had a terrible sense of direction. Whenever the two of us went on an outing together, it usually involved me taking a few wrong turns. I always needed to reassure him that even if we got lost we would make it to our destination.

I was matched with Micheal by Big Brothers Big Sisters of Greater Sacramento when he was eight and I was in my mid-twenties. There had been a surplus of women willing to be Big Sisters, and a deficit of men willing to be Big Brothers. The organization decided to try "cross-gender" matches, setting up women to be mentors to young boys.

Many of the mothers who had enrolled their sons in the program chose to hold out for a male mentor, but Micheal's mother wanted another adult in his life who could guide him through what was shaping up to be a tough childhood. She didn't mind that it was me. Donna — a bright, warm woman not much older than I — was working full-time as a dental assistant while raising Micheal and his older sister. Donna's ex-husband (Micheal's dad) was in prison.

When I first met Micheal, he looked like a child painted by Norman Rockwell for a 1950s cover of *The Saturday Evening Post*. His light brown hair was cut short, with a cowlick on the back of his head. His enormous, sky-blue eyes were framed by long lashes, aptly conveying his bashful nature. A smattering of freckles covered his upturned nose and rosy cheeks.

The folks at Big Brothers Big Sisters had warned us during our weeks of training that it was not unusual for "Littles," as they're called, to be wary of the adults with whom they're matched. The Littles figure the "Bigs" will eventually disappoint them, like most of the grown-ups in their lives already have. The Littles usually asked for material possessions; they figured as long as another adult was going to bail on them, they might as well get a video game or toy out of the deal first.

This was true of my relationship with Micheal, at least for the first few months. When we went to the zoo, he always begged me to buy him a stuffed animal at the gift shop. Then, after I bought the stuffed animal, he wanted me to buy him a Happy Meal at McDonald's. When I said no, he'd turn gloomy and give me the silent treatment.

The dynamic changed when I left my job as a substitute teacher. My dreams of becoming a journalist had started to materialize in dribs and drabs — with a Saturday morning gig reading the news at a country music radio station, a job as overnight producer on Monday and Tuesday at Sacramento's public radio station, and a paid internship for a television news service during the daylight hours of Tuesday, Wednesday and Thursday.

That left Thursday night as the one free block of time I had to spend with Micheal. No more visits to the zoo or McDonald's or miniature golf.

Instead, I would visit Micheal after work and help him with his homework. We even built a model of one of California's missions from sugar cubes. Each subsequent Thursday, Micheal seemed more and more excited to see me when I'd arrive for an evening of long division and sentence diagramming.

Several months later, I got hired full-time at the television news service and resumed normal working hours. I now had the time (and financial resources) to take Micheal somewhere fun again.

I soon discovered it wasn't just our schedule that had changed, but the dynamic between us. Micheal now trusted I wasn't going to flake on him. He rewarded my consistency by believing in me. Every outing to the movies or mini golf was appreciated just as it was. He never again asked for extras.

That trust was tested when the two of us made our way out to San Francisco to watch a preseason football game.

Micheal had won the tickets (and VIP parking) in a raffle at the annual Big Brothers Big Sisters picnic. I picked him up early from school on the day of the game and we made the drive from Sacramento to San Francisco, crossing a few toll bridges along the way. Micheal watched with great interest each time we pulled up to the tollbooth to pay.

The game itself was uneventful. We stuffed ourselves with hot dogs and Sprite and licorice. We bundled up to stay warm in the wind tunnel that was Candlestick Park. When it was clear the 49ers would take the game, we strolled back to the VIP parking lot.

Making our way from the stadium back to the road that would lead us over the bay and onto the freeway to Sacramento was tricky. Micheal and I usually didn't plan our outings for after dark, and I think this fact, combined with my disorientation, worried him.

Yet he asked me only once if I knew where we were going.

"Not just yet," I answered. "But I promise you I will."

And I did. We were soon crossing the Bay Bridge, and the tension in the car eased.

I then heard a rip of Velcro. Michael was opening up his wallet. He removed two crisp $1 bills from his wallet. He put the seat back a few notches and prepared himself for a snooze, but not before carefully sticking the bills in his clenched left fist, as if he were placing flowers in a vase.

"This is for the toll on the bridge on the way back. You paid for all the food, so I want to pay for this." He yawned. "But I'm too tired to stay awake until then. Just take them from my hand when it's time.

* * *

It's been fifteen years since that night. I saw Micheal just a few months ago, when he flew down from Northern California with his girlfriend to visit my husband and me in San Diego.

I was excited to meet Amanda, Micheal's girlfriend, and to show her a framed picture I kept on our mantelpiece. The photo was taken on the floor of the State Assembly at the Capitol in Sacramento on "Take Your Daughter to Work Day." Micheal was at least a foot shorter than I was in the picture — very different from the tall, handsome young man he is now.

Amanda and Micheal came for dinner, managing our three hyper dogs as we welcomed them into our home. I took Amanda aside with the photo in hand.

"Isn't this adorable?" I asked. "Can you believe it's the same person?"

Amanda smiled. "Oh, I've seen this picture before. Micheal has it framed in his house."

~Beth Ford Roth

Unexpected Blessings

Weave in faith and God will find the thread.
~Author Unknown

When I opened the large manila envelope and read about an opportunity to volunteer with the September 11th Families Association as a docent for the 9/11 Tribute Center, I had no idea what amazing adventures, opportunities and blessings lay before me. To be honest, as I held that envelope I didn't know what a docent was. I had to look the word up in the dictionary. My next thought was that I was not even a member of the Association. I hadn't joined any groups in the four years since Bruce's death in the line of duty on September 11, 2001.

As I traveled into New York City for my first interview, I was nervous. I knew nothing about lower Manhattan or the World Trade Center. I had only been to the World Trade Center twice in my whole life. I barely knew the September 11th timeline of events. Growing up in New Jersey, the "stomping" ground of my youth had always been from the Port Authority to Columbus Circle, for auditions and dance classes, or Greenwich Village for acting lessons. But all of that was a lifetime ago. In recent years my trips into the city had been to take my girls to the Rockefeller Center tree lighting or a Broadway show or up north to the Bronx Zoo. Traveling into lower Manhattan was new and scary. What was I thinking?

Actually, I knew exactly what I was thinking. The 9/11 Tribute

Center's mission was "person-to-person" history and I knew I could do that. I could tell Bruce's and my story. I had already told "our" story many times, but that was in churches or at ladies' groups. This was a whole new thing, but I knew I had to try.

A few weeks after the interview, I attended a two-day training session. I felt like I was going to throw up the whole time I was driving into Manhattan. I was sure I was in way over my head. "Lord, I am willing to try this, but let me know you want me to do it."

As I timidly entered the room for the training session, I scanned the faces, looking for Rachel, the person who had interviewed me. *Wait! That's Bruce's captain from Squad 41. Wow! Thank you, Lord. Someone I know. A nod from God.*

The training was going along nicely and then it was mentioned that you shouldn't get political. Well, that was fine; I am not political. Then a fellow trainee commented that "you shouldn't get too religious either." I cautiously raised my hand. "If we aren't allowed to mention God I will respect that, but to tell my story I need to mention God because God is a big part of my story." The response was "if God is your story, you can mention God." *Wow! Another big nod from God.*

So I started volunteering. I studied, read, practiced and led walking tours around the World Trade Center site. I discovered where to park and where to get coffee. When the Tribute Center galleries opened in September 2006, I started speaking to school and other groups in the center as well as leading the walking tours. I watched the World Trade Center site go from an empty hole in the ground to a beautiful memorial and vibrant neighborhood. I have led or supported more than four hundred tours in nine years and spoken to various groups.

One group that stood out was composed of teens from Lebanon, South Africa, Ireland and Israel. It was a humbling experience to speak with these young people of multiple faiths. As I sat on the floor of the Tribute Center, I shared my story and taught them about the original World Trade Center and the events of September 11, 2001. I was struck by the fact that it was July 4th. Exactly thirty-five years earlier, on July 4, 1976, Bruce and I had visited the World Trade Center observation deck. I remembered the date because everyone had discouraged us from heading into the city on such a busy day—America's 200th birthday. There was very little traffic and I only remember it because of the date's significance.

When I tell my story while leading walking tours, I say "There are three things that have gotten me through my personal loss in the midst of an international tragedy. The first thing is my faith. God has gotten me through. And the second is the fact that my husband was a New York City firefighter. It was his job to go into those buildings. A job that he loved. The third thing is family and friends. We don't do life alone. I have a wonderful family and great friends. I also have many new friends through volunteering with Tribute who never met Bruce but know his story. They do life with me."

When I started doing tours, I only had my story and that was enough. But now I know the stories of my fellow docents—other family members, survivors, fire responders, rescue workers—who saw things no one should ever see, and downtown residents who couldn't go home for months. I believe the story of September 11th is like a mosaic made of little pieces. They don't connect like a puzzle but they lie next to each other to make the picture of what happened on September 11, 2001—hundreds of thousands of experiences that come together to tell the story.

Being a docent has been an unexpected blessing for me. I love giving tours and am awed by my fellow docents and everyone at Tribute—an amazing group of people. I am blessed by the number of visitors who take the time to come on walking tours and learn not only the history but the individual stories. So on Monday I will talk to two school groups, lead the 1 p.m. tour and then help out with the 3 p.m. tour. To quote one of my fellow docents: "I will get my volunteer on."

There have been even more benefits for me. My decision to pursue this volunteer opportunity led to two trips to Japan to share my 9/11 story with survivors of the Great East Japan earthquake and tsunami. I was humbled and blessed beyond measure to be able to share my story as an avenue to encourage others. As I help others, my healing continues.

~Ann Clark Van Hine

3

Everyone Is Helping Everyone Here

The word "funny" is a bit like the word "love" — we don't have
enough words to describe the many varieties.
~George Saunders

'd lost Mrs. Lawson, which wasn't good, because she was ninety-two years old, used a walker and was depending on me to get her back home. The problem with these stores is that they're so unbelievably enormous, so when one of my senior charges doesn't arrive back at the bus at the appointed time I start to worry. And then I start hunting.

This all started a few months ago when I ended up with some Involuntary Time Off From Work (also known as unemployment). I quickly realized how isolating it is to be unemployed. All your friends and acquaintances are somewhere else during the day. The world starts to feel a bit unreal, as if you are not really part of it.

I knew I had to do something apart from job hunting. I'd always enjoyed being around seniors so I figured that driving seniors to grocery stores would be a good use of my time.

That is how I found myself in a store like this one. Harsh lighting. Thirty long aisles. One missing comrade.

I started doing a "serpentine," which is how I often find items for myself in a mega-store like this: starting at Aisle 1 and winding down consecutive aisles until all thirty have been covered.

After I cleared all the aisles I started looking through the checkout aisles. Note to self: It would've made more sense to start there.

Mrs. Larson is the arts-and-crafts master in the group of ten who I take shopping. She knits all kinds of things for her grandkids and displays them to other members on the bus. Knowing that I like to read and write, she even knitted a bookmark for me as thanks for driving her to this store each week.

I checked my watch and realized that my Search and Rescue mission had taken ten minutes. If I found Mrs. Lawson soon I'd be able to drop everyone back at home and get the bus back to the center in time for the next driver to do his rounds. If not, I'd have to call into the office. I really didn't want to do that.

I swung past the last self-checkout machine and noticed a woman standing at the other entrance to the store. She was leaning on one of those four-pronged canes and staring out into the parking lot. Mrs. Lawson.

I laughed and chided myself for forgetting about the second entrance to the store. Another note to self: The new Search and Rescue plan is second door, then checkout aisles, then serpentine.

I walked up to Mrs. Lawson and said, "Hey Mrs. Lawson, the bus is in the other lot. Hold on a sec and I'll be right back." She grinned with relief and shook her head.

I ran back to the bus, fired it up, and rolled toward the other side of the store. None of the other nine people complained about the additional wait. That's one thing I've learned from doing this job — seniors have learned from time and experience that mistakes are just that, and there's no need for blame and recrimination. They've also learned that it makes no sense to always be in a hurry. It's funny; you start a job like this thinking that you're the one providing services and helping others. But the others help you just as much, if not more.

Halfway across the parking lot Mrs. Roberts started singing. She's the gregarious one, the one who acted on Broadway long ago. From behind me I heard her chant: "Tom lost Mrs. Lawson, Tom lost Mrs.

Lawson."

Soon the others joined in. I glanced in the mirror and saw four pairs of seniors singing, laughing and bumping shoulders. They looked like schoolchildren on a field trip.

I flashed a faux expression of menace and barked, "Don't make me pull this bus over!"

As we pulled up to Mrs. Lawson, the bus dissolved into howls of laughter. I joined in, which is something I hadn't done enough lately. But my senior citizen buddies were there to help me with that, too.

~Thomas Sullivan

Humdrum No More

*A child who does not play is not a child, but the man who does
not play has lost forever the child who lived in him.*
~Pablo Neruda

Have you ever been busy but unfulfilled? I have. My daily life revolved around raising my youngest daughter, who I had just before my forty-fifth birthday. I juggled the usual home and gardening chores, grocery shopping, animal care and church activities. Throw in a retired husband and a father who came to live with us and you have a smorgasbord of chaos. The weight of the world rested on my shoulders.

But then Janette walked into my life. Well, actually, she danced into my life. I met her at our community clubhouse, where she facilitated a ballet class. The corners of her eyes crinkled and her eyes twinkled when she approached me about joining the class, which I did reluctantly. When the eight of us got together for our first class, the creaks, groans and exasperated wails filled the small room.

"Oh my gosh. Do *what* with my toes?" moaned Sally.

"You've got to be kidding. You want me to put my tree-sized leg on top of that bar?" chimed in Betty.

"I may need to purchase Depends for the next class." Alice held her legs together, ready to explode with laughter.

When Janette suggested after the class that I should join her dance troupe, I knew God surely intended this whole idea as a joke.

.Ie went on to explain that her troupe consisted of three other ladies who entertained with song and dance at convalescent and assisted living homes. She said. "It is so rewarding to bring a little joy into the lives of these people who seldom have visitors. You have lots of talent and catch on to the routines fast." With a limp hand wave, I promised her I'd think about it.

I left the clubhouse and sat in my car. I thought back to my younger years when I dreamed of becoming a famous dancer and singer. I had attended dance classes from first grade through high school. All I ever thought of as I paraded and belted out songs around the house was that Fred Astaire needed me. I threw my head back with a sigh and said, "God, you really do have a sense of humor." My humdrum routine life was about to become a lot more joyful.

We were known as Triple T, even though eventually there were five of us. I began to feel a new purpose in my life. The long-lost love of song and dance made it back into my life just as the gray hair started to come in at my temples. My life was no longer humdrum.

I organized my chores and my life so that I could practice with Triple T three times a week. The music uplifted my spirit and I enjoyed the fellowship of women who enjoyed my same passion.

The biggest blessings of all came from the audience we entertained. I rejoiced when I watched a wheelchair-bound woman tap her toe to an old favorite, and I loved hearing the laughter of a resident who hadn't spoken in months. When we directed sing-alongs, some of the strongest voices came from the frailest residents.

Yes, we renewed the hearts of our audience, but truth be told… it was my heart that was renewed. I was transformed. And using my long-lost passion to bring others joy and fellowship allowed me to offer my family more of myself too.

~Alice Klies

Saying Thank You

What we keep, we lose; what we give away, we keep forever.
~Axel Munthe, The Story of San Michele

"'m bringing a book with me," I called to my father as we headed out the door. We were on our way to his VA medical appointment and I was bracing myself for a long, tedious day. My father had just come to live with me in California, and I had no prior experience with the Veteran's Administration. When he was living in New Jersey, Dad received all of his medical care through the VA there. He said that treatment there was a lot like going to the Department of Motor Vehicles—long wait times, redundant paperwork, apathetic staff and government bureaucracy. I expected a similar experience as we pulled up to the clinic in San Jose. In my haste, I forgot to take the book with me when we left the car. As it turned out, I never would have had a chance to read it anyway.

Upon entering the clinic, I was immediately impressed by the neat décor and welcoming lobby. The colors were soft and pleasant and the furniture looked new and comfortable, though very few chairs were occupied. I wondered where all the vets were waiting. We found our way to the proper department and Dad gave his name and information to the receptionist. She greeted him warmly and assured him that a doctor would see him shortly. Before he was able to take a seat, my father was escorted to an exam room—three minutes ahead of his appointment time. The receptionist explained that I would be able to speak with the doctor at the conclusion of the exam and she directed me to the coffee corner where I was offered a complimentary cup of coffee by a friendly volunteer.

"Is it always like this?" I asked.

"Like what?" he replied.

"Quiet. Calm. Orderly. I don't see any lines; there doesn't seem to be anyone waiting. Don't any vets come here?"

"Oh, plenty of vets come here." He smiled. "It's just that they're well taken care of. This isn't like those other clinics that you read about in the paper. They run this place pretty good."

We were out of there in under ninety minutes complete with blood tests and medications. Dad's comprehensive exam had taken almost a full hour — an absolute luxury by any contemporary medical standard. In each department, the staff was friendly, helpful and displayed genuine regard for my father and his concerns. It was apparent that the employees and volunteers actually enjoyed their work and took great pride in providing the best service possible for America's retired servicemen.

Over the next few months my regard for the VA clinics and hospitals grew as I followed my father through his appointments and procedures. I had never given much thought to our nation's veterans and I didn't consider myself overly patriotic, but the dedication to service and genuine regard for patients demonstrated by the VA staff propelled me to want to be a part of such an honorable organization. I had no medical skills or administrative inclinations, and very little time, but I did have one thing that I could share: my art.

On my first day as a volunteer art teacher I was introduced to ten men seated around a long table, most of whom were in their seventies and eighties. They shared their names, branch of service and whether or not they served during wartime. One of the vets was a World War II soldier who had taken part in the invasion of Normandy and had recently been honored by the government for his dedicated service. Another was a flight surgeon who spent his civilian years as a medical doctor. I was humbled by their accomplishments, dignity and quiet pride. When they completed their introductions I did what I was instructed to do during orientation—I thanked them for their service and dedication to preserving our freedom. I thanked them for giving me the opportunity to work with them.

Despite thirty years as an art teacher, designing activities for the group was a challenge. The activities had to be engaging, but could not be too difficult or frustrating for arthritic fingers and dimmed vision. The projects needed relevance or they would easily be dismissed as "kid stuff."

We began by making crafts to be sold at the yearly Day Respite fundraiser. Positive encouragement, praise and participation by the Day Respite staff helped boost morale and motivate the men to continue creating. We displayed their work on the walls of the Day Respite room, and throughout the clinic lobby and waiting areas. The men took great pride in their work and each week I would notice that they were paying closer attention to detail and taking more time with their projects. One day, while completing a complex design, one of the vets looked up and said, "If someone had told me twenty years ago that I would be sitting here today coloring I would have told them that they didn't know what they were talking about. But there's something to this, you know? It kind of makes you feel good."

It makes me feel good, too. The vets believe that they are on the receiving end of my volunteer services. Perhaps they don't recognize the exchange of joy that takes place during each visit. It is truly rewarding to be able to bring the gift of the creative process to a group that has long forgotten the joys of making art. On that first day, when I thanked the vets for their service, I realized that nothing I could offer these men would ever equal their efforts protecting our American freedom. But for two hours each week, with a little paper and paint and glue, I take them on an adventure that allows them to experience the joys of creative expression and the magic of art.

~T.A. Barbella

The Teacher Learns the Lesson

Education is not filling a pail but the lighting of a fire.
~William Butler Yeats

Laughter rang out as the cake knife in Raúl's hand cut through the thick white frosting. It was a small graduation party. Only Ed, Max, Raúl and I were there. There were no caps or gowns. "Pomp and Circumstance" was not played, nor were diplomas handed out.

But a celebration was in order.

All three men, each over the age of fifty, had achieved a first in their lives.

They could read.

Overcoming decades of embarrassment and a lifetime of covering up their illiteracy, these three men, along with four others, had signed up for a free three-month course, taught by me, at a local church in the Oak Cliff section of Dallas, Texas.

Volunteering was nothing new to me. I had been doing it since childhood. Collecting mittens for children, singing carols to seniors, being a Sunday school teacher and Special Olympics coach... I gladly carried on my family's multi-generational motto: "To whom much has been given — much is expected."

Unlike other countywide classes, which were filled with immigrants and refugees, mine was to be conducted with all native-born Americans.

I wondered how someone born here couldn't have been taught to read. Since my earliest years, reading had been a joy — from the nightly stories read aloud by my parents to my adult practice of falling asleep with a book in my hand.

However, on my first night as a reading teacher, as my car's headlights illuminated the church's parking lot, I was far from feeling curious or excited.

I was just plain scared.

The neighborhood was beyond seedy; it was dangerous. Just driving the two miles off R.L. Thornton Freeway I had witnessed numerous people leaning into parked cars for drug transactions and other illegal activities. I was so nervous that I decided to scurry inside the building with all my supplies in one trip. When I dropped everything with a crash, doors flew open and people looked out to investigate.

My new students scrambled to help me as I entered the classroom. I had seven students, all male, who ranged in age from thirty to sixty-three.

At twenty-four, I was the youngest person in the room, and the palest.

"Not exactly the entrance I wanted to make, but thank you for your help."

Aside from my klutzy entrance, the class went well and everyone returned the following week. I was still afraid of the neighborhood, but my students helped me. Ed had been waiting in his car to help me carry in the supplies and Max walked me out and stood by until I started my car.

By the following week, and all the remaining ones, I realized Raúl's battered, bright blue pickup truck trailed directly behind my car as I drove through the war zone. When I turned safely onto the freeway I would honk my thanks with my horn to be followed by a blast of the song "La Cucaracha" from his.

By the end of the first month, four students had quit but my gallant trio of protectors remained. Their determination to succeed combined with their natural intelligence and the results were amazing.

"I take the bus every day to work," said Ed. "Have done for over thirty years. Just yesterday I figured out what the words 'Emergency Exit' mean."

Max reported that he was able to understand much of Monday's newspaper sports article on his beloved Dallas Cowboys' win over the Washington Redskins. Previously, his break time was spent pretending to read in the hope his co-workers would never discover his shameful secret. Max also reported that his six-year-old granddaughter had asked him the name of America's first president. "Pop Pop came to the rescue," he laughed. "I pulled the newspaper out, pointed to the word 'Washington' and spelled it for her."

As our final night came to a close, hugs were exchanged, jokes were made about my less than graceful first entrance and then Raúl took my hand between his rough and calloused ones: "You gave me a future. You gave me a new life."

I looked into his smiling brown eyes, which were wreathed in wrinkles, and felt overwhelmed and humbled. I thanked him for allowing me to help him.

Being so young, I did not grasp the full wisdom of his simple statement until my own gray hairs appeared, lines streaked out across my forehead and an economic downturn robbed me of my work and financial security.

Now I'm the age of my former pupils and my future needs a restart button. I realize that limiting my destiny because of my age or my lack of skills is as ridiculous as being held back by fear. A future with many wonderful opportunities could belong to me as long as I have the courage to seek it out and work for it.

Like Ed, Max and Raúl, I am determined to make a new life for myself.

They taught me well.

~Linda J. Bottjer

Shared Challenges

*We should look to the mind, and not to the outward
appearance.*

~Aesop

As I entered the building two burly security guards framed the doorway. I had known this library was on the wrong side of town, but security guards in a library? My heart sank a little more than usual. Since losing my job I had become accustomed to that sinking feeling. Applications ignored, interviews that didn't go well... fighting the weariness, I pulled myself together.

"Remember why you are doing this," I whispered to myself.

Volunteering had been the idea of the overworked employee at the job centre. "You've got some great skills but perhaps it's time to consider retraining. It's an ideal opportunity to try something new." She'd pushed the list towards me. I scanned the opportunities: charity shop assistant or dog walker.

"I love dogs," I'd said.

"But would you want to work with them, all day, every day?" I had to admit I was no fan of cold weather. I moved my pen further down the list, then stopped at the line that said, "Teaching computer skills in a library."

"Your IT skills are good, perhaps a route into teaching?" I knew she had spent more time with me than she could really afford so I nodded. Why not?

As I entered the main library I looked around. A large portion of the building was devoted to rows of computer stations. People sat at every one of these stations, absorbed and quiet. It felt like a college exam hall.

I was interrupted from my thoughts by a round, eager face. A friendly hand was thrust towards me.

"Hi, I'm Stephen. I look after this project. Glad you could make it."

Pretty soon I was put to work; no lengthy inductions here. There were too many learners and not enough teachers. Stephen led me down the rows of computers until we reached Jenna. My first view of Jenna was of her back as she hunched over the computer, shoulders rounded stiffly.

"Jenna's part of the job club — been trying to get a job for a while. She'll succeed because she keeps trying." Stephen introduced us. It turned out that Jenna was trying to get a job cleaning hotels. Her last job had ended seven months earlier when the owners went bankrupt.

Jenna was fighting back tears of frustration while trying to attach her CV to an e-mail. As we worked through the steps necessary to do this, her face brightened and her shoulders relaxed a little. When we had finally sent out three applications she sat back.

"I just hope this works. The things a six-year-old needs…" Her voice trailed off.

Before we could spend time chatting, Stephen noticed my work was done, bounded over to me, and ushered me to the next client.

Ray was an elderly gentleman whose son lived far away and had sent him an e-mail with an attached video of his grandchildren. Ray did not know how to open the attachment and watch the video. A few quick clicks of the mouse and Ray was happily playing and re-playing. I asked if he wanted me to show him how to do it for himself but he didn't.

"Oh, don't worry about Ray," one of the other volunteers said. "He comes every week with the same problem. I think he likes the company as much as anything." I looked at Ray as he clicked again on the mouse. He gave me a quick wave, then returned to the screen.

I thought about my family close by. I had been thinking of moving away to find work, but surely it wouldn't have to come to that?

I was a little afraid as I approached Allan. He had a shaved head, dark sunglasses, and a tattoo of a python snaking down his neck and disappearing under his shirt. His huge bulk covered the small chair. I pulled up a seat and sat next to him.

"Hi, I'm Penny. Can I help?" I felt nervous. Did it come across in my voice? Out of the corner of my eye I could see the security guard was watching.

"I want to write a letter." His voice was gruff. I started to show him how to work the computer. As I clicked he watched the characters appear on the screen. I passed the keyboard to him. His large hands started to move over it but then stopped.

"Who is the letter to?" I asked.

"My wife. I've been out of prison now twelve months. I want to tell her I've been straight and clean."

His large fingers once again moved around the keyboard, then started to clench into fists. I showed him what to do again. He looked down. "I can't write."

I mentally kicked myself. How could I have been so stupid? It was obvious now that he had said it. I took the keyboard from him. As Allan relayed his story I typed. Between us we managed to put the words together to show how he had changed, how he had stayed out of trouble, and to ask his wife if she would see him. As the empty page filled with letters Allan discarded the dark glasses. His hard shell gave way to vulnerability and animation as he told me his story.

When I left the library that day a weight had lifted from me. It was late afternoon and the air was beginning to turn cold as I made my way home through the rough side of town. My footsteps, though, were light. I had a new sense of purpose and a different way of thinking.

Later that evening I curled up in a chair next to the fire and reviewed the day. As I took a sip of my soup I thought about Jenna struggling to feed her child. I thought about Ray captivated by a video of his far-away grandchildren. I thought about Allan desperately trying to find his way back to the life he had once had. But what I thought about most was how alike we all were — just people joined together in taking those first steps to make a difference to our lives.

I had entered the library as a teacher, hoping to share some of my skills with others. That day, through volunteering, I was the most fortunate student of all. I had emerged with the knowledge that to struggle alone through life's challenges is a lonely process, but to make that journey with others can make facing even the hardest challenges rewarding.

~Penny Black

The Accidental Volunteer

Music expresses that which cannot be said and on which it is
impossible to be silent.
~Victor Hugo

My sister Rose had suffered from mental and emotional problems for many years. She was ten years older than me and she had lived with my parents since she became ill. She managed her own physical needs and did simple household tasks, but she needed my parents to provide structure. When they died, she became my responsibility.

At age sixty-six, Rose moved to the city where I lived with my family. We found a wonderful place for her to live — The Gardens Assisted Living Facility. She was thrilled.

"Oh! It's like a wonderland," Rose had exclaimed as we entered a spacious foyer. The living room and dining room were airy and welcoming. Everything sparkled, and so did Rose's eyes! It was a new facility where residents each had individual apartments. The common areas included a lovely dining room and living room, as well as an activities room, library and outdoor courtyard. An aviary covered one wall of the living room; the chirping and tweeting that greeted us made the room especially inviting. Rose moved in the following week.

I was relieved. With our busy work schedules and two of our five children still at home, I couldn't imagine Rose moving in with us.

The Gardens had opened just in time. Rose loved the place, and it was close enough for me to visit often.

And that was a problem. Yes, I could visit easily. But to what purpose? After the first few minutes, Rose withdrew into her private world and our conversation fizzled out. I don't know if she was uncomfortable with silences, but I was. Sometimes I brought craft projects to engage us for a while. Or I took her out to lunch, also a short-term distraction. Sometimes we joined other residents for the weekly Bingo session or for current affairs discussions. But mostly I sat in her apartment and, after a few minutes of chitchat, stared at the walls or the floor as she became increasingly oblivious to my presence.

Then one day I had an idea. "Rose, would you mind if I ask the activities director whether I can bring my guitar once a week and have a sing-along for the residents?"

Her eyes lit up. "I think she would appreciate that. And the other residents would like it. Music brightens the days here."

I knew Rose would enjoy it, too. She relished showing off by having something others didn't. And a sister who could sing and play the guitar would certainly qualify.

I broached the subject with my husband. His response was definitely not positive.

"Will the activities director expect you to be available on the weekly schedule long term? Do you want that big a commitment? Won't you get sick of performing every week?"

"I can always find an excuse to back out. But it beats sitting there staring at Rose. I'll keep my guitar picking skills honed, if nothing else."

Erin, the activities director, welcomed my offer to visit every week to perform folk songs and lead a sing-along. Thus began my twenty-year volunteer stint at The Gardens. Erin named it Toni-Time, and that name persisted through a number of directors after her. I suspended visiting for a few years when we moved to the Texas Gulf Coast to escape winter, but we missed the Ozark hills and changing seasons, so we returned to Missouri. I resumed my weekly sing-alongs. Rose was delighted and so were the other residents. And so was I! Living away, I realized that my singing sessions at the Gardens were fun, rewarding times for me, too. Sometimes I wondered why the residents seemed so eager about Toni-Time every Monday.

"You're the best activity we have!" enthused Linda.

"Yes. We love when you come and sing, and we love you too," said Elise as she beamed.

"They like you so much because you remember their names," said Sandy, one of the nursing assistants.

I started to add to the sing-alongs. I told stories occasionally or asked trivia questions. Sometimes we recalled favorite Christmas memories or what our first grade classes were like. And we found we still remembered our teachers' names! We sang. We reminisced. We laughed. And when we needed it, we cried together.

I reminded my husband that his concerns were unfounded and that I was right as usual. "See! I knew it would work out. I love performing. The residents enjoy my visits and Rose knows I've come to see her. She's especially pleased that she can brag to new residents about the singer being HER sister."

Rose died five years ago at age eighty-six. She was at peace, and so was I: I'd fulfilled my responsibility.

For a time after Rose passed away I spent Mondays doing whatever I wanted to do. No obligations. No commitments. Only freedom. Then one day I realized how much I missed my friends at The Gardens. They were more than friends. They were family, as Rose had been.

All it took was a phone call.

"We'd love you to come back! The ladies miss you and still talk about you."

The response convinced me. I recognized my own need for the wonderful friendships I'd found. Seeking to do something for my sister and for her fellow residents, I'd found a loving community and become a part of it.

I'm eighty years old now and can't go every week, so I go every other Tuesday. We sing songs. We exchange stories and share memories. We laugh and we cry.

I know that if I am ever alone and need a place to live, there's a place I can go where people will remember my name.

~Toni Somers

A Lesson in Humility

The wings of angels are often found on the backs of the least likely people.
~Eric Honeycutt

heard the familiar drip-drip-drip sound as I opened the door to the daytime homeless shelter. Even though it occupied the first floor of a four-story building, I had to strategically place buckets when it rained or snowed. The building was close to being condemned. But still, it provided a place for the homeless to come inside and have coffee, a brief respite from the December winds along the Allegheny River in downtown Pittsburgh.

Rules were few and mostly in place to maintain peace and a semblance of cleanliness despite the shabbily furnished structure. One of the rules: If you left the shelter, you took your belongings with you. On this particular cold, wet December day, only a handful of people wandered in and out. Most sought refuge across the street in the bus station where it was warmer and drier. It was a miserable day and my relief staff person called in sick, leaving me there alone from 8 a.m. to 5 p.m.

A client named Mary sat on the well-worn sofa and leaned over the coffee table, counting her coins. I sat at the desk feeling guilty that I had the only space heater.

She said, "I know it's against the rules, but can I leave my bags here for five minutes? I'm just going over to the bus station and I'll be right back." Since she was the only person there and I was the only one in charge, I agreed, reminding her that she had to return for her bags.

True to her word, Mary came back within minutes and set a Burger King bag on the desk in front of me. "Here," she said. "You can't be here alone all day and not have something to eat." Then she pulled an orange from the pocket of her old coat. "They gave me two of these this morning before I left the night shelter. You take one. Vitamin C is good for you."

I felt humbled. I knew that to refuse her gift would deeply offend her. I also knew that she had spent the last of her money to buy my lunch. I asked Mary to share the hamburger with me, but she refused, insisting I needed it more. She smiled as I took the first bite. I realized that in accepting her gift I gave her something — pride that she could be generous with what little she had. She had no idea, of course, that she gave me much more than a hamburger that day.

~Linda Rettstatt

10

The Best Job of All

I know from experience that you should never give up on
yourself or others, no matter what.
~George Foreman

B
ack when I was in my twenties, I worked in an office in Philadelphia. Each day I boarded the train with my coffee and book, struggling to keep my eyes open so early in the morning. I'd push through the hustle and bustle of the city to my office, and then I'd spend my day there crunching numbers and attending meetings and dealing with clients. My work at the office had its fulfilling moments, like when I got kudos from a client or received a hard-earned promotion. And I was grateful to have a well-paying job at a time when some of my friends and family were not so lucky. But in the end, this job was just about making a living. I wasn't enjoying "corporate America."

But it was different on Tuesdays. On Tuesday nights I walked several blocks to a nearby community center to my "other job," a job that was a world apart from the number-crunching career I had during the day. I'd make my way to a large room with high ceilings where I was greeted by shouts of excitement — "Miss Maggie is here! Miss Maggie is here!" This unbridled enthusiasm came from a group of kids who were all mine to teach, connect with and inspire for the next two hours. You see, on these Tuesday nights, I coached volleyball for athletes of the Special Olympics.

As I entered this large room one particular Tuesday night, most of the kids came running. "Miss Maggie! Can we start warming up?" I had taught the kids the importance of warming up before starting their volleyball lesson, and they were eager to show me that they'd learned well. I gave them a nod and watched them begin their moves.

Looking around, I noticed that Brian was sitting in the corner by himself, as usual. He came from a family that struggled greatly with what they referred to as his "condition." Unfortunately, this caused him a lot of anger and sadness.

As the other kids started to exercise, I walked over to Brian and sat down. I said hello, but he gave me only an angry mumble in return. I asked how he was doing, and I got a scowl and a headshake for an answer. I had gotten this type of reaction from Brian before, so it wasn't a surprise. With a limited ability to fully understand and cope with the negativity in his life, Brian often shut down and struggled to communicate at all. Any response at all from him was a positive, and sometimes an angry mumble or scowl was the only response he could muster. And even though he insisted on coming to the lesson each week, Brian's permanent place seemed to be in the corner, alternating between watching the other kids and resting his head on his knees.

Working with Brian each week, I knew I had to be patient, and this experience taught me a valuable lesson in the power of compassion and perseverance. As I gained Brian's trust and he started to respond to me, even when the responses were mumbles and scowls, I knew that I had to stay positive and make sure he knew that I was there for him no matter what.

On this particular Tuesday night, as I had done so many Tuesday nights before, I simply gave Brian a gentle squeeze, told him that we'd love to have him join us, and made my way over to the other kids. Once the kids had warmed up, I began my lesson. I was not a volleyball expert by any means, but I had a good understanding of the game, and it was enough for me to teach these kids the basics. The reality was, even with my limited knowledge and skills, there were no easier kids to teach. Sure, there were the occasional squabbles and silly antics that all kids get into, but more than anything these kids were thrilled to be there, learning a sport.

As the volleyball lesson progressed, I saw movement on the sideline. Brian had come out of his corner and was moving closer, intrigued by how much fun the other kids were having. Hesitantly, he approached me and asked if he could play. On this night, Brian had finally decided to move past his anger and take part in the fun. I put my arm around him and replied with an enthusiastic yes, and in return he gave me the slightest hint of a smile. He joined the other kids, and they readily welcomed him. I watched Brian forget, at least for a moment, the things that made him so sad and angry as he enjoyed learning volleyball with his friends.

At the end of that Tuesday night, as I watched Brian and the other kids leave the volleyball court together, I knew that this truly was the job that mattered. I knew that I was making at least a small difference in these kids' lives, and I knew that the difference they were making in mine was great. No office job, no client praise or promotion, no paycheck could ever compare to the fulfillment I received every week from my "other job," my work with Brian and the other kids of the Special Olympics.

~Maggie Hofstaedter

Chapter 2

Volunteering & Giving Back

A Family Affair

11

A Hero's Welcome

*The joy of meeting pays the pangs of absence; else who could
bear it?*
~Nicholas Rowe

stared at the flight board. It estimated landing time as 5:45 a.m. I
checked my phone. It read 7 a.m. Toby Keith's "American Soldier"
played in the background for at least the tenth time.

"My feet hurt," my seven-year-old complained.

"Why do they have to fly in before the sun comes up?" my teenager wondered.

"These soldiers just spent the last eighteen months getting shot
at while defending our freedom. The least we can do is show our
gratitude when they come home," my husband explained.

The announcement thundered over the loudspeaker: "Flight 348
from Kabul to Dallas has landed." We cheered and gathered around the
entrance while a volunteer at the Dallas/Fort Worth airport explained,
"These soldiers were fighting on a battlefield in Afghanistan less than
twenty-four hours ago. This is the first time they've touched down on
American soil in over a year. Do not attempt to hug or touch them. If
they reach out to you, it's okay to reciprocate. But it can be alarming
if a crowd rushes toward them."

We stood behind the roped-off perimeter, gripping our flags and
straining to see the first group exit the plane. A single soldier stopped
short at the entrance, glanced around and broke into a huge grin.

A blanket of flags waved through the air and applause erupted as he strode past the crowd. Veterans stood in a salute and Boy Scouts shouted, "Thank you."

The next guy peeked around the corner. He slunk past with his head low, never making eye contact or accepting gifts from volunteers.

The next soldier must have heard cheers before rounding the corner. He ran out with his hands in the air slapping palms like an NBA player celebrating a victory. Other soldiers followed him, openly wiping tears.

During the lulls between welcoming the next group, we offered our cell phones to service members. They called relatives and said they'd made it home safely. This time gave us an opportunity to listen to their anecdotes and learn about their families. We heard stories about their passion for freedom and their loyalty to our nation. One young soldier handed my phone back, hugged me and thanked me for what she called "your generosity."

My generosity? A soldier who volunteered to spend a year and a half fighting terrorists in Afghanistan thanked me for my generosity?

Several awkward seconds ticked by before I could manage a response. "The honor's all mine. And thank you."

~Belinda Cohen

12

The Difference Maker

What counts in life is not the mere fact that we have lived. It is what difference we have made to the lives of others that will determine the significance of the life we lead.
~Nelson Mandela

As a kid I had the chance to spend a lot of time with my grandparents, all amazing people to whom I attribute so much of who I am today. Sadly, my last grandparent passed away when I was first becoming a parent myself. Their passing caused me to really think about how I would raise my own kids, without my grandparents' life experiences and wisdom to teach my kids everything, from how to make perfect homemade biscuits to how to fix anything to be better than it originally was. This reality caused even more stress, knowing that my kids would be responsible for the next generation and the next, and that my grandparents' influence would end with me.

When my firstborn, Kylan, was five, we wanted him to focus outside himself and material possessions, so we sponsored a child and got him a pen pal named Haruna, in Uganda. Haruna was also five and we thought they could share stories about growing up in their respective parts of the world. There were no expectations—just a desire to give Kylan a more worldly view. So the process began of getting to know his pen pal and the differences of growing up in Africa.

As Kylan's parents, we encouraged him to save a little bit of money to send a birthday gift to his pen pal, to hopefully make a difference and brighten his day. Kylan started fundraising with a lemonade stand, which wasn't quite as profitable as he was hoping, in spite of the fact that he was in a suit and top hat. So we moved on to idea number two, to recycle scrap metal. Because of the influence of his great-grandfather he knew that there was often value in things that others didn't see. As parents, our only rule was "not to say no." We wanted to give him an outlet for his ideas, and if it meant hauling scrap metal then we hauled scrap metal.

Kylan created and printed flyers about his pen pal and his desire to help Haruna and his family. He distributed them around the neighborhood and before long, scrap metal was showing up at our house. We were given everything from metal shelving to cans to computers. Over the course of the first two years Kylan raised around two hundred dollars. With that much money, not only was he able to send a birthday gift to Haruna, he was also able to buy a goat or livestock for the village.

Kylan is very driven and very compassionate. So when he wanted to do even more we completely supported him. Kylan thought that if he could get his school involved, he could make an even greater impact. Like any good entrepreneur, Kylan made business cards for his company, named "Metal Mission," and requested a meeting with his principal. His principal was so impressed with his desire to make a difference that she started telling his story and it spread like wildfire. The next thing you know, we were sponsored to go to Africa, and found ourselves on a plane headed halfway around the world to meet Haruna and have the experience of a lifetime.

But the real story began after we returned. The first thing Kylan said when we got home was, "This changed me, Mom. I know it changed me." I didn't know where this journey would lead, or how Kylan would feel after going to Africa. Would he feel that he had accomplished all he'd intended and move on? Or would this feed the fire that had been sparked four years earlier? That spark is now a blazing fire.

Kylan felt that if he could share his story then maybe he could inspire others to make a difference. He began by telling kids at his school about the experience, and found himself being asked to speak at other schools, but even that wasn't enough. With this simple idea and a lot of support, Kylan started a youth movement called the Difference Maker Movement. By sharing his story along with the values we have raised him to follow he hopes to inspire other Difference Makers. Those values became the mantra for his work. They are:

Life isn't about keeping score.
It's not about how many friends you have.
It isn't about who your family is, or what kind of car you drive, or where you go to school.
It's not about how you look, or what clothes you wear, or what kind of music you listen to.
It's not about if your hair is blond, or if your skin is light or dark.
It's not about what grades you get, how smart you are, how smart everyone else thinks you are, or how smart the tests say you are.
Life is about who you love and who you hurt; it's about who you make happy or unhappy; it's about keeping or losing trust.
It's about friendship.
It's about what you say and what you mean.
It's about the person you are right now and the person you have the potential to become.

Most of all, it's about using your life to touch other people's hearts.

To Kylan, a difference maker is anyone that, no matter their age or income, can make a difference to someone; the person whose life they impact could be a neighbor, a friend, or someone around the world, like Haruna.

The Difference Maker Movement is gaining momentum. We have a website: www.iamthedifferencemaker.org. The idea of the site is to have a place where we can share other Difference Maker stories around the world. We are coordinating Difference Maker Days, which are focused activities for groups to provide help to those in need. We are also working on after-school programs called Difference

Maker clubs. These Difference Maker clubs will give kids an opportunity to apply problem-solving principles to issues faced around the world. The goal of each club will be to develop products to address the problems. These products will be created using school resources and materials donated by local manufacturers.

My proudest moment has been watching my son throughout this experience. Seeing him stand up in front of kids and adults and watch that spark that is in Kylan spread to others; to hear kids talk about who in their life they are going to impact; to have parents ask me how to get their kids to become Difference Makers.

I watched Kylan sit in the front of our van, during our travels around Africa, for four hours waving to kids in the villages we passed. He would be surrounded by kids in each village we went through; they would touch his hair and skin. He would teach little kids how to give high-fives and play Frisbee. Kylan is changing the world in ways I never imagined, and he has changed me, too. I think my grandparents would approve. Next we need to work on homemade biscuits. He is only nine after all.

~Sumer Sorensen-Bain

Handled with Care

Life begins at the end of your comfort zone.
~Neale Donald Walsch

"**M**om, I need twenty service hours for this school year," my daughter Piper said, her voice quavering. As an introvert, Piper had struggled with volunteer work in the past — not from a lack of compassion, but from fear of new situations and talking with strangers. That evening, while researching volunteer opportunities on the Internet, we stumbled across multiple postings: assisting disabled children with sporting activities, reading books to hospice patients, visiting nursing home residents, and babysitting children at a women's shelter. They were all great causes, but Piper's anxiety grew with each suggestion that required interaction with people she'd never met.

Exasperated from her stream of no's, I searched the list again. "Wait, what about boxing food for the food bank?"

She asked, "Just boxing food?"

"Yes."

"So I don't have to talk to the people getting the food?"

"I don't think so," I said, unsure of all of the details but hopeful that she'd feel comfortable.

"You'll come with me, right?"

I nodded and registered us for a shift at the St. Louis Area Foodbank. Honestly, I feared the work would be boring, and how beneficial could it be to merely pack food? But I wanted to support my daughter, so I volunteered.

Arriving at the agency, Piper walked behind me, using me as her shield. The woman at the front desk directed us to the warehouse. I glanced at Piper, fearing she'd ask to leave. "It'll be fine," I assured her.

The warehouse manager pointed to the break room. "Have a seat, and I'll be in shortly to give you instructions."

When he joined us, he said that a group of thirty volunteers had canceled, and there'd only be five volunteers for the afternoon shift. With that, the tension in Piper's shoulders eased. But as we watched a video on the mission of the agency, Piper looked uncomfortable.

"What's wrong?" I asked.

Piper whispered, "One out of six people fear they won't have enough food to last the month?"

The term "food insecurity" was foreign to us; we'd never had to choose between paying for housing or medicine or food — a tough choice that many faced according to the statistics flashing on the screen. As the video continued to portray the growing hunger crisis in our country, especially for children, I watched Piper blink away tears through my own misty eyes. While we knew that people struggled with receiving proper nutrition, we didn't realize how much hunger there was in our own community.

"Let's do this," I said, energized by the video, and Piper boldly followed.

For the next three hours, we packed boxes of cookies, candy, and snacks donated by local stores — not quite the "we're-going-to-fight-hunger" experience we were primed for. At the end of the shift, we didn't quite know how we felt about our volunteer hours because the boxes lacked substantial nutritional value.

The warehouse manager must have read our faces. "I know that today's deliveries weren't exactly nutritional," he said, "but we make good use of all donations. The next job will be more like regular meals." He handed us a slip of paper with our cumulative numbers for the evening: 174 cases and 2,958 pounds of food passed through our hands. Despite it being snack-type items, Piper and I took pride in the pallets of boxes that would be shipped to agencies within a hundred-mile radius of the warehouse.

"You know, Mom, everyone deserves a piece of candy or a cookie every now and then," Piper said as we made our way home.

She was right, I thought. Everyone did deserve a treat.

"When do we go back?" Piper asked.

I winked. "The day after tomorrow."

"Good," she said. "That was fun."

That evening, as I opened my pantry door and viewed the myriad food choices, a twinge of guilt flashed through me. My biggest concern: Do I choose the mild or medium-spiced salsa? My shelves lined with food could feed several families. How many times had I said, "We have nothing to eat in this house" and then made my husband drive to the store for more choices?

That evening, our family offered a special mealtime prayer for those who sat at a sparse or empty table. Piper discussed the staggering number of hungry children as we enjoyed our hot, nutritious meal — a rediscovered blessing.

Never a fan of early rising, Piper surprised me with her eagerness to return to the food bank for a morning shift. This time, she led us through the doors and made her way to the break room without hesitation. Later, she beamed as the manager took roll call for the volunteers, referring to the two of us as "veterans."

Our group of about twenty volunteers dispersed to several workstations. Piper and I spied the Gaylord boxes, brimming with food gathered through food drives and smiled, knowing the morning's work would help provide hearty meals to those in need.

As background music played, we separated canned goods, paper goods, and food in plastic or glass containers. We needed to check expiration dates and the quality of the packaging for the safety of those seeking food assistance — something we wouldn't have thought to do as consumers who purchased food straight from the grocery store. We had entered into an unfamiliar realm filled with concerns that hadn't pertained to our lives. We'd been spoiled. Sheltered. Privileged.

We soon chatted with other volunteers, sharing items to top off boxes, holding each other's boxes closed while securing them with tape, and assisting each other with the labeling. Piper now conversed freely with those around us: We had become a community of helpers focused on delivering food to those who sought relief from hunger pains.

At the end of our shift, the manager offered a tour of the facilities. Piper turned to me. "Can we go?"

"Sure," I said, happy that she wanted to learn more about the agency.

As we toured the warehouse, the cooler and the freezer, we realized the number of man hours involved in running a food distribution center and how the behind-the-scenes folks played an integral role in getting the food from the warehouse to people's dinner tables. Without volunteers, the food would remain on the pallets.

These days, when we pull out from the food bank's parking lot, Piper and I know that we're an important link in the pipeline from those donating food to those benefiting from the donations. Most likely we'll never meet those we serve, but that in no way diminishes the importance of our service. Hunger is nondiscriminatory, and we can only hope that, if life ever hands us misfortune of such magnitude that we must seek food assistance, that the volunteers boxing our meals will do so with the same care and pride that Piper and I feel upon finishing our shifts.

~Cathi LaMarche

Feeding the Spirit

Happiness often sneaks in through a door you didn't know you left open.

~John Barrymore

The heat of the day lingered as the sun began to set. My wife and I gathered up twenty of the 110 bags of popcorn we had just finished popping, along with a small cooler packed with various fruit juices. We walked the short distance from the dining hall to the Infant House.

It was movie night, and fifteen excited children, ages six and under, had gathered in the living room to watch *Ice Age* in Spanish. As the movie began, three-year-old Daniela climbed onto my lap. For the duration of the movie, she lay back against my chest. She would reach up and rub my chin, look up with her beautiful dark eyes and smile, then turn back to watch the movie while rubbing the back of my hands which held her. My many cuts, bruises, smashed fingers and sore muscles from the week's construction projects became badges of honor because of the loving touches of this little girl. The amazing thing was, this experience was six years in the making and nearly did not happen.

I had been pressured into participating in this weeklong mission trip to a Mexican orphanage. I had resisted going for the previous five years. My work at a major Fortune 500 company was extremely demanding, my skill set did not fit the requirements of the scheduled mission activities and I didn't speak Spanish. When a lack of volunteers threatened to cancel the time at the orphanage altogether — an orphanage whose kids had counted on the group's arrival and service for the last ten years — I caved and signed up.

The first morning in Mexico I awoke very early and slipped out of my dorm room to the dining hall. As I entered, I smelled the aroma of hot coffee coming from the kitchen. Through a screen door, I could see an eighty-cup coffeemaker with the ready light illuminated. I turned the doorknob — locked. I looked for another entrance, but there was none, so I walked over and sat alone at one of the many tables.

Shortly, an older gentleman entered and unlocked the screen door. I started to rise, but he motioned for me to remain seated as he entered the kitchen. Soon he returned with two cups of hot coffee and handed me one. He introduced himself as "Ed the Cook" and pulled up a chair. He thanked me for coming and asked if it was my first time at the orphanage. After my less-than-enthusiastic yes, Ed smiled and challenged me to put my heart into the week. He said he sold his stateside diamond business and came to live at the orphanage because he wanted to "work where Christ was working" — and Christ was surely working in this place. I told Ed if he would keep the coffee hot I would accept his challenge. He did and I did.

Our team of nineteen adults worked through the day renovating an old structure into a three-bedroom apartment for a new mission family. In the evenings, we played with the seventy-two kids. I soon realized that enthusiasm and commitment trumped both lack of skill and language barriers. I began to enjoy the experience immensely. Then little Daniela showed me why I needed to make volunteerism a routine part of my life.

I learned volunteerism was the simple act of providing a service without expecting anything in return. If your world was like my world, it was complex and seemed to run at hyper speed. The demands of work and rearing children left little time to volunteer. Returning from Mexico, I realized I needed to look at my surroundings and watch for opportunities to offer a helping hand. "Heroic" volunteerism, such as international mission trips, is wonderful, but so is helping an elderly neighbor roll her trashcan to the curb on trash day, or listening to a grieving mother who just lost her son, or serving a meal at a homeless shelter. It can change lives. Opportunities abound; all we have to do is say yes. And I started saying yes.

As I approached retirement I had the normal misgivings about how I would spend my days. But because of volunteering, I was confident I would find a way to stay engaged. The day I retired, I visited a co-worker in his office. I told him it was my last day of work and I would miss our association. He smiled, draped his arm around my shoulders and said, "No, this is your last day of working for monetary gain — your work to fatten your bank account and feed your retirement fund. Now you will get to do God's work, the really fun work that feeds your spirit. The work that puts smiles on strangers' faces and deposits joy into your heart. Your real work is just beginning, and it will be an exciting time."

How true his words have become. No amount of money can feed the soul like stretching out a helping hand. The volunteer world has opened new doors to fulfillment and supplied new friends at every turn. I experienced one sterling example at a local VA hospital one day when I stopped my six-passenger golf cart behind an aging Ford sedan with a license plate displaying a Purple Heart military award and a Disabled Vet symbol. The car door opened and a walking cane appeared. Very deliberately, an elderly man emerged from the driver's seat.

"It takes me a while, but I'll make it," he said with a smile.

"No hurry… take your time, and be careful," I replied as I watched him place his WWII Veteran cap on his balding head.

He walked slowly to my cart and asked if he could sit next to me. I smiled and nodded yes as I read IWO JIMA monogrammed next to PEARL HARBOR on his hatband. I was humbled and honored to have this man at my side.

"God bless you for being here to help an old man like me. Not sure I could have made the long walk to the hospital on this cold day. How often do you work here?" he asked.

"I volunteer at least once a week for an entire day."

"You are a volunteer? They don't pay you for this? Bless you even more!"

"Oh, my pay is the greatest. I get to meet heroes like you. And, I get more God-bless-yous and Great-to-see-yous during my shift here than I will get the rest of the week."

The aging vet smiled, and we had a lively discussion about his military service as I delivered him to the hospital door. He thanked me again and said he hoped I would be available to take him back to his car.

The loving touch of a small child with an uncertain future; the smile and reminiscing of a hero nearing the end of his earthly life… simple actions that fed my spirit and had life-changing effects on my soul. All I had to do was anticipate an opportunity to serve and say yes.

~K. Michael Ware

15

Taking Back Our Story

The robbed that smiles, steals something from the thief.
~William Shakespeare, Othello

O n the morning of 9/11, I woke up extremely happy because for weeks I had been planning a surprise for my husband Joe, whose birthday is September 11th. I kissed him and our sixteen-year-old daughter goodbye that morning, not knowing that within two hours our world would change. I was caught in an evacuation in midtown Manhattan when I heard from Joe, who was with the NYPD. He told me we were under attack, that he'd brought home our daughter and that I should get home before the city shut down. He made me promise not to respond even though I was also a first responder.

We heard from my husband again at around five that day. Something was so different about him. He explained the darkness, he talked about where he was headed and his voice cracked as he said, "Baby, this is bad. It's really bad." He told me he loved us and that he would take his next break at ten as he was heading towards World Trade Center Tower 7. It wasn't long after that my daughter and I watched television in horror as Tower 7 collapsed. By two in the morning, having heard nothing, I started talking about his funeral.

My husband finally walked in around five that morning but he was not the man I had kissed the day before. He was injured and had refused treatment because he was afraid they would not let him go back in to look for survivors. We were relieved he was alive, but the sadness would continue. We had lost friends, and attending funerals was a regular part of our lives in the weeks following.

My husband didn't speak about that day, formerly a day for celebrating his birthday, for years. I knew we needed to do something, so seven years ago, when my volunteering days at my daughter's school were over, I decided to volunteer at the World Trade Center site with the 9/11 Tribute Center. Finding this organization was a godsend to me.

I was accepted into their volunteer program and began working alongside other 9/11 families, survivors, residents and first responders. The experience at first was very emotional, but at the end of each visit I would feel that I had accomplished something.

I began doing walking tours of the World Trade Center with other docents. We welcomed visitors. We'd share our personal stories about that day, and the visitors would end our tours with hugs and warm thoughts.

After being with the organization for three years, I convinced my husband to become a volunteer docent, too. He resisted at first, thinking it would be too emotional for him, but eventually he tried it and was astonished when, after he led his first tour, one visitor — a tall, husky man — came up to him and hugged him. I watched as my husband hugged the man back. This is not the kind of thing my husband does. Yet there I was watching a transformation begin. A year later, my husband would toss into the garbage the story he wrote and read from during tours — because he couldn't look people in the eye as he told it. He was finally ready to look at the visitors while he spoke to them.

A group of docents invited me to lunch one day. We had time between tours and thought it would be fun to get away from the sadness for a little while. The group was made up of women who were brought together by a tragedy, who had lost a husband, a son, a daughter. Some had been displaced because they lived near the site. Some were first responders and recovery workers. Lunch became a standing date. We were all there week after week telling our stories to the world. Then we'd meet up to continue the healing process via food, dessert and great conversation.

We don't see each other every day, but when we do come together it is always to talk about the good things in our lives. We have not let 9/11 define us. We define 9/11. I have felt so fulfilled doing these walking tours, speaking to school groups and talking individually to visitors about that day. But most importantly by honoring and remembering those who were taken from us.

We now give tours on the Memorial Plaza, and I end each and every one holding up a picture of New York's new skyline. I share with all of the visitors that fourteen years ago, those that committed this horrific crime did not think we would be standing on a memorial, a labor of love, talking to each other about hope rising from the ashes. The visitors nod their heads in agreement as they wipe their tears away. I remind them that they knew this was not a tourist attraction, that they came to honor and remember. What they don't know is that in coming they have helped those of us who volunteer get closer to healing from the horrors of that day.

I was told during one of my very first tours that my story would change at some point and I never quite understood what that meant — not until a day two years ago when we got the news that my husband was one of many 9/11 first responders who developed lung cancer and other respiratory diseases from time working at the site.

I thought for sure my husband would not continue to volunteer, but he did. At one point he did not want to because he felt people would feel sorry for him. But we decided we would tell "our" story together on the tours as we honor all those that are sick or have died.

It has become our mission to share not only our story, but to tell all those that come to the memorial to live good lives, to be kind to each other, to honor and remember, and to understand that in spite of a day that began with hate and destruction the world stood tall and strong.

~Sonia M. Agron

16

Healing Hearts

The greatest healing therapy is friendship and love.
~Hubert H. Humphrey

"Mommy, don't go," my three-year-old screamed as I walked to the door. My fifteen-year-old leaned against the kitchen counter with his arms folded across his chest, not screaming, but glaring at me as I pried his brother off my legs.

"You're mad at me too?"

"You spend all your time taking care of other people's kids, but what about us?" Dylan shook his head and stomped away.

Was that true? Did he really think I cared about other kids more than I did my own? I'd spent the better part of a week two hours from home in Jacksonville, arranging for a seven-year-old boy from the Dominican Republic to have surgery to correct a congenital heart defect. I had at least another week of twelve-hour days before I could fly the boy back to his mother.

I was stunned and a little hurt. How could my own child not understand that the work I was doing was saving lives? Then the answer hit me. He didn't know, because he had never seen what Healing the Children actually did. Dylan had heard the stories, but had never once looked into the eyes of a child and understood the hard truth—that without our help, the child would likely die.

"Get dressed. You're going with me," I said, without considering what a disaster taking him with me could turn out to be.

I spent the drive explaining the case to my son, who pretended to ignore me the entire time. "His name is Hector and he's seven. He only weighs thirty pounds and is very sick. The kids in his village call him 'Blue Boy' because his skin and nails are blue from lack of oxygen in his blood. He has a heart condition called tetralogy of Fallot, which could kill him. It's a miracle he's still alive. Kids in the States get this condition fixed before they turn one."

I went on to explain that Hector's village didn't have electricity and he was pretty scared being in an American hospital surrounded by machines. Hector came to the United States alone and had been staying with volunteers before he was admitted to the hospital for surgery. It took a team of volunteer medical staff and lay people to get him to Florida and care for him while he was here. Still, Dylan seemed unimpressed.

About a block from the hospital, we stopped at a convenience store for water and snacks. When he got to the register I asked why Dylan had one large and one small Slurpee. He told me that all kids loved Slurpees and the small one was for Hector. I doubted the little guy would be able to drink it, but remained silent. This was the first interest Dylan had shown in being there. I wasn't about to ruin it.

I stopped at the nurse's station to check on Hector's progress while Dylan went to the room. Our patient was recovering physically, but the nurse was concerned that he was struggling emotionally. She said, "Kids usually bounce back fast, but he hardly speaks and never smiles."

Imagine our surprise when we heard laughter from three doors down. I entered the room, with the nurse on my heels, and found Dylan sitting on the edge of Hector's bed wiping chunks of frozen drink from Hector's belly. Both boys were giggling and Hector was squirming away from the cold mess.

"I told you he would like a Slurpee. He's having a hard time with the straw," said a grinning Dylan.

I spent the remainder of the day speaking to doctors and watching my normally taciturn son play with a special little boy. Hector didn't speak a word of English, and Dylan didn't speak Spanish, but neither let that get in the way. They communicated with their own form of sign language and laughter. Unlike the adult volunteers who couldn't quite reach him on his level, Dylan didn't get frustrated or give up. It was truly amazing to watch them interact, as if it were the most natural thing in the world. Perhaps to the two of them it was.

Dylan took Hector on a wagon ride through the hospital. Wolfson Children's Hospital uses special wagons instead of wheelchairs for some of their patients. I had never noticed how the kids loved those wagons until that day. Seeing a kid in a wheelchair was always difficult, but seeing one in a wagon looked almost normal.

We took Hector outside for the first time since he was admitted to the hospital. I stood holding my breath as Dylan encouraged him to crawl out of the wagon and onto a tricycle. I hadn't thought to ask how much physical activity he could tolerate. Even if I had, I doubt I would have had the heart to stop him when I saw the delight on his face. Riding a tricycle is no big deal for an American five-year-old. However, for a kid who normally couldn't cross a room without being exhausted, riding a tricycle is nothing short of a miracle.

On the way home that night, Dylan broke down in tears. "Is Hector going to be okay?"

"I think so. He has a hard road ahead of him, but the surgery gave him a fighting chance," I answered as my throat tightened with emotion.

"Can we adopt him?"

I looked at my son and shook my head. "He has a family waiting for him."

"Mom, I took one look at his big brown eyes and…" Dylan paused and wiped his eyes. "Can I go with you tomorrow?"

"Of course."

The remainder of the drive was filled with laughter and hope. Dylan recalled some of the special moments he'd shared with Hector and made plans to bring video games and a portable DVD player the next day. He accompanied me to Jacksonville every day until it was time to say a tearful goodbye to Hector.

Over the next few years, Dylan volunteered with Healing the Children numerous times. We were able to bring several children to the United States to receive lifesaving medical treatment, but that only saved their little bodies. What saved their hearts was the caring and love of countless volunteers. Volunteers like a formerly moody teenager who never again complained about his mother's crazy work schedule.

~Kathryn M. Hearst

17

It Takes a Village

*Don't give up. There are too many naysayers out there who will
try to discourage you. Don't listen to them. The only one who
can make you give up is yourself.*
~Sidney Sheldon

When the world was really first introduced to HIV/AIDS
in the early 1980s it was called "Gay Flu." I was working as the Media Specialist at a local four-year college
where there were many gay professors and students. I
knew I couldn't ignore the sexual activity, gay or straight, on campus, so I called Trojan's parent company and convinced them to
donate a 3-pack of condoms for every student at the school (discretely kept in my office). That was just the beginning. I decided to
bring AIDS education programs to campus as a volunteer. I made
enemies of some of the faculty and administration because they
refused to acknowledge the need for such programs, but I also
made many friends and raised the kind of awareness that could
save lives.

Fast forward to 1987. I left my job at the college to join the
staff of Centennial Comprehensive Health Care Center (CCHCC).
As the clinic social worker, I started coordinating a healthcare program for the homeless and working poor. Soon after I started I won
a grant to work with HIV patients, both gay and straight.

CCHCC was a 501(c)(3), a private, non-profit center. No

patient was ever turned away. However, the funds to pay decent physicians were not readily available. The clinic was failing financially, and it was difficult to have to watch such a vital resource for an entire county disappear. To sacrifice the quality of care because of cost was unacceptable to me. Bad health care is worse than none. CCHCC was on the verge of having to close its doors forever.

Working at the clinic was as much about my family as it was about me. My family stepped up to create some wonderful fundraising events and served as my personal volunteer team. We decided to hold a charity golf tournament, and my husband and father became an expert tournament-organizing duo. Even my kids helped!

The magnitude of an event like this should have been beyond what two volunteers could do, but it was a huge success. Participants all got three meals, gift bags, raffle prizes and games on the course, so everyone went home smiling.

My husband worked for Roche Pharma and got them to send AIDS educators to speak at champagne breakfasts before the tournaments. The breakfast educated many participants, who asked great questions and came away with less fear and some great information they could share with others. By year two we had a corporate sponsor and raised over $10,000. Not only that, but we educated a hundred more golfers. I was so proud of my family and the clinic staff, who all volunteered to make this successful. By year three there were more golfers trying to sign up than we could accommodate.

At the same time we created the Funny You Should Bid Auction, named by my husband to dovetail on Comic Relief. When I wasn't doing my real job, which by year two was Executive Director of CCHCC, I was on the phone with celebrities, television writers and movie producers. Comedy Cabaret's Andy Scarpati not only volunteered his venue, but the Friday night before the auction he donated the proceeds from the cover charge to the clinic. Movie stars, national radio personalities, athletes, sports teams and TV show cast members sent amazing autographed items. Local businesses were beyond generous. This became a labor of love for all the donors and volunteers, not to mention the comedian auctioneers who donated their time and talent.

When I inherited CCHCC, we couldn't even pass our audit. Thanks to the efforts of my family and staff, plus all of our dedicated volunteers, we were able to not only start an HIV clinical research study for the patients, but also buy updated medical equipment and add a training program for fourth-year medical students, many of whom returned after their three-month rotations as volunteers! We had finally turned our clinic into a place where people could receive the best quality of care, even when they were in the direst of financial straits. We also treated inmates at the local prison, which not only used CCHCC services but let my husband and me bring in a Passover Seder. This is what we did as volunteers together. This is the example we wanted to set for our son and daughter.

My volunteers continued to work with me, as well as all of our new donors. Thanks to my husband's hard work, my patients always had what they needed; we never ran out of supplies. I was able to attend meetings dealing with all manner of diseases, and the pharmaceutical representatives let me take their display products and ship them back to the clinic. Doors were open to my patients by specialists who would take them pro bono. Even the building, which had had its mortgage in arrears for years, was donated to us by the builder. We paid our bills, expanded our hours and services, and delivered surplus food from local markets to shut-in patients.

Unfortunately, eventually I was diagnosed with Lupus—in a way, the opposite of HIV, causing an overactive, not under-active, immune system. I came out of remission after eight years and was forced to retire early. I was bedridden and heartbroken. I found other ways to give back, but the 24/7 days were a thing of the past.

Volunteering is not a solo activity in my world. For me, it took a family, a staff, a community, and dedicated friends and strangers, who all shared my vision and passion for quality health care. I went from being a lone AIDs educator and activist in jeopardy of losing my job for being outspoken, to being a social worker at a bankrupt clinic actually working with sick patients, to being the executive director of a successful community health care center. The success of CCHCC did not belong to me. It really did take a village.

~Judy L. Davidson

18

The Circle of Volunteerism

Success doesn't happen in a vacuum. You're only as good as the
people you work with and the people you work for.
~Casey Kasem

During our homeschool group's tour of a local radio station, we observed a massive soundboard. Eleven-year-old Jeremy's eyes widened. I knew what my son was thinking. All those switches and buttons and knobs — it looked like a little boy's paradise.

Station owner Reverend Lane finished the tour with the statement, "If anyone is interested in learning more about radio, we'd love to have you volunteer with us."

Jeremy looked up at me, a hopeful smile lighting his face.

I patted his shoulder. "We'll see."

With Attention Deficit Disorder and two learning disabilities, Jeremy was both a delight and a challenge to teach. I couldn't have asked for a sweeter child, and he was very bright, especially when it came to technology. Because he was a kinesthetic learner, however, I had to come up with hands-on approaches to presenting information. Maybe volunteering at the radio station was just what he needed.

A few weeks later, Jeremy started at the station. He quickly picked up running the soundboard, and we enjoyed hearing about his adventures in radio. Before long, terms like legal ID, dead air, and PSA (public service announcement) became household words. When

Reverend Lane asked Jeremy to take a break for the summer so they could train new personnel, our son could hardly wait for fall so he could resume his "job."

The station's new DJ, Danny, took Jeremy under his wing and gave him opportunities to test his new skills. He joked with Jeremy as an equal and seemed to enjoy their time together, causing our sometimes-shy son to blossom. Jeremy told us one day that Danny leaned back with his hands behind his head and said how nice it was having Jeremy there because he could relax and let "our youngest DJ" run the show. Danny's words boosted our son's confidence so much that we had to peel him off the ceiling that night.

When I stopped by to pick up Jeremy one afternoon, Reverend Lane asked to speak to me. I entered his office with trepidation, fearing that Jeremy's two years of volunteering were coming to an end. I was right.

"I wanted to talk to you before I mentioned this to Jeremy," Reverend Lane began. "We'd like him to take over the Sunday programming for us. Our current DJ is leaving, and Danny thinks Jeremy could handle the job."

I stared at him. "You want him to work for you?"

"Yes. We can't let him talk on the air until his voice changes," he said apologetically, "but he'll air your church's live service at eleven and play prerecorded programming until three."

"But . . . but," I stammered, "he's just thirteen."

"I know," Reverend Lane said, misunderstanding my concern. "It means someone will have to stay with him each week. No one else is in the office on Sundays, and we wouldn't want him here by himself."

I took a deep breath. If the owner trusted my thirteen-year-old to run his radio station one day a week, who was I to argue? "Sure. I'll stay with him."

Thus began my two-year volunteer job. Jeremy and I would attend Sunday school each week and then race over to the station in time to get the church service on the air. We ate lunch while listening to our pastor preach, and afterwards Jeremy began the afternoon programming.

Sometimes the afternoons stretched out endlessly before me. I dusted or vacuumed the reception area, contributing where I could, but mostly I sat with Jeremy. It was a wonder to watch him. I soon learned why Danny said an hour of DJing consisted of fifty-five minutes of boredom interspersed with five minutes of sheer terror. Whenever a program CD wouldn't play or something else went wrong, I panicked while Jeremy quietly slipped in some music to avoid "dead air" and figured out what to do. Only his time volunteering at the station could have given him the composure and expertise to handle the many problems that cropped up each week.

Of course, Jeremy never really stopped volunteering. He and his dad put together a website for the station and initiated live audio streaming before streaming was even popular. Jeremy also rounded up members of his 4-H youth club for a service project, cleaning up the garden in front of the station. They trimmed bushes, pulled weeds, and planted flowers. Reverend Lane's wife was especially thrilled with the results. Shortly before he graduated from school, Jeremy recorded a PSA to promote 4-H's many opportunities for youth development. It thrilled several young 4-Hers who heard their voices on air for the first time and gave Jeremy experience in directing, recording, and splicing together a radio spot.

In all, Jeremy worked for the radio station for seven years, starting with the two years he volunteered as a preteen. No, he didn't become a DJ, but the friendships, skills, and experience he acquired bolstered his confidence and buoyed him through college and into the workforce.

As we found, volunteering is not only a family affair but a community effort. Though Jeremy started out as the volunteer, others volunteered their time to train him, nurture him, and oversee his efforts. By giving of themselves, Reverend Lane, Danny, and others took a shy little boy and built him up to become an employable young man whom they in turn employed. What goes around comes around in the circle of volunteerism.

~Tracy Crump

19

The Greatest Gift

Stop this attitude that older people ain't any good anymore!
We're as good as we ever were — if we ever were any good.
~Dolly Parton

I saw the nursing home out of the corner of my eye as my family and I carried boxes from the moving van to our new apartment. The place my mom had found for us was a nice apartment, and I was happy that it was in a quiet neighborhood with trees and a nearby park. What I hadn't noticed when she showed it to my brothers, sister and me was that there was a nursing home for senior citizens right across from it.

I was in my teens then, and since my grandparents had passed away years ago, I really had no daily contact with older people. I was more interested in my own life. Old people weren't on my radar. I figured they weren't very interested in me, either.

I walked to the bus stop down the road to go to school, so every morning I would walk past the nursing home. Invariably, four or five people would be sitting on iron chairs on the porch. They would always call out and wave to me as I passed by. I didn't really know what to say to them, so I just pretended I didn't hear them.

One day I came home to find my mom frosting a chocolate cake in the kitchen. "Is that for dessert?" I asked, my mouth watering.

Mom shook her head. "I baked it for the people at the nursing home," she told me. "I found out from some of the nurses that they love cake, so I decided to bake them one."

"You went over there?" I asked.

My mom nodded. "I go over two or three times a week after work to visit with the residents. Some of those people don't get many visitors. We sit and talk and play cards."

"You mean you volunteer there?"

She nodded. "They're great people. I enjoy it."

I was amazed. My mom wasn't old. What could she have in common with the people at the nursing home? I had a hard time imagining spending any time with them. They seemed so confused all the time I figured they wouldn't even know I was there. So I shrugged, told myself there wouldn't be cake for dessert, and went to do my homework.

A few weeks went by. One Saturday morning my mom told me she had a cold and couldn't go to the nursing home. She asked if I would go in her place.

"You want me to go inside that place and talk to those people?" I really wanted no part of that. I was happy my mom liked volunteering, but it wasn't for me.

"Someone should go," she said. "Your brothers and sister have other work to do today, and I wouldn't want the folks at the nursing home to think I forgot about them."

I moaned and groaned about it, but in the end, I agreed to go. I figured I'd tell the nurses there that my mom was sick and couldn't come and then leave. But when I stepped inside a nurse listened while I explained why my mom couldn't come, then smiled at me.

"Your mom called and told us you'd be coming over to visit with our residents. Why don't you go into the recreation room and say hello?"

I really didn't want to do that. The whole place smelled strange, and there were old people everywhere. Some walked around, some were in wheelchairs, and I saw that some were in their beds in the rooms that lined the hallways. I was very uncomfortable, but I had promised my mom so I decided to give it a try.

In the recreation room I sat down next to an old man who was staring at a checkerboard on a table. "Are you playing checkers?" I asked.

The old man looked at me. "Do you see me playing with anyone?" He sounded kind of grouchy, but then I figured it might be because he had no one to play checkers with.

"May I play?" I asked.

He looked at me. His eyes seemed suspicious, but then he nodded and made the first move. I had always liked to play checkers, and considered myself a fair player, but this guy was good! He won the first game, and as we set up the board for another, he told me he'd been a teacher before he retired.

"Really? That's something I'd like to do someday," I said as I moved a checker.

"You have to study very hard," he told me. Then he told me about his teaching days, and some of the other things he'd done in his life. He'd been a pilot in the Air Force, worked on a farm, and even worked in a circus! I couldn't believe he'd led such an interesting life. We played several more games while he shared more stories about his life.

By the time I left that morning, I had met a few other residents and learned that all these people were individuals who had done many things in their lives, and who still hoped and dreamed and laughed, and treasured spending time with others. I think I saw them as real people for the very first time that day.

I went back after that, again and again, and my brothers and sister came, too. We spent lots of time there throughout the years we lived next to the nursing home. I made many friends whom I'll always remember, and I learned that sometimes the greatest gift you can give others is your time, your understanding, and your love. It's a gift that is never wasted.

~John P. Buentello

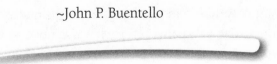

20

Amy's Treat

Never get tired of doing little things for others. Sometimes, those little things occupy the biggest part of their hearts.
~Author Unknown

The phone vibrated and her name appeared on the screen. "They found something, a little blip," she said, and then, trying to put me at ease, "Don't worry. They'll go in and zap it. It will be alright." Eighteen months later, the cancer that had returned first as a blip and then with a vengeance ended her life.

Amy's disease and prognosis were stunning for us all. This should not happen to a fit, kind, well-loved and respected individual who by her very nature made so many lives around her better.

I recognized true courage and was awed that, in spite of pain and fear, Amy's humor and compassion remained. In the middle of a life interrupted, she continued to display a concern for others. She once said, before sitting down to a lovely meal in a waterfront cottage on a small island in Maine, as family and friends gathered to celebrate her forty-sixth birthday, "Wouldn't it be nice if everyone with cancer could have a special day like this?" It was said at a time when being self-absorbed would have been both understood and excused. But that was not Amy. For those of us there, in the midst of all that beauty, in all the magic of a perfect day, what was not lost was the fact that Amy was terminally ill. I am certain that every one of us wondered whether this would be her last birthday. And yet, in that moment,

Amy was not thinking of herself, nor of us, but of others who shared with her a diagnosis of cancer.

With her passing, Amy's family and friends, along with her medical team at the Seacoast Cancer Center, contributed thoughts and ideas so that we could create a foundation that was most like the individual we hoped to honor. We wanted to fulfill her wish that "everyone with cancer could have a special day."

We decided to call our non-profit "Amy's Treat." Everything fell rather smoothly into place. The arrival back in our lives of an attorney friend who specializes in non-profits, coupled with a whole lot of effort by a dedicated team of volunteers, saw to it that in March 2008, less than six months after Amy passed away, Amy's Treat became a registered 501(c)(3) non-profit. Our mission is to provide solutions to the day-to-day difficulties of living with cancer and to offer unexpected "treats" to renew the spirit.

Since its inception, Amy's Treat has remained an all-volunteer non-profit and has helped thousands of people whose lives have been altered by cancer. It has given out more than a million dollars' worth of direct aid, services, and access to a "special day," like box seats at a Red Sox game or money for a woman to purchase a new dress for her son's wedding. We also grant bucket-list wishes, such as we did for one terminally ill young man who was able to speed around a NASCAR track in a race car just like he had watched so many of his racing heroes do.

Of course, what we really want is to have Amy back. This is the next best thing. To be able to turn one of the more heartbreaking events in a lifetime into something that not only honors the memory of a good person, but also makes a kinder cancer journey for others, has been a gift. Helping to launch this group and devoting hours of volunteering to assure its continued success has changed my life in ways that I never thought possible. To stand in the reflection of the indomitable spirit of someone facing one of the most frightening set of words one will ever hear—"You have cancer"—puts one's own worries into perspective. It reminds me of all the ways I should be grateful.

Volunteering for Amy's Treat has restored in me a once wavering faith in the thoughtfulness of humankind. We would not be successful without the generosity of so many people who will never meet the person or families that their checks and donations will ultimately benefit. It has humbled me to witness many kindhearted acts, such as receiving ten quarters taped to a card from the seven-year-old son of a woman whose car payment we had made, on which he had printed in neat penmanship: "Thank you for helping my mom. Hope this helps someone else." Numerous Amy's Treat recipients who have passed on and wanted to pay it forward named our non-profit as the recipient for their own memorial donations.

"Wouldn't it be nice if everyone with cancer could have a special day like this?" Amy said. Because she lived and because she died, many have. I think she would be pleased with how it all turned out.

~Lenore Rogers

21

Service with a Smile

Judgments prevent us from seeing the good that lies beyond
appearances.
~Wayne W. Dyer

t was an early Saturday morning, about 5:30 a.m. My mom called to me. "Austin, get up! Time to go and serve the homeless!" I dragged myself out of bed.

I started serving the homeless when I was eight years old. I didn't know these people would make such a big difference in my life.

Two Saturdays a month I go to the church and help get things ready for breakfast. When the gate is opened, people come rushing in to get coffee, juice or milk. They take their seats while breakfast is prepared, and then we begin to serve. We each grab two plates and carry them down the line as the plates are filled. Each person receives two pancakes, a scoop of eggs, hash browns, and two sausages. I walk to the tables where the people are sitting and set the plates before them. I always make sure to smile. After I've served them, I ask if they need anything else and bring them whatever they ask for. Some say thank you, some don't, but I don't care. I'm there to serve them.

When I first started serving I was a little scared. Some of the people were wearing clothes with patches on them and shoes with holes in them. They were not that clean and their teeth were yellow or missing. At first I stayed close to my mom most of the time, but after I got to know these strangers I realized that they were nice, friendly people. And the inside of them was often nicer than the outside. I started talking to my new friends and realized that there was no reason to be scared. After serving for a few months, I started to look forward to seeing the same people each week.

Take Cowboy. He always puts me in a good mood. When I see him, he always says, "Austin! How are you?" I've often heard him say that I am a really hard worker. This makes me feel really good inside because I know I'm making a difference in someone's life. There's a guy named Larry who has a lot of piercings and tattoos — even tattoos on his face! I would feel a little scared if I saw him on the street and didn't know him, but now that I do know him I've realized that he's a very nice guy. He even works at a church and helps others, too.

Then there's Curtis. He's a really big guy. Every time I see Curtis, he is very talkative. He always has a big smile on his face. Curtis has a friend named James. James is even taller and bigger than Curtis. When I first saw him, I thought, "Whoa! Is he a nice guy or not?" He looked really tough. But as soon as I met him, he said — in a deep, deep voice — Hello! What's your name?" I knew that we would be good friends.

All of these people make my day much better. When I don't see one of them, I wonder if they are okay. The past two years have made a big difference in my life. I do this because it is the right thing to do. When I serve people I want them to know that someone cares for them and that they matter — they are not just "homeless" — they are human beings. Serving makes me happy, but even more importantly, it teaches me to love and respect others and helps make the world a better place to live.

~Austin Nicholas Lees, age 10

Chapter
3

Volunteering
& Giving Back

Lessons Learned

22

Just Twenty Hours

I don't believe an accident of birth makes people sisters or brothers.... Sisterhood and brotherhood is a condition people have to work at.
~Maya Angelou

Freshman year of college. World History class. My professor has just dropped a bombshell on the class. Thirty percent of our final grade will be based on an assignment that is going to take, at minimum, twenty hours to complete. The assignment? Community service.

"We are all part of a community. Whether or not a community succeeds is largely dependent on how citizens treat each other. So go out into your communities — get involved, but do it in a way that you don't get paid. Making cookies and taking them to your neighbor doesn't count. It has to be something that is actually going to take some time, and I can assure you there are plenty of ways to help out in your community. It is my belief that this assignment will change your life. It is only for twenty hours, but you might be surprised what can happen in those twenty hours."

Some people in my class grumbled. I wasn't particularly irritated by the assignment, but I was trying to figure out how I would find the time. I was going to school only part-time because I was working full-time to pay for college. I eventually just shrugged my shoulders and thought, "I'm just going to have to make it work."

After doing some research, I found an after-school tutoring program for kids held in a former elementary school. I filled out my paperwork, paid the fee for a background check, and a week later got a phone call saying that I had been paired with a fourth-grade boy named Steven.

He was small for his age, wore glasses and was a Harry Potter fan. He was a little on the quiet side for the first few weeks, but it was obvious he was a very bright boy. He didn't need a tutor as much as he needed a friend. I don't think he was bullied at school or anything like that; it seemed that his classmates mostly ignored him.

We met twice a week for two hours, so it only took me five weeks to complete the necessary hours for my class. When I started, I only intended to complete the required hours for my assignment. But when the hours were done, I realized how small a sacrifice it had been for me to tutor Steven. I still had sufficient time to do my schoolwork, my full-time job, and even spend time with family and friends. But most importantly, I liked Steven. And I could tell that he had already grown attached to me. There was no way I was going to back out on that kid.

Most days, Steven finished his homework in half an hour if he even had any. That meant we could do other things. We played *Jenga* and air hockey. He mentioned he was a *Star Wars* fan, so I brought my sister's *Star Wars Monopoly* game so that we could practice math skills and play a nerdy game at the same time. We read the fourth *Harry Potter* book together and wondered what was going to happen in the final three and argued over whether or not Snape was a bad guy. In the winter, we had snowball fights. When the second *Star Wars* movie came out, I got permission from his grandparents to take him to the movie. We were both totally disappointed by it, but we still had fun. I got him an R2-D2 keychain. He called me a dork, but that keychain was quickly attached to the zipper on his backpack.

As the end of the school year approached, Steven started to get a little depressed. I finally asked him one day what was wrong. He said, "I don't want the school year to end."

"But, Steven, I thought you didn't like school." He had told me on numerous occasions that he didn't.

"I don't."

"Then why don't you want the school year to end?"

He was quiet for a second, and then said, "Because when the school year is over, I won't see you anymore. We won't come here and you will forget all about me."

I felt like crying. "Steven, I will never forget you."

"But we still won't get to see each other like we do."

"No, we won't." I had signed an agreement stating that at the end of the school year I wouldn't seek to have a relationship with the child I tutored. It hadn't seemed like a big deal nine months before and I understood the reasons behind it. But now that the school year was coming to a close, I realized it really did stink that I wasn't going to be able to hang out with this awesome young man anymore. He had become so much more than just a kid I spent time with to fulfill a class requirement. He was like a little brother. "I'm going to miss you, too, Steven, but I promise I will never, ever forget you." I don't think I really made him feel any better, but I knew that I couldn't lie to him and say that we were still going to see each other on a regular basis.

We were supposed to have one last day together, but on that day, the supervisor of the tutoring program called to tell me that he had been offered a new job and was leaving, so never mind, no tutoring today. I called Steven to tell him the news and he was heartbroken. "But I got you a present!" So I got on the phone with his grandpa and he told me to come over so that Steven could say goodbye.

I ended up staying for about an hour. He had gotten me a teddy bear with a pink bow tied around its neck. I handed him paperback copies of the first two *Harry Potter* books. Then Steven gave me a school picture and a note. The note read, "I will never forget you. You were my best friend this year. I will remember you always." It was probably the most heartfelt note that I have ever received.

It took me some time to get used to not heading over to that old elementary school and seeing that sweet, smiling boy waiting for me. But then I realized I had a young boy in my life about the same age, with a sweet smile of his own, a boy I didn't see enough: my own brother.

I had been so busy being an adult that I really didn't pay him any attention at all. And then I realized I hadn't been spending any time with my younger sister, either. I had a brother and a sister who I loved and cared about, but when I actually took the time to think about it, I realized I wasn't really friends with them. Other than the obligatory nightly dinner routine and going to their various school functions, I didn't spend any time with them. I had just spent nine months getting to know a kid, but I couldn't say the same thing about my own brother and sister.

It was time to change that. I started going on weekly dates with my brother, even letting him pick what we did. Sometimes that meant playing *Pokémon* games, something I abhorred, but the look of excitement on my brother's face made it worth it. I started inviting my sister to do things with my friends and me. Sure enough, in less than a year my siblings became much more than just my siblings. They are my best friends. I don't know if I would have ever become as close to them as I am now if it hadn't been for that assignment from my history professor.

I still think about Steven. He's at least twenty years old now. I wonder what he's up to. I wonder if he even remembers me. But mostly I am grateful that even though we didn't get to continue our friendship, it was because of that friendship that I realized I was missing out on having relationships with my siblings. My professor was right: A lot can happen in just twenty hours.

~Nicole Webster

23

A Little Lipstick

Beauty, to me, is about being comfortable in your own skin.
That, or kick-ass red lipstick.
~Gwyneth Paltrow

"Now if you could just put on a little lipstick that would make me so happy." That was the second thing Mr. Stolarz said after opening the door. The first thing he said was, "Oy, my girls are here," while beaming the brightest, somewhat impish smile. My friend and I volunteered for "Meals on Wheels," an organization providing food to the elderly and shut-ins.

Two things stood out about most of our clients: they were lonely and grateful. The institutional-type food was mediocre but it was clear not many cared about that. They were thrilled to have companionship, even for only a few moments. They made the most of the time we were able to spend with them, given our task of having to make many stops between 9 a.m. and 11 a.m. They'd tell us about their children who lived far away, and those who lived close but didn't come around to visit often. Even the people who saw their children frequently would admit "frequent" was not enough when the rest of their days were so empty.

Sometimes I'd pick up a framed and dusty photo from a breakfront shelf and say, "Is this you? You look beautiful." They loved talking about their long ago wedding or about the grandchild who had performed in a dance recital then but was now in law school.

Mr. Stolarz was different. He had no framed photos and no stories about his wedding long ago or about any grandchildren. His prized possession, the only decoration in his small, sparse apartment, was in a beautiful, ornate, gilded wooden frame hanging on an otherwise bare wall.

"You know Spielberg? *Schindler's List*?" he had asked while pointing at the frame. "You know he's Jewish?"

In the frame was a signed letter from Steven Spielberg thanking Mr. Stolarz for participating in his Holocaust documentary, *Shoah*. Mr. Stolarz had survived the Nazis and their death camps. When Spielberg's organization reached out to him he shared his painful personal story. He told me he rarely spoke about it but was willing to have it recorded for the documentary toward the mission of "Never Again."

He recounted his ordeal as a teenager ripped from his family and imprisoned in a concentration camp, never to be reunited with any of them. That's the story he told to the documentary producer and it was an honest account of his life. What he didn't share was that as much as losing his family in that horrific way broke his heart, what was almost as painful was being torn from his passion. He had wanted to be a rabbi. He wanted to study the Torah and serve others. He had begun his studies just before the war and was a few years into it when he was sent to the camp. By the time he was liberated, he was quite ill and near death. He somehow made it to America, where he knew no one and had to start his life anew.

He worked in a factory and made just enough to pay for food and shelter. He was alive and okay, but before he knew it, he was no longer young and didn't have money for school. He was never going to be a rabbi. He was heartbroken, happy to have survived but sad to have lost everything that mattered — his family and his calling. He didn't want to be bitter, but some days he couldn't help it. That's why being part of the *Shoah* documentary meant so much to him. If he couldn't devote his life to service and teaching, at least he'd leave a legacy larger than his single experience. With *Shoah*, his story would be woven into the stories of other survivors and as such he would be a small part of changing the world in a meaningful way. "Never again," he'd explain, "never again."

I looked forward to seeing him each week. He'd often share some personal philosophy and ask me what I thought, similar to what I imagined a conversation with a rabbi might entail. Sometimes he'd try to teach me something using a story about his family, but usually without too much detail. I wondered if he had trouble remembering the little things about his adolescence because the big ones were so insurmountable. Regardless of what we talked about, one thing was always the same. He'd take my hand, look directly into my eyes, smile, and thank me for visiting him. I know volunteering is something we do to help others, but sometimes I wonder if it isn't selfishly motivated, at least in my case. Seeing how happy he and the others were about these visits made me feel great. Was I helping them or myself?

After about a year of visiting him, he said, "Debby, why don't you wear any make-up? You're a pretty girl but even a pretty girl could use a little help."

"Mr. Stolarz," I replied somewhat sarcastically but smiling, "you're lucky I brush my teeth and show up at all at this hour. I have to get up really early to pick up the food and get it to everyone. Don't push your luck!" I didn't tell him it made me laugh to hear him use the word "girl" in reference to fifty-five-year-old me. But he was well into his eighties, so to him I was, in fact, a girl. My husband thought his lipstick request was a bit perverse but I understood why it mattered. He was old but he wanted to feel like a man for whom a woman would put on lipstick.

The week after he told me a "little lipstick" would make him "so happy," just before knocking on his door I applied a lovely shade of rose-colored lipstick. I must've been quite a sight wearing my lipstick along with my gray sweatshirt, baggy black sweatpants and sneakers.

"Debby," he smiled expansively after opening the door, "you look beautiful. A little mascara wouldn't hurt either."

I didn't get a chance to find out whether he'd have another

request after the mascara. When I arrived a few weeks later, having applied mascara and lipstick, he didn't answer when I knocked on his door. I returned to the lobby to inquire, worried he might have been hospitalized or worse.

"No," they explained, "he's okay but he doesn't live here anymore. He fell a few days ago and had to move to an assisted living facility." They didn't know which one.

I knew I'd miss him and hoped he had the presence of mind after his fall to take his *Shoah* letter with him.

I volunteered for a while longer but never met anyone quite as compelling as Mr. Stolarz. Sometimes when I apply make-up, I think, "Here's to you, Rabbi Stolarz." I hope that's not blasphemous.

~Deborah Drezon Carroll

24

You Can't Save Souls in Shiny Shoes

Vital lives are about action. You can't feel warmth unless you create it, can't feel delight until you play, can't know serendipity unless you risk.

~Joan Erickson

Before studying at university I took a year off to be a volunteer with The London City Mission. Of all the varied activities I helped in, it was the work with the homeless in Charing Cross that made the most lasting impression.

Twice a week we would go to the City Mission Hall, preparing soup and sandwiches for the homeless, sorting out the clothes store and then spending time with them — playing cards and dominoes or simply offering an ear as they recounted their stories and experiences.

The rapport I built up with them never left me, and two years later, whilst commuting, I had a chance encounter with a homeless man in Waterloo Station. He was a broken man — an alcoholic with a penetrating sadness in his eyes, who looked at least sixty even though he told me he was in his forties. After I bought him a coffee in one of the station's cafés, he showed me photographs of his family — three beautiful children and a loving wife — and he made a surprising request. He had been on the streets for three years, following the breakdown of his marriage due to his addiction. He had not heard from his children since they had emigrated to Canada to be with his ex-wife's extended family. His wallet was empty, save for the photographs and a Post-It note with a phone number — his wife's. He was too embarrassed to speak to them directly, but asked me if I would ring the number to see if it was still the correct one. "Just let my wife know that I am sorry and I think about the children every day," he pleaded.

Nervously I made the call and my heart sank, not because it was the wrong number, but because as soon as I explained the reason for the call, all I could hear on the other end was sobbing. I apologised for causing undue pain, and his wife replied, "No, thank you so very much. We have been so worried. Tell him we love him. The children miss him, and we just want him to get his life back on track. Maybe one day we can visit when he's in the right place." She gave me her address and, shaken, I returned to the stranger and shared the news. I made some more calls and got him in touch with the relevant agencies that could help him.

I have no idea what happened to him, whether he got it together, whether his story ended happily or in tragedy. But from that moment on I felt a personal connection to the homeless. I joined numerous charities wherever I lived, until in one place I found a complete lack of services: It was Poole in Dorset, the end of the train line, and consequently a place where numerous travellers ended up. A seaside town, it came with the false hope of summer work. And its wealth caused an even greater rich/poor divide than in Central London. Grants and government funding for the homeless were restricted at the time to areas considered to be in multiple deprivation, and in this town the poor were hidden, forgotten — assumed to be a tiny minority.

In fact, the town's policy was to hive the homeless off to the neighbouring town of Bournemouth. Many homeless people I spoke to resented this move, preferring to sleep rough in a town to which they felt a greater affinity. And so, I resolved to establish a coordinated voluntary approach to the problem.

At the time one church did a weekly soup run, and a group of nuns provided a twice-weekly lunch, but there was nothing the rest of the week and no joined-up work with other services to help them find longer-term solutions. Making connections with churches, charities and relevant health and social care departments, we started a nightly soup run under a bridge near the town centre. Expecting just the two or three folk we had encountered in the high street and the car parks, we were surprised at how quickly the word got about and the sheer numbers of needy people.

The council did an annual homelessness count, which had the previous year reported a single figure number of street homeless. Consequently, rough sleeping was not seen as a priority in their housing strategy. Speaking to the outreach team, I suggested the count be carried out by our volunteers and at a more suitable time, shifting it from nine o'clock (which was before many of them had even bedded down for the night) to after midnight. We were able to take the council worker to those hidden places we had found out about through the soup runs. The officially recorded numbers were over four times higher that year.

The work really began to blossom from that point on, and we soon established a drop-in centre and clothes bank. We provided a neutral place for people to link up with valuable services like housing officers, drug and alcohol support workers, adult educators and a health visitor.

It was often soul-destroying work; things rarely turned out the way we hoped. But in the midst of the heartache there were so many lighter moments. These very often came from the kindly yet sometimes-inappropriate donations people provided. Like the time we were donated a bulk load of uniforms. They turned out to be postal workers' outfits and we had to recall them for fear that one of our clients might start impersonating a postman. There was the bulk load of sweet Kendal Mint Cakes that were served alongside the soup. A great source of energy for long, cold days and nights, but some of our clients needed a dentist and not solid bars of sugar. Or the perfume, insensitively called "Tramp." Best of all were the potted plants that our volunteers ended up placing besides the sleeping bags of some clients, in stairwells, on derelict shop porches, and under the bridge.

A touch of home on a harsh pavement.

Of all the gifts that the homeless received, it was the offer of friendship, a shoulder to cry on, and a non-judgmental ear that touched them the most. Building up trust was essential if they were to accept our help. The day centre and the soup run were theirs. We broke the divide between them and us, without compromising professional boundaries. We gave them a place around the table alongside the top brass of council officialdom in their strategy and planning meetings. Their views came to be heard, and made a difference.

I moved to the North twelve years ago, where I continue to volunteer. I am a board member for my local council's social housing provider, where I constantly remind the directors to always consider the most vulnerable in their policies and procedures.

To this day, something the man said to me in that station café shapes the way I approach volunteering: "You can't save souls in shiny shoes."

~Paul Driscoll

25

Brand-New Socks

If there is to be any peace it will come through being, not having.
~Henry Miller

I spent two weeks in 2007 as a seminary student at Ghost Ranch in Santa Fe, completing a course in transcultural ministry. We'd been invited to join a group of people who took water and breakfast to a local park where day laborers gathered, hoping to be chosen for work. We pulled up and let down the tailgate of the truck carrying the bottles of water and the rolls we handed out to the immigrant men who gathered around us. My classmates and I spoke with the men, hoping to learn more about their stories. My friend Kim and I ended up in conversation with a Mexican man in his forties named Natal, handsome with his long black hair. He wore a T-shirt and faded jeans. Next to him, on the low wall where he sat, rested a large backpack and a bedroll.

Natal spoke very little English and we spoke even less Spanish. Nonetheless, we had a wonderful conversation, ranging from the difficulty of finding work to artwork, from Santa Fe history to Natal's "beautiful home," as he described it. As we sat under the protection of the Virgin of Guadalupe, whose image was carved into the metal roof of the gazebo so that her shadow appeared on the concrete floor when the sun shone through, Natal told us of his travels in search of work. He had traveled all over the U.S. and Canada, taking jobs where he found them, meeting people, and seeing the sights. He told us he'd especially loved Oregon.

He was filled with praise, too, for the beauty of the Sangre de Cristo Mountains outside Santa Fe and for all the history in the town. We agreed that the area was stunning. He grinned and told us it was important to appreciate beauty. Then, he invited us to visit him in his home in the mountains. When we demurred, Natal assured us that it was only a twenty-minute walk from the park. He wanted to show us the beauty of the trees and have us smell the freshness in the mountains. He wanted to be a good host.

Natal introduced us to some of the men in the park. They told stories about their lives and asked us about ours. I felt such an awareness of my own privilege as the conversation proceeded. I had engaged in a gratitude practice for years, writing in a journal each night about the things for which I was grateful. However, this experience was really a wake-up call for me, a reminder that I could never be grateful enough for what I had.

We continued to talk and it became clear that Natal's "home" was a clearing under the trees. His bed was the bedroll he carried with him, spread on the ground under the starlight. He loved it there and wanted to share it with us. We declined, telling him that we were honored by the invitation, but that our classes would keep us too busy to make the trip. He told us that we could find him in this park any morning and that, if we found the time, we could come for a visit anytime. I was very touched by the appreciation in this homeless man's voice for his "beautiful home," and sad that he didn't have an actual home. It made me think about all the faults I was always finding with my own home, a 1923 bungalow with central heat and hot water in a suburb of Cleveland. What a whiner I was!

Natal's love of his "home" was in sharp contrast to my griping about the water in my pipes not heating up fast enough, about my bedroom ceiling being too low, about not having central air conditioning, about my lack of a fenced yard. What a brat I was!

If I was amazed by his appreciation for everything he had, I was completely floored by what happened next. I have always hated socks and it was a warm June day, so I was wearing palm tree–printed sneakers with no socks. In the midst of conversation, Natal noticed that I had no socks on my feet. He pointed and asked if I needed socks. I looked at my feet as though they had just grown there. He commented that I wasn't wearing socks and that I must need socks. I quickly told him that, no, no, I didn't need socks. He looked a bit offended, opened his backpack, pulled out a package of socks, and showed me. He assured me that they were clean socks, brand-new.

He thought I felt his socks weren't good enough for me, so he wanted me to know they had never been worn by anyone. Brand-new! Good enough! I told him I was honored he would give me his socks but that I truly disliked wearing socks. Natal thought I was crazy, telling one of his companions in rapid-fire Spanish that I was a *loca*. However, he accepted that I wasn't disturbed by the idea of wearing his socks; I just didn't want any socks at all.

What he didn't know was that I was absolutely astonished, touched and humbled, almost to the point of tears. This man who had so very little, the sum total of his possessions a backpack and a bedroll, was offering me his brand-new socks. Here I was, a minister-in-training, going along to the park to help these poor men who had so little. There Natal was, ministering to me, with an open heart and an open backpack. I have never forgotten his appreciation for the world or his generosity. We volunteers sometimes think we are the only ones with something to give. Let's not forget that we are never the only ones with something to give — and many times, when we reach out to help others, we receive more than we give. What a blessing for us.

~Daria Schaffnit

26

Through the Looking Glass

We can only be said to be alive in those moments when our hearts are conscious of our treasures.

~Thornton Wilder

"You have pretty hair." The woman sitting to my side on the old trailer porch, made of weatherworn wood and surrounded by clutter, squinted up at me.

I touched a few of the stray ends sticking out from beneath a baseball cap. "Oh, thanks. It looks better without the cap."

She nodded, her own hair graying, and her eyes tired. Fifty-eight. Only eight years older than I, although I might have guessed older.

For the past four days I'd forfeited my usual morning hair ritual. Instead, I woke, combed out the matted mess I'd slept on, and stuck a baseball cap over the top of my head... the only grooming necessary for a day's labor in the rural coal-mining county where I planned to spend a full week.

Working on homes in Appalachia took me as far away from my comfort zone as I could go. From others who'd done this volunteer work before me, I understood they slept on air mattresses in humid gyms, worked in the scorching summer sun and ate whatever could be provided on the limited budget the organization was able to provide... with no second helpings, either. I heard it wasn't uncommon to find large spiders or snakes while crawling under a trailer to do plumbing work or some other repair.

Let's face it, sleeping in anything less than a decent hotel wasn't really my thing. But that year an urge to experience all these inconveniences wouldn't go away. And every person who ever went said they'd definitely do it again.

So I went. My group was assigned to fix a trailer that needed aluminum siding and other repairs. The first few days, we worked quietly on our tasks. We installed an underlayment on the house exterior, learned how to use the electric saw, measured and hammered pieces of siding that fit together like a large jigsaw puzzle. The homeowners treated us kindly; they were a couple who suffered from health issues, making it hard to earn a living.

Initially, it was awkward. My cheeks hurt from smiling too much, probably a way to cope with the discomfort of facing another person's poverty.

Their kindness didn't go unnoticed. Each day by noon we were all sweating from the humid August heat. The woman would invite us inside to cool down in front of the fan. She offered us cold drinks and snacks, but we always brought our own lunches and left the remaining sandwiches with her.

One day, while we enjoyed our noon cool-down inside the house, I walked over to study some photographs on the hallway wall.

The woman joined me. "Oh, those are my grandkids. And that one," she pointed to a pretty young woman. "That's my daughter."

Her eyes brightened as she shared details. Her parents' wedding photo. The latest grandchild. A nephew. I followed her back to the living room, her steps slow, her head bent as she stared at the carpet. Before we neared the others, she lifted her head and turned to me. Tears filled her eyes and her voice cracked. "You know, I never believed I'd need the kind of help that you people are bringing me."

Tears immediately welled in my own eyes and I blinked to stop them. My response stalled, because admitting I saw her struggle didn't feel right. Finally, I found words that felt right. I put my arm around her shoulders and gave her a hug. "We're happy to do this."

Nobody chooses to be poor. Health issues, losing a job, the death of a primary wage earner—any one of these can cause a monumental change in the way someone lives.

Little things I'd noticed all week took on clarity: Broken appliances and rusty chairs belonged in a junkyard, not sitting on someone's property. Those items remained because it costs money to get rid of them. Overgrown weeds around the house's exterior and small pieces of discarded trash served as a reminder that being poor is depressing, making it easy to lose interest in maintaining your surroundings.

The day we were scheduled to leave a few of us sat on the porch again, talking with the woman. Being there now felt comfortable, because the people who were once strangers had become friends.

She touched my arm. "What do you use on your skin? It's so nice."

"Thanks. I just wash it, put on a little cream." I rattled off the name of a skin care product, not super expensive in my world, but not plain soap either.

"And your teeth. They're so nice, too. Straight, white."

I thanked her, but her words made me think about my appearance. Not a day goes by that I don't find something wrong when I look in the mirror.

My hair isn't quite right today.

My face looks fat.

Why are my eyes so puffy?

Is my nose growing as I get older?

The list goes on. But her kind words showed me a blessing I normally don't see in the midst of complaining. How I've had great dental care my entire life, a healthy diet filled with fruits and vegetables, and the use of some fine skin care products. Trips to the beauty shop for a nice haircut every six or seven weeks are well within my household budget, and even money for good hair care products.

Now, when I look in the mirror and feel the urge to complain, I'm reminded of my week sweating in the hot southern sun and the words of a very wise woman who'd fallen on hard times. A week when I got as much as I gave. And, on occasion, I still make the occasional complaint, but I'll never forget that the view in the looking glass can change depending on where you're standing.

~Sharon Struth

27

A Very Special Special Olympian

*Most of the important things in the world have been
accomplished by people who have kept on trying when there
seemed to be no hope at all.*
~Dale Carnegie

The professor was searching for student volunteers for a Special Olympics event. As the sign-up sheet went up and down the rows I started to come up with my excuses. Maybe it was the distance to the college where the event was to take place, or the early hour that volunteers had to report for duty. Whatever the reasons that made me hesitate, I am thankful to this day that I ended up volunteering. If I had missed this event I would have missed one of the most unforgettable moments that I have ever witnessed.

I arrived at the volunteer tent bright and early. My assignment was simple. I was to stand at the finish line and wait until the event was over, then take the results to the announcing booth. Standing at the finish line, I was able to witness many amazing efforts and close races. I was most impressed by the effort each athlete put into his or her event. What also impressed me was the sincere joy each athlete expressed while participating. Sometimes the joy of participating in a sporting event can get lost in the intense competition of winning and losing.

Then a miraculous moment happened right before my eyes. A group of athletes were lined up to run a short sprint. One of them was in a wheelchair, a little girl with a huge smile wearing bright bows in her hair. Her smile filled the stadium that day. I couldn't help but smile back at her.

The gun sounded. They were off. Runners sped up the track with all their might. My eyes searched for the little girl with the bright bows. There she was, pumping her arms with every ounce of energy she had. Her efforts were getting little result, but that did not stop her. I noticed as she got closer that she also had an injured arm. But that did not stop this bright star. The race was long over but the young athlete kept pumping her arms. The crowd of spectators focused on her. They started to cheer passionately for this amazing girl. That made her pump her arms even harder!

As she neared the finish line the noise of the crowd was thunderous. There I stood cheering, with tears falling down my cheeks and chills going up my spine. I wish you could have been there to hear the roar as she passed the finish line.

After all these years, I can still hear those cheers. I wish I could thank that remarkable athlete for what her efforts taught this unmotivated college guy. I grew up a lot that day because of the tenacity of that little girl in the wheelchair. I was reminded that day of a verse from the book of Ecclesiastes that states, "Whatever you do, do it with all your might."

I wasn't making the most of the abilities and talents so graciously bestowed upon me, so whenever I get that lazy bug that buzzes in and out of my life, I remember the heroic athlete with the bows in her hair and the joy in her heart.

~Edward Tooley

28

Never Too Late

Being stubborn can be a good thing. Being stubborn can be a
bad thing. It just depends on how you use it.
~Willie Aimes

I stood at the end of a long hallway in the rehab unit of a local nursing home. A nurse warned me — a middle-schooler — that Howard, the stroke patient in the room to the left, was cranky and rude on a good day. On a bad day, I could expect to be sworn at. I went ahead and invited Howard to join us for our recreation program that afternoon. He replied with angry, unkind words telling me to never come back.

I've always appreciated a challenge. Howard didn't break my heart like sweet Mrs. Quattlebaum, who told me each day that her son would be in soon to visit; her son never came. In a place full of hard stories, end-of-life stories, stories of loss and leaving, Howard's story became a welcome relief. I didn't feel pity or sadness when I walked into Howard's room. I was livid.

He was relatively young in comparison to the other residents, maybe in his early fifties or a bit younger. He had been a wealthy and successful business executive in New York City, and he had chosen a rehab center a hundred miles away so that none of his former peers could see the shell of a man he'd become. Instead of diving in to physical and occupational therapy, he refused to go.

When I first met Howard, I was told that he never got out of his hospital gown into his own clothes, even though the therapists and nurses urged him to. Each time I visited him in the early days, he would be in bed, in a gown, unkempt.

I spent my summer days at the center, helping residents get to recreation programs, passing out mail, reading letters to the many residents with vision trouble, organizing an entire closet of recorded books from the local society for the blind. After I met Howard, I decided to invite him to the recreation program every single day, regardless of his response.

I had a grandmother who also had suffered a stroke, but she didn't have the positive prognosis that Howard had. I was angry that he was willing to throw his life away without even trying. The therapists told me again and again that if Howard would just come to therapy, he would recover almost all of the functions he had lost in his stroke. So each day I braved Howard's verbal onslaught and invited him to do puzzles and play bingo.

As the therapists and nurses saw me persevere with Howard, they asked me to bring him to his therapy appointments. He wasn't exactly warm but he usually held back his verbal barrage and curtly told me, "No," he did not want to go to physical therapy. One day, after many attempts, Howard finally said, "Yes."

Howard started warming up to me, telling me pieces of his story. He started shaving and getting into brightly colored tracksuits. He began to clean up after meals so that the crumbs and bits of egg no longer speckled his chin and chest. He told me about his life in New York and the shame that drove him far up the coast, away from those who knew him as a powerful man. Looking back on it from an adult perspective, I'm sure confiding in a twelve-year-old candy striper was safer and easier than talking with any of the adults at the center. Perhaps that was why my persistence finally bore fruit.

Howard shared how he had never married. He talked about his niece, whom he loved very much. He hadn't been in touch with her since his stroke. After a lot of insistence on my part, he dictated a letter that I happily mailed to her. Soon she was writing back and eventually making plans to visit.

I remember the day he was waiting for me with a new photograph resting in his hands, eager to show me the portrait his niece had sent. Howard also began to contact former friends and colleagues who had wondered where he was. The last day of my work there that summer, Howard was sitting in his wheelchair in the hallway near the nurse's station, standing out in his bright red tracksuit, cheerful and smiling and ready to greet me when I arrived. He was no longer a prisoner in his room at the end of the hall, no longer the resident that everyone was afraid of.

I don't know who had a greater impact on the other: me with irritating persistence asking Howard to join life again and stop wallowing in self-pity or him teaching me a profound lesson — it's never too late to start again. Howard wasted months of his life after his stroke, refusing any help offered to him, ignoring the pleas of medical professionals assuring him that he could live, and live well, if he would work hard at his recovery. Somehow, in the face of a chubby and stubborn seventh-grader who had signed up as a volunteer in response to her own grandmother's stroke, Howard met his match and made significant changes.

Labor Day came and school started; my afternoons at the center were over for the year. When I returned months later to visit, Howard's room had a new name on the door. The director of the recreation program told me that he had left the center, able to live on his own again. It really wasn't too late to have a fresh start.

~Elizabeth Peterson

Art Appreciation

Every child is an artist. The problem is how to remain an artist
once we grow up.
~Pablo Picasso

"Look at this! MaryLou can't even draw a straight line." The art teacher held up my paper for the whole class to see and spoke loudly as he poked fun at my attempt to sketch a landscape in perspective. That mortifying experience made me decide I hated art.

Later in junior high, when art class became optional, I opted out. In high school I chose music classes rather than art classes. I eventually became a teacher and freelance writer, but for many years had as little as possible to do with the art world.

During the first months of my retirement I saw an advertisement for volunteers to act as tour guides for children visiting our city's art gallery. The retirement advice books I'd read said this was the time to try something completely outside your comfort zone. Volunteering at an art gallery certainly fit into that category for me. I sent in my application.

Because of my experience as a teacher they let me train for the job, and in a few months I became a certified volunteer.

I've volunteered on nearly a hundred tours now. I'm always inspired by the delightful and imaginative responses to art by the children I shepherd around the galleries. I've learned that if I affirm and express interest in kids' ideas they grow more confident about responding in a personal way to the art they see. I help with workshops in printmaking, painting and collage. I've discovered by praising children's efforts at creating their own art that I can help them feel like they are real artists. I want them to love art and not have the kind of negative experience I did.

I've had the chance to give tours to exchange students from Japan. I've guided a group of teens from all across Canada who were attending a national youth conference in our city. I've spent a day with twenty-four three-year-olds from a nursery school. I got twenty-four hugs after we'd explored the galleries together and they'd created their own paintings. I've done tours for gifted students and for children with learning and behavioral challenges. I've given tours to families and school classes, day camps and daycares.

I love hearing children's positive comments and good questions as we tour the art gallery:

"This is so much fun."

"Why does that artist use the color blue so much?"

"An art gallery is an awesome place."

"Why is that statue naked?"

"This is the best field trip I've every been on."

"Is a photograph art?"

"I think I could draw like that."

In the process of watching so many young people discover the joy of art, my love and appreciation for art has grown immeasurably. I've written posts about art exhibits on my blog that have attracted hundreds of readers. One of my blog posts was published in a professional art journal. I've even taken online courses in art education from the Museum of Modern Art in New York.

Now whenever my husband and I travel to a new city he knows we will need to set some time aside for a visit to an art gallery. I've written a resource book for tour guides, providing tips on how to approach certain kinds of art with children. But most astonishing of all, I've decided I'm ready to be an artist myself. I'm taking drawing lessons!

Being an art gallery volunteer has enriched my life and changed my attitude towards art. I wish my old art teacher were still alive so I could let him know that I've turned into an art lover.

~MaryLou Driedger

30

The Old Woman in a Shoe

Education is not preparation for life; education is life itself.
~John Dewey

was riding a New York City bus, scanning the advertisements above its windows, when a special request caught my eye. Volunteers were needed for a brand-new educational initiative in inner-city schools to help underprivileged students.

I went to an introductory meeting. Various positions were available. I didn't seem to fit anywhere, since I had no experience in education.

The director was adamant. "Let me think," she said. "No way I'm going to let an able, willing volunteer walk. I will find something for you." And so she did.

I had submitted extensive personal and family information and references. When we initially met, the director commented on the excellent colleges that my two children attended. I mentioned how convoluted the entire admissions process had been, and based on that, we found my fit.

There was a small experimental "pocket" high school in mid-Manhattan with a number of immigrant children and students who were born in the U.S. of immigrant parents. These kids would become the first generation in their families to attend college, but many of their parents didn't speak English and had no experience with the college admissions process. That's where I fit—I could help the students choose schools and wend their way through the application process.

On day one I was ensconced in a tiny corner of someone else's office and twenty-seven students lined up to see me. A nursery rhyme popped into my head. I felt like the old woman in a shoe who "had so many children she didn't know what to do...." My one-day-per-week of volunteering suddenly jumped to two!

The next few months were hectic. I wasn't just guiding the students—who by term's end numbered over fifty—I was also formulating new protocol. But more than that, I was becoming aware of the special needs and challenges affecting inner-city students' abilities to navigate the college admissions process.

These kids had no quiet place in their tiny apartments to complete applications. Many of them worked full-time jobs. They didn't have the money for the application fees, and they needed help filling out the forms to get the fees waived. They didn't have money for postage. They couldn't afford college visits, so their choices were based solely upon photos and information in brochures. They would need financial aid and jobs wherever they went. The list went on and on.

This scenario was so far removed from the rituals of private prep classes, independent college advisors, and school visits with which I was familiar that I often worried if any of my students would actually be accepted. I began to covet the training "real" college advisers had, even though I had a growing understanding of my students' difficulties, at times detailed in truly harrowing application essays.

Then there were cultural and religious issues—fathers who refused to allow highly qualified daughters to attend college; parents who were afraid to let children enroll in out-of-town schools; parents who insisted on same-sex schools; parents who felt higher education was unnecessary because no one in their extended families had ever attended. I started having meetings with parents, with their children translating. I never imagined all the variables in this volunteer position. But I learned so much—about different lifestyles, cultures, and religions; economic hardship; why families emigrated; how they adapted; how U.S. systems both helped and hindered them.

We finally got all the applications in and the waiting began. As early decision acceptances came in, the entire school started buzzing. Seniors who hadn't planned on college started making appointments to see me. Then juniors started visiting. It was terrific! I was just as thrilled with each student's acceptance, and just as sad with each rejection, as when my own children received their notifications. I had literally become that nursery rhyme's old woman in a shoe with many, many children.

A poster was hung in a hallway listing the students' names and schools as they got their acceptance letters. A few were accepted to two or three schools. Incredibly, every single student who applied was accepted somewhere. I was ecstatic.

But there was a new worry about "my kids." Most had never left home, or even been out of the city. Would they be able to adjust to their new surroundings, far away, without family or friends? Unbelievably, only one freshman didn't make it through her first term.

The following semester, before Christmas, a few college freshmen returned to the school to speak to the new senior class. And so a tradition was established: each year the college students would return and share their experiences with their peers.

In the end, though, I do believe that I was the one who benefitted the most. I became more patient, more aware, more understanding, more tolerant. This "old woman" of nursery rhyme fame, with "so many children," learned never to question anyone, their motives or their actions unless I had first, personally, walked in their shoes.

~Marsha Warren Mittman

31

A Shaky Beginning

Plant flowers in others' gardens and your life becomes a
bouquet!
~Author Unknown

To this day I can recall my dry throat as I put a hesitant hand on the door handle of that plant nursery. Gosh, how I hated asking for things, but flowers and greenery for the senior housing patio area were desperately needed. I had volunteered, given the seniors my word and made it my mission, so I was determined to overcome my shyness and ask for a donation of plants. The little plot of land where the residents gathered to chat and get some sun was just hard-packed dirt. Red geraniums and cheery yellow mums would brighten the garden, but there was no money in the budget for little extras like that. My grandmother had lived there until she had passed away the prior year, and now my aunt resided in the front building. I often dropped by to visit with her and some of Gram's friends. That's how I had become aware of the pathetic patch of dirt that should have been a flowerbed.

I was in my twenties and struggling, and my salary at the travel agency didn't go very far. The reality was they mostly paid me in travel. I promised my aunt and the other ladies that I'd get some flowers donated to them, but I was terrible at that kind of thing. The night before I planned to visit the nursery, I hardly slept.

I remember how the handle of the door grew warm under my

hand as I stood gathering the courage to open it. I don't actually know how long I was out there, but I know I was frozen in place for a while. Finally another customer came behind me and I had no choice. A pleasant little bell rang as we stepped inside the cheerful greenhouse. We were greeted by the earthy smell of soil and green growing things mixed with the sweet aroma of gardenias that were shelved by the entryway. There were wind chimes gently swaying among the hanging plants, and rows of painted pots and plant stands. With such a large garden out back, surely they could spare a few plants. I was even willing to take the scraggly ones and nurse them back to health. The warm air in the room made me a bit dizzy. I fanned my face as I looked around.

"Can I help you?"

I turned to see a tall good-looking man wearing a gardening apron. He had a dirt smudge on his cheek and a trowel in his hand.

"Yes," I stammered. "I'm looking for the owner, Rita Stanley."

"I'm Rita's son, Mitch." He held out his hand but quickly drew it back when he realized he was wearing gardening gloves.

I wasn't ready to deal with a handsome man. Or any man. I thought I would be talking to, or rather pleading with, an older woman. That was the only thing that made my feet move through the door. The back of my neck began to feel clammy and I knew my face was flushed.

"I'll come back when she's here," I said, inching backwards, gauging how far the door was from where we were standing.

He studied me as I hopped from foot to foot and finally said, "If you're looking for work, I'm afraid we're not hiring."

"Oh, no, I'm not looking to work here." It must have been the way I said it because he looked a bit taken aback. Maybe I had insulted him. I don't know, but after a lot of stammering on my part and an awkward gesture toward the rows of blooms I said, "But if I were, this would be a wonderful place to work. I was… I just…" I looked up at him and was chagrined to see that he seemed amused. He had a grin on his face as he leaned against the counter, arms crossed, waiting me out.

Words came out of my mouth, gunshot fast, before I could stop them. "Look, my grandma lives in the senior housing property." No, that was wrong. I backtracked. "I mean she used to, she doesn't anymore, but my aunt does. And I was thinking… you know, the weather is really nice out and…"

"Yes, that's true," he said.

"And the seniors like to sit outdoors on a nice day."

"Also true." He had shiny dark hair that hung over his forehead. I tried not to stare. I looked up at the ceiling so I wouldn't lose my nerve. Why was this so hard for me?

"And there is this little plot of land there that's bare."

He nodded. "I see."

"A few flowers would really brighten it up so I thought I would…"

He held up his hand. "I get it. You want to fix it up with some plants and flowers."

I sagged with relief. "Yes."

"Well, come out back." He indicated a set of glass doors with his gloved hand. "We have a lot of annuals on sale."

At those words my heart sank. All that and it wasn't the thing I had come for. "Oh, thank you, but I was hoping to, you know, get some flowers… donated." That last word was barely audible but I got it out. A few beats passed as I stared down at the floor. When I finally looked up he was grinning at me. "I can tell you don't solicit flowers for a living."

"Well, that's pretty obvious, don't you think?"

His smile got wider as I confessed, "I just hate asking for things, I'm terrible at it." I tucked a strand of hair behind my ear and hoped he didn't see the tremble in my hand.

"You're not so terrible. I think you're sweet. We'd be happy to put some flowers in the senior garden."

"You would?" I had done it! I almost did a little happy jig, but caught myself in time. "Thank you so much," I managed to croak out.

"Come on, I'll help you pick out some low maintenance ones."

I started to follow him but he stopped abruptly in the middle of the garden door. "But there's a condition."

Uh oh, I thought. Now what?

"After I deliver these flowers, you have to let me help you plant them, and then go for coffee with me."

I smiled and began to relax for the first time since I came into the nursery. Now that was something I wouldn't be terrible at!

After that I managed to get donations for the senior center for Christmas that year. That started me on a life of volunteering. I'm now an officer in the local chapter of the Lions Clubs International. Once you experience the pleasure of helping others your life becomes richer, your heart becomes lighter, and you find hope in the goodness of the world.

~Jody E. Lebel

Hookers

A person without a sense of humor is like a wagon without springs — jolted by every pebble in the road.
~Henry Ward Beecher

My wife is the volunteer coordinator for our local police department. One of her tasks is to arrange for citizens to tour the police department. These tours are extremely popular, especially with seniors, Scouts and special needs groups. My wife and her volunteers do a tremendous job making these tours interesting, utilizing canine officers and even letting people examine the jail cells, unless they happen to be occupied. But every now and then my wife receives a comment that makes her shake her head. She recently took a call from an irate mom. The conversation went like this:

Ring...ring....

"How may I help you?"

"Are YOU the volunteer coordinator for the police department, the one responsible for tours?"

"Yes."

"Good. I want to register a complaint. I'm very upset about what happened when my six-year-old son toured your building with his Cub Scout troop last Thursday."

"I participated in that tour and remember it well. What seems to be the problem?"

"Nothing, unless you think it appropriate to expose small children to the harsh realities of life."

"I'm sorry, but I don't know what you're talking about. What's your son's name and what does he look like?"

"He has blond hair, blue eyes, and his name is Donny."

"Did something on the tour upset Donny?"

"No. Something on the tour upset ME! How dare you bring impressionable children into contact with — hookers! What were you people thinking?"

My wife was nonplussed for a moment, but eventually managed to spit out, "Let me assure you that your child was not exposed to hookers. We don't bring visitors into the cells if they're occupied."

"So you're saying my Donny is a liar when he says an officer let him play with hookers?"

A pause. "Does Donny wear Spiderman shoes?"

"As a matter of fact he does."

My wife started laughing.

"I hardly think this is something to laugh at."

My wife did her best to compose herself. "I remember Donny. And yes, he did have fun playing with hookers. But not in the way you're thinking. Donny was fascinated with the hookers hanging from an officer's work belt. Most people call them 'handcuffs' but little Donny referred to them as hookers because they hook hands together."

Silence on the phone.

Finally, "Well, keep up the good work."

~Stephen Hayes

Chapter 4

Volunteering & Giving Back

The Spirit of Christmas

33

Where Do Those Toys Go?

We make a living by what we get. We make a life by what we give.
~Winston Churchill

I always wondered where the toys go. Those toys collected for Toys for Tots — where do they go? Are they whisked immediately to the North Pole and entered into inventory at Santa's workshop? Do the elves collect them, wrap them and take them to the UPS Store to send them to families around the world?

My question was answered this past December when my family and I volunteered with United Way of Martin County in Florida. I'm sure my eyes were as wide as a child's on Christmas morning when we entered a building at the fairgrounds and saw thousands of toys and games lined up, along with hundreds of bikes and helmets.

For years, a core group of volunteers have led this massive Christmas effort to make sure that families have the opportunity to give to their own children, just like you and I give to our children. When I asked the lead volunteer why she does this year after year, tears welled up in her eyes. She shared a story about a shopping trip at Walmart when a family that received toys from the Toys for Tots drive had recognized her. That mother told the volunteer how special their Christmas was and shared that it was only possible because of the toys they got from the drive.

The volunteer understands hard times herself. She and her family had some difficulties in the past. The kindness she received during those months helped her family get back on their feet, and volunteering to bring Christmas to others was her way of paying it forward. I realized that the volunteers all had their own stories, which were just as powerful as those of the families they were serving.

Every family that came to the fairgrounds to pick out Christmas presents had gone through a big process just to get there. They had to fill out an application before they were approved and assigned a time to show up. The parents needed to request time off from work to make the appointment. This happened 3,000 times. That was the number of families that made their children's Christmas wishes come true with the help of Toys for Tots and United Way of Martin County.

You may wonder, like I did, how they managed to deliver Christmas to so many families in just forty-eight hours. Their system was flawless. They started by dividing the toys into boy and girl categories. Then the toys were organized by age. Massive tables were covered with unwrapped toys, allowing the families to see what they could get for their children. Toys continued to flow in, and the numbers continued to be crunched. Using simple math, they took the applicants they had and divided the toys by the needs listed. This generated a number that the shopping volunteers could fulfill. The majority of the gifts were for young children; hence, the day of the event each child was allowed three small gifts, one major gift, and every half hour there was a drawing for a new bike and helmet.

Our daughter Michelle shared with me that they were instructed to spend as much time shopping with their clients as possible. This was the one time that the family could shop for their children and not have to worry about the cost. Michelle told me about one mom she worked with, both speaking Spanish, as they laughed and worked their way down the packed tables of toys. She said the mom was so careful picking out toys for her three small children that it took almost an hour to get through the process. When they were checking out her full cart, the mom had a complete breakdown. She hugged and thanked my daughter and all the volunteers for showing her compassion and kindness through this difficult time.

Our son John had a similar experience. His shopper was lucky enough to have won a bike and helmet. If you won the bike raffle, you had to give back the "major" gift that you had selected. This system is really fair. But John's shopper took it to a new level. Not only did she give back the major gift that she had chosen for her child, but she announced that she was giving the bike to a family down the street that had a son with no toys. The bike would be a perfect gift for him. This was the most touching story. It didn't matter how much she and her family were in need, she was sharing her win with the family down the street. How selfless!

During Christmastime, when we focus on our families and ourselves, I truly enjoyed giving to someone else. This organization has me hooked, and I know our family will be back next year to help out. I learned a few things along the way. It is respectful to buy Barbie dolls that look like the families in your community. Moms were asking for dolls with dark complexions. I learned that Toys for Tots also serves a teenage group, and they had the least amount of toys, mostly cologne for the boys and nail polish for the girls. I will shop differently next year to help that group of kids. I learned how dedicated the volunteers are to this particular project and after spending the day with them, I understood why.

If you have never volunteered at a Christmas event or a soup kitchen, I encourage you to give it a try. I have never been so fulfilled and wrapped in the Christmas spirit as I was that day.

~Carrie Morgridge

34

Live Every Minute, Love Every Second

The best way to cheer yourself up is to try to cheer somebody else up.
~Mark Twain

When my daughter Audra was fifteen, her best childhood friend lost her fight with leukemia. My husband and I watched as Audra entered one of the darkest seasons in her life. My heart felt like it was being torn out as I sat helplessly watching her navigate the tidal wave of grief.

The first thing we noticed is that she began stifling anything that brought her joy; her reasoning was that her friend Ryleigh could never have fun again, so she shouldn't either. She withdrew from her normal activities and friends and spent most of her time in her bedroom. She was overwhelmed with guilt that she was still alive and her friend wasn't. She was also deeply remorseful for being too afraid to go to the hospital when she was given the opportunity to say goodbye to Ryleigh.

A month after the funeral, I received an e-mail from our local chapter of the American Childhood Cancer Organization asking for volunteers for their annual Christmas party. It was something our family normally would have jumped to volunteer for, but this year I wasn't sure if the timing was right. Within days, I received two more invitations and could see that they were desperate for volunteers, so I signed us up.

The party was designed to celebrate childhood cancer patients, survivors and their families. It was an entire day of food, gifts, crafts and dancing.

The day of the event we all walked into the venue tentatively, but Audra was the most reluctant and on the verge of tears when we entered the room with all the bald and pale kids. She stood in the background observing and pouting. She was angry with me for making her face these sick kids and she was making sure I knew it.

There were many volunteers that day who handed out presents to the kids, led group games and served food and drinks, but the special surprise at this party were the many costumed characters that roamed the room bringing smiles to the kids' faces.

Halfway through the event the party coordinator came to my daughter, a little frantic. The volunteer that was supposed to dress in the cuddly panda costume had gotten sick and couldn't come, so she asked my daughter to put on a giant panda costume and visit with the kids. With a little coaxing, Audra agreed, and I watched in awe as that amazing costume transformed her. She walked out of the room a sulky teenager and walked back in with the enthusiasm of a college mascot.

As a panda, Audra went from table to table inviting the children onto the dance floor. She coaxed the shy ones and jumped up and down cheering for the excited ones. When she made it to the dance floor the DJ began playing the funky chicken song and she led the whole group of chicken-dancing kids.

She danced for hours with the kids. The children were mesmerized by the giant panda and took turns holding Audra's hand while they danced. A sea of bald heads and ones with newly grown hair surrounded the panda.

As everything was winding down and the parents were gathering their sugar-filled Christmas miracles, one little girl came running back up to Audra. She had a princess crown atop her bald head and fake jewels dangling from her ears and neck. Her big brown eyes were sparkling with delight as she gestured for the panda to bend down to her. Audra squatted down to her new friend's height and the little girl wrapped her arms around her, squeezing her tight, and said "I love you, Panda."

Our family stood watching this healing moment and feeling so grateful that Audra was able to experience something so special. All of us felt like something big had happened for her—and it had. Hiding behind the costume allowed her to let loose and have fun with the kids. She watched as the sick children forgot their medical problems and played like normal children again.

It was while in the costume that something clicked for Audra. She realized her friend would have wanted her to live—and live fully!

After the party, Audra began volunteering for other childhood cancer events, and she has truly enjoyed each chance she's gotten to help the kids. With Audra's insistence, we have made volunteering for the Christmas party an annual tradition.

Ryleigh's motto was "Live every minute, love every second!" Audra has embraced that now, and we know Ryleigh would be pleased.

~Jennie Bradstreet

35

Christmas Eve Service

*Gratitude can transform common days into thanksgivings, turn
routine jobs into joy, and change ordinary opportunities into
blessings.*
~William Arthur Ward

"Merry Christmas!" Annie called out as soon as I
entered the Fellowship Hall. When she saw the
cookies I carried, she angled her head toward the
kitchen. "You can drop those off with Gary."

Every church, synagogue or house of worship has an Annie
and Gary. They're the couple who help without being asked, step
forward when others step back, and make congregational life run
smoothly. But there's a twist to Annie and Gary's volunteering: Annie
chairs committees, organizes fundraisers and takes center stage.
Just as warm, but quieter, Gary supervises coffee hour and washes
dishes after potlucks. This might be common among my peers, but
not in the previous generation. I wondered—did Gary mind doing
"domestic" chores?

"I like being back here," he said, standing at the oversized kitchen
sink. Wearing a chef's apron, he rinsed and loaded dirty cups and
plates onto racks and ran them through the church's heavy-duty
commercial dishwasher. Sleeves rolled up, hands soapy, face pink
from the steamy hot water, Gary seemed happy. "This is my calling.
This is the best way I know of serving people. The work is spiritual,

especially when there's a full congregation worshiping upstairs and you're all alone down here."

He made it sound so easy and serene, but it wasn't. Week after week, Gary handled the many tasks associated with coffee hour: operating the industrial-sized coffee machine, laying out the snacks for kids and adults, setting up tables and chairs so people could linger after the service—a service Gary rarely got to attend in its entirety. He either came in late, slipped out early, or never made it upstairs at all.

Until I got to know Gary I took his labors for granted. Like other parents with young children, I volunteered in Sunday school and felt that was enough. As my girls got older and could manage for themselves, I began helping out with coffee hour. Eventually I learned my way around the kitchen and grew to enjoy the quiet Gary talked about. Missing a service now and then was fine, but not Christmas. Never Christmas. I couldn't imagine missing a Christmas Eve service.

Except the reception following Christmas Eve service was the church's most crucial coffee-hour event. Attendance doubled, and the tradition of members dropping off home-baked cookies, cakes and treats meant someone had to stay downstairs to receive the goodies. Then there was the long to-do list: make the holiday punch; lay out linens and napkins; cut up the coffeecakes, fruit cakes, rum cakes; arrange slices and cookies for serving; and brew coffee.

The reception volunteer missed out on all that made Christmas Eve special—the carol sing-along; ringing the jingle bells as the children paraded around the sanctuary; passing the light during the "Silent Night" candle ritual; seeing the darkened sanctuary lit by the glow of two hundred dancing flames. Missing these traditions would mean missing Christmas, I thought. Not me. I wouldn't.

Fortunately, I was never asked to make that sacrifice. You can guess who did it.

But not even Gary could be two places at once. The year my husband was president of the congregation, Gary announced he'd be out of town Christmas Eve. Jim explained the jam he was in. I listened stony-faced with arms crossed. Finally, he just said it: "Would you organize the cookie reception?"

My look would have dimmed even Rudolph's shining nose. "You're kidding, right?"

"I can't ask anybody else. You know what's involved. And I bet your mother would be willing to help."

"But the service ends at eight, and there'll be people in the Fellowship Hall until nine. It'll take at least forty-five minutes to get everything cleaned up and put away. And my mother can't drive after dark; I'll have to take her home. That means I won't get home until close to eleven. I'll miss Christmas Eve with the girls."

"I'll pick your mother up before church. And I'll get the girls to bed and help them set out milk and cookies for Santa. I really need your help."

I felt aggrieved and put-upon as I arrived at church an hour early on Christmas Eve. Not wanting my mother to miss out too, I shooed her away as the service started. "I need you up there to make sure the girls don't get burned by hot wax," I told her. "You have to help them with their candles during 'Silent Night.'"

Alone, I somehow felt better. The music filtered down from above, setting a steady rhythm for the work ahead. I rinsed out the punch bowl and poured in lemon-lime soda, fruit juice and sherbet. I draped three banquet tables with colorful tablecloths, then artfully arranged Christmas-themed paper napkins. I moved evergreen boughs from the windows to the tables and nestled votive candleholders among them. When the coffee machine's ready-to-brew light went on, I put the big industrial filters into the metal baskets and filled them with ground coffee.

Each simple kitchen task, familiar to me after years of volunteering, took on the majesty of ritual. I began to understand what Gary meant about service to others being spiritual.

The rumble of footsteps in the stairwell broke my reverie. The Fellowship Hall was soon standing-room-only. Mounds of cookies and sweets were reduced to a few scattered crumbs on empty plates. The large room echoed with holiday spirit, the joy of fellowship and community. I felt an unexpected ownership of this moment, as if this were my home and I was responsible for everyone's good cheer.

The reception came to a close and a steady stream of members and friends filed into the kitchen to drop their glasses and cups into a sink topped with soapsuds. I'd hoped to get a head start on the dishes, but I kept needing to stop and dry my hands to receive hugs, thanks and praise.

An hour later I locked up the church and drove my mother home, giddy with success and relief. We exclaimed over the holiday light displays we passed, and I added a few extra turns to the trip to see the most spectacular houses. After dropping her off, I followed my usual route for the twenty-minute crosstown drive from her house to mine. Yet tonight, the roads I'd taken hundreds of times before were completely transformed.

Every street was lined with glowing paper bag luminarias. I'd never been in this part of town on Christmas Eve and had forgotten the neighborhood's longstanding tradition of lighting the way in the spirit of the season. This was a magical moment I'd never witnessed because I'd never ventured outside my usual routine.

I drove home filled with the joy of a different kind of Christmas Eve service — not the service that I'd missed, but the service I'd offered to others — and how it had made this night the most memorable Christmas Eve of all.

~Linda Lowen

36

The Power of Giving

Christmas is the spirit of giving without a thought of getting.
It is happiness because we see joy in people. It is forgetting self
and finding time for others.
~Thomas S. Monson

The e-mail came from a friend who is always doing something interesting, unusual or rewarding. This time, it was an invitation to participate in a Christmas Day visit to a Lutheran assisted-living facility in our community. The mission: help the staff in whatever way we could because, as Jewish families, we don't celebrate Christmas ourselves.

Christmas can, in fact, be a somewhat odd day for those of us who are Jewish. Most years, the formula is familiar: a newly released movie and Chinese food.

We almost said no. We'd already made plans, and this suggestion sounded a bit daunting, as the unfamiliar often does.

But after some conversation, my husband and I decided to take on the three-hour shift together at the familiar building on our town's Main Street, a building we'd walked past often.

Of course, the motivation was not only that we could be of help to the staff; we also could hopefully interact with some of the lonely souls who were not slated to have visitors on Christmas Day.

My husband always had the gift of easy communication and connection. As a long-time writer I, however, had been shielded behind the written word.

I'm a tad shy, and I was more than a tad nervous about this Christmas Day visit.

"These are strangers," I reminded my easygoing husband. "We're Jewish. We don't even celebrate Christmas. What will we talk about?"

Vic made short shrift of my anxiety. "We're human!" he said. "Humans find ways to communicate."

We got our first challenge at the entrance to the Lutheran home, where a lone elderly man sat in a wheelchair. We greeted him with the standard "Hi," but got no response.

He seemed so alone, and what touched us so much was that he was holding a small American flag in his hand. There he sat, on Christmas Day with his flag. But after several attempts at conversation, it struck us: He had lost the gift of speech. A stroke, perhaps, or some other infirmity.

I don't know what made me do it, but I stepped up close to his wheelchair, smiled and pointed to the flag. And I gave it a thumbs-up.

Suddenly, a smile as radiant as the sun spread across an old soldier's face.

Mind you, we don't know that he was one, but he seemed straight out of Central Casting as a World War II vet.

In that moment I knew we'd made a very good decision.

All around us were people in wheelchairs — some surrounded by families, some alone. There were staffers bustling around, leaning over to whisper something sweet or funny or just friendly. These are the amazing men and women who sacrifice their own Christmas Days to be there for the forgotten or the needy.

Suddenly, religion didn't matter a bit. Nor did shyness. All that mattered was the privilege of being a part of this day.

To pause to say "Merry Christmas!" To shake a hand. To offer a cookie.

But there was so much more to come.

We were ultimately assigned to the area where the Alzheimer's and dementia residents were finishing lunch, many of them slumped in their wheelchairs, a few with some small spark of awareness.

We'd been advised to meet these residents at eye level, to approach them from the front, never from behind, and to expect anything from total indifference to anger to a blank stare.

We got some of each.

But gradually, as we knelt down to try to connect — as we smiled, patted a shoulder, held a hand — there was a glimmer of something.

Eye contact. A hesitant smile. A word or two.

In some ways, that was a most difficult, even exhausting experience. But oh, the amazing rewards.

There was the tiny lady whose sweet face showed delight when we wished her a Merry Christmas. Her nails had been polished, her white sweater was clearly for special occasions, and her ability to connect and respond was in there somewhere.

So we talked without words. And yes, that's not just possible — it's amazing.

I handed her two soft little plush teddy bears that were available to these residents to have and to hold. She cuddled them close to her heart.

We repeated this again and again with men and women who didn't care what religion we were or why we were there, as long as we let them know that they were worthy of a smile or a touch.

And then we discovered the lady with a cap of silver hair who began to call us "Mommy" and "Poppy," and reminded us that we used to make Christmas pudding together. She was, she told us, seventeen years old.

Good for her! Maybe that's how she felt on this Christmas Day in her late senior years.

Our most astounding moments came with her.

The background music piped into the activity room was Christmas music, and almost instinctively my husband began singing along to the words of "I'm Dreaming of a White Christmas." Then I, the world's most self-conscious singer, joined in.

Then, suddenly, there was a third voice. Our silver-haired lady friend was singing every word of "Jingle Bells," and then of "Silent Night."

There we sat, two Jewish Christmas visitors and a sweet woman with a voice like an angel, singing together on Christmas Day.

Unlikely? Definitely.

Uplifting? Absolutely.

Meaningful? Certainly for us.

Hopefully also for the residents of this place, five blocks — and light years — removed from our lives.

When we tiptoed away, we noticed that our new friend had fallen into a peaceful sleep, with just a hint of a smile on her lips.

We left knowing that we'd just experienced our very own beautiful, wonderful Christmas miracle.

~Sally Friedman

37

Just Words on a Screen

The words of kindness are more healing to a drooping heart
than balm or honey.
~Sarah Fielding

started volunteering with the hotline because of the recession. I was fresh out of college, liberal arts degree in hand, and living next to one of the biggest job centers in the country — Washington, D.C. It didn't matter. It took four months, twelve interviews and fifty applications for me to find a job.

That June, with no end in sight to the long silences and rejection letters, I decided if I couldn't work, I still needed to do something, if only to keep myself sane. I liked the hotline because (aside from the in-person training) I could volunteer entirely remotely, which meant I wouldn't have to worry about gas money and could schedule my own hours.

An online hotline for survivors of sexual assault and domestic violence — I knew it wouldn't be the cheeriest work, but I didn't really know what I was getting into, even after the cultural competency training and PowerPoint presentation and the jittery roleplaying exercises with my fellow trainees. How could any of us really know what it would be like?

Three weeks after signing up, I sat down at my computer for my first session. I logged into the portal for volunteers. I created my pseudonym for the site — we weren't allowed to give any personal information — and checked in with the session supervisor, Anne Marie. She welcomed me and, less than a minute later, the site chimed to let me know that a visitor was in the waiting area.

"Do you want to get that?" Anne Marie asked. I gulped. "Yeah, okay," I typed. My hands were shaking.

All at once, my inner critics started howling. What did I think I was doing? How was I at all qualified to help someone who'd had such a traumatic experience? What if I made it worse? What if they hurt themselves?

It didn't matter. The chat box opened. My visitor was there, just a blinking line on a screen, but I pictured her — or him — sitting in front of a computer, just like I was, nervous and waiting.

"Welcome to the online hotline," I typed. There was protocol to go through — things each visitor had to know about safety — before we could address what brought my visitor to the site that day. As I went through them step by step, I started feeling like less of a fraud.

I won't say my anxiety immediately eased that afternoon, but by the end of the first hour my hands had stopped shaking. "Good job," Anne Marie wrote. "Ready for more?"

It helped, I think, that there were a lot of rules guiding us on the hotline. We weren't counselors or legal experts. The most important thing was for visitors to feel supported and listened to, but we couldn't spend more than an hour on a conversation. Repeat visits were highly discouraged — the hotline isn't a substitute for therapy. It was always good to provide resources, but only if the visitor agreed. We weren't supposed to use the word "rape" unless the visitor did first. Visitors were never "victims" but rather "survivors," even if they didn't think of themselves that way.

The majority of our visitors were women, many of them well into middle age. Some had been assaulted or abused years ago, even decades ago. Some of them came looking for support groups or advice. Some simply wanted someone to listen to them. Many were depressed. Others had recently experienced a "triggering" event, which is to say they saw or heard or felt something that brought their experiences back vividly and painfully. Occasionally, they would sign in at the beginning of an anxiety attack and we would jump into averting it. "Put your feet firmly on the floor. Tell me about the walls of your room. Are there pictures? What are they?"

Then there were those who were only weeks or days or hours from the event. They needed information above all else. These visitors were shakier and often vague about why they were on the hotline. "It wasn't your fault," I typed every time. Sometimes they would argue. I was stubborn about it: "You don't know what would have happened if you'd done something different. No one can know that."

The worst sessions — the scariest ones — were the minors. Many of them still lived with their abusers. We brainstormed about adults they could confide in, ways they could stay safe. Sometimes they were in immediate danger and emergency services had to be contacted. These visitors were frightened and they were alone. "I'll talk to you until the police come."

I volunteered with the hotline for two years. I stuck with it even after I got a job and went on to grad school. It wasn't the kind of volunteering that ever seemed fun or easy, not like walking dogs for your local animal shelter or collecting school supplies for disadvantaged kids. It took attention, and most days the hotline was busy, one visitor after another for two to four hours. Sometimes I'd sign off feeling emotionally and psychologically bruised. But at the same time, I felt productive.

It felt the most tangible one night on December 24th. I had been working on the hotline for almost eighteen months. I didn't deliberately sign up for Christmas Eve — I was just trying to finish my hours before the holidays. It was a late-night session. Everyone else in my family had gone to bed. There were only a couple of us on the hotline. It wasn't a high traffic block. I put on a podcast and picked up a book. Twenty minutes in, the site chimed.

"I'll take this one," I told the supervisor.

After we went through the formalities, my visitor told me she was dreading the next day because everyone would be celebrating with their loved ones and she felt so alone and abandoned. Her story was common enough: When she shared what had happened to her, many of those close to her didn't believe her story and her confession caused conflict among her friends and family. They blamed her, she said, even though she had only told the truth.

We talked a bit about support groups and how she might reach out to her community again when she felt comfortable. I helped her make plans and goals, an oddly common activity on the hotline. It seemed like a productive session, but then she said: "I still don't know what to do tomorrow."

"Maybe you could volunteer somewhere," I said. "Is there a homeless shelter in your town? I'm sure they're shorthanded."

She thought of a soup kitchen that would likely need help; it seemed to make her feel better. I went into the exit formalities, reminding her about safety even though she had said she was safe enough.

"Thank you," she said at the end of the session. "Thank you for being here tonight."

I felt embarrassed. In a way, it seemed like so little. I'm a night owl; I would have been up anyway. All I had done was type words on a screen. But if it had helped, then that was something, wasn't it? "Have a happy holiday," I said.

"You too."

~JK Patt

38

Santa's Secret Shop

We worry about what a child will become tomorrow, yet we
forget that he is someone today.
~Stacia Tauscher

December 8th through December 12th. That's what I read pulling out the reminder card as I retrieved my mail one cold, blustery day before Thanksgiving. "Time for Santa's Secret Shop again and volunteers are desperately needed! A home-cooked lunch will be provided each day for the volunteers."

"Has it been a year already?" I asked myself as I quickly scurried back into the house. "Do these kids really care about Santa's Secret Shop?"

Ever since I retired, my days were filled as a volunteer reading-tutor, helping out with school events, running errands for people, taking people to appointments and babysitting. I didn't realize how often people needed help. I glanced at the card once again to check the dates on my calendar. I had nothing listed for a couple of those days. I could do it again. But why did I always choose to help out during the busiest times of the year? There were so many other things I could be doing to prepare for the holidays. I hadn't started my shopping or my baking. But there I was, scheduling time to help someone else. I felt a bit like Scrooge — I didn't want to do it, but I knew I would feel guilty if I said no.

The day arrived for me to show up at the elementary school and help with Santa's Secret Shop. There were a variety of jobs waiting for the volunteers, from cashiers and gift wrappers to helpers assisting students choosing gifts for each family member or helping them count their money. Within the first hour, I couldn't help but share in the kids' excitement. They made the place come alive. They made it as magical as the North Pole!

I helped kids carefully count their money to make sure they had enough money to purchase the gifts they painstakingly chose for each member of their families. Even the family dog was included! Lots of time and love went into their thoughtful decisions.

No matter what job I had at Santa's Secret Shop, I always enjoyed myself and the lessons the kids taught me about giving. It wasn't the cost of the gift, but rather the love that went into choosing it. It didn't matter to them that they spent ninety-eight cents on a potholder for Mom and four dollars on a flashlight for Dad: They knew in their hearts that they were choosing gifts they felt their loved ones could use.

I wished I could be more like that. Every year I try to even out the number of presents for everyone and the amount I spend. That detracts from the joy of giving. Another lesson I learned from these kids is that they can always find everything they need right there in that shop. There's no running around from store to store trying to comparison shop or going on endless searches just to pick out the right toy or sweater. These kids always found something for everyone on their lists right there in that school gymnasium.

The most important lesson I learned was from a little boy when school was canceled due to snow one year. This little boy was so disappointed he called the Santa's Secret Shop coordinator in desperation. He begged her to open the shop so he could buy his dying grandfather a gift. He could have gone to any dollar store or some other place that carried inexpensive items, but he wanted to purchase something he had seen at Santa's Shop the day before on Preview Day — the day all the kids come down, one class at a time, to write down the names and prices of the items they wish to purchase. The coordinator knew she had to find a way to that rural school, regardless of the road conditions, and open that shop for him.

The boy and his parents met her in the unplowed parking lot. Once inside, he went right to the gift he wanted and then asked her to wrap it. He and his parents went straight to the hospital. The boy proudly gave his grandfather the gift and even helped him open it. The grandfather held it in his hands and died shortly thereafter. He was buried with his Santa's Secret Shop gift.

Why do I volunteer? It's the lessons like these I would have never learned had I not been a volunteer. It's the yearly reminders of the true joy of giving. Above all, it's what Santa's Secret Shop means in the eyes of a child.

~KoAnn Rutter

39

Right On Time

Even when you do not feel big hearted, you can give yourself
permission to act that way.
~Lama Willa Miller

still remember the autumn our YWCA special events committee volunteers spent months soliciting gifts for the residents at
our WomenShelter, a refuge for victims of domestic violence. We
gathered to wrap and label them a few days before Christmas.

We marveled over the candy canes, chocolate-covered cherries,
and popular toys. Then, as we affixed bows to the foil-wrapped toiletries, legwarmers and scarves, we realized that we lacked one thing
to make Christmas morning magical: Santa.

"We really need Santa. We can't take the children from the shelter
to the mall to see him. I heard them wondering if he can find them so
far away from their homes."

"I can be Santa's helper," I volunteered. I was a psychiatric social
worker at the Los Angeles County residence for abused kids, and I
had agreed to work the holiday, but I didn't have to be there until
shortly before noon. I'd be free Christmas morning.

"Look," I told the group, "Let me ask my friend, John. He's tall,
has a deep voice, and I know he'll be in town."

John and I had started to date soon after he graduated from an
inpatient alcohol rehab program. I knew he was meeting some of
his former group on Christmas at an Alano club, a center for AA

members and families. "We'll be sharing our experiences, strength and hope," he had said, "and with any luck, a decent turkey dinner." He claimed it would be his first sober Christmas since his teens.

I headed toward the office phone. John listened while I explained what we needed. "It won't take more than a couple of hours. You just have to help me carry in the presents, talk to the kids, hand everybody a candy cane and be jolly. Will you do it? Be our Santa?"

"One thing I've learned in AA," he said, "is to grab every opportunity to make amends. Some Christmases I wasn't there for my own kids. This would be a chance to make Christmas merrier for other kids. Just one caveat... don't call me Santa. I've lost twenty pounds, I'm not particularly jolly, and when I did take my kids to see Santa, sometimes he'd have booze on his breath."

I frowned. "But I'd counted on being Santa's elf. I have a red angora sweater and white pants and a Santa cap with bells."

"You'll just have to be Kringle Bells."

"Kris Kringle will do. And thanks." I hung up the phone and rejoined the group.

"He'll do it!" Everybody sighed with relief.

"I've never really understood why you want to be such a do-gooder," he'd said when he learned I spent many Saturdays volunteering for the shelter.

"Why is that hard to understand?" I'd asked.

"You could have fun on your days off. You could go to the movies, listen to your Billy Joel albums or walk on the beach."

I'd laughed. I couldn't imagine anything more satisfying than watching these children and their moms opening presents that holiday in a safe house.

Early Christmas morning, John and I piled the bags of gifts into the back of his old Chevy and drove through the fog-cloaked streets to the shelter.

"I'll go in first and make sure everybody's dressed and ready," I said, as we pulled up in front of the duplex the YWCA maintained for the program.

A woman in a faded chenille bathrobe answered my knock, eying

me warily. "I'm here with the Christmas gifts," I announced. "Santa…
I mean Kris Kringle is stuffing some presents in his sack. We may
have to make several trips."

"Kris Kringle?"

"Yes," I said, nodding my head to rattle my bells. "And I'm his
faithful elf, Kringle Bells."

"No Santa? The children will be so disappointed."

"Well, they won't know the difference. He's dressed in a Santa
suit, just without a pillow, and he's promised to say 'ho, ho, ho.' Just
don't call him Santa."

"Oh, whatever," she said, looking hesitant. But when John
stepped up on the porch, her puzzled expression quickly changed.
I'd hesitated to tell him so, but even with the twenty-pound weight
loss he still looked like Santa Claus.

The children gathered as John began to read the gift tags.

"Thank you, Kris Crinkle," said one angelic-looking preschooler.

"Thank you, Kris Wrinkle," echoed an older boy, with a slight
smirk.

"Thank you, Kris Tinkle," lisped a toddler. John ducked his head
to hide a grin.

When John drove me home he said he wanted to stop by later that
evening. "I have a little present for Ms. Kringle Bells," he announced.

That night, John handed me a small package wrapped in silver paper. "Before you open this, I want to tell you that last night,
Christmas Eve, I really wanted a drink," he said. "I actually got in the
car to drive to a bar. Then I remembered I had to take the presents
to the shelter this morning. I drove to an AA meeting instead. You
helped me maintain my sobriety… what a gift that was."

I hugged him and then opened my package. It was Billy Joel's *The
Nylon Curtain*.

John and I chatted about how our respective Christmas Days had
gone. Then a certain tune started up.

"Listen to this one," I said, catching my breath. It was my favorite.

The Piano Man started out with the opening phrase of his
Christmas song, a huge hit, "She's Right On Time." We both hummed

along with the chorus.

"Hey, Kringle Bells," John said, his voice soft, unusual for him. "Thanks. You were right on time."

"You're welcome, Kris Tinkle Wrinkle Crinkle." We burst out laughing.

Our romance didn't last, but our friendship did. Each time we reconnected before he died a few years later, John, still sober, reminded me of that magical Christmas when Kringle Bells showed up right on time, right where she should be, volunteering on Christmas morning. With a formerly reluctant costumed recruit grinning right beside her.

~Terri Elders

Christmas Promise

Because that's what kindness is. It's not doing something for
someone else because they can't, but because you can.
~Andrew Iskander

C hristmas Promise began more than twenty years ago. Three
women started it, one of whom was a teacher who asked
the children in her first-grade class to write letters to Santa.
Those letters launched the program.

Christmas Promise is not a governmental program. It is not a
church program, though it is non-profit. It is not advertised or promoted; it is secret. There is no paid staff. No gasoline reimburse-
ments, no lunch, nothing. One local golf course hosts a fundraiser in
September. All the money goes to Christmas Promise.

A person can select one family and buy for the whole family. The
gift giver takes the gifts to Christmas Promise and the program wraps
and delivers them. Christmas Promise might also decide to add to
the gifts.

Everything from office space to wrapping paper to gifts is
donated. Some local companies send their staff over to spend an
afternoon wrapping gifts. Once they are introduced to the program,
those people will often return to help on their own time.

In 2013, 254 families were recipients of Christmas Promise. The
families are nominated by individuals familiar with the secret program — teachers at low-income-area schools, clergy, ministers and so

on. It doesn't matter how many kids are in the family and no family is on the list more than one year. No family knows or suspects they are going to receive anything. Everyone living in the household receives a gift, even grandparents.

Families don't get cell phones or laptops. They get basic needs, like warm clothes, blankets, pajamas, books and games. Additionally, stockings for homeless children and adults are filled with toothbrushes, toothpaste, hand cream, tissues, and other items that most of us don't think of as luxuries. Over four hundred backpacks are filled with pencils, paper, crayons and books.

Many of the families receive specific requests. One little boy asked for warm socks for his father so that he could go out and get a job. Another child wanted "bug shampoo" (the teacher wrote that he had lice). Another child wanted something for his mother who has four children and only one job. The letters the kids write are heartbreaking. One little girl asked for nothing for herself; many of the kids don't. They ask for items for their parents, brothers and sisters.

There are more than sixty men who grow white beards to deliver carloads of toys and food. Yes, they wear the requisite costume! The Santas report back to the office after finishing their Christmas Eve deliveries and volunteers get letters describing the Santa experience. The letters explain how grown men break down and cry. Each Santa delivers to four or more families in a specific area. They sometimes have to go back (fully costumed each time) until they catch the family at home. Since no one knows they are coming, deliveries can be a challenge.

This is Christmas at its best. This year I am making doll clothes for the program. I have purchased twelve dolls, and they all need shoes, pajamas and dresses. Any donations are appreciated. And if you'd like to help wrap packages after Halloween, I'll show you where to do it and help you get started. You won't feel like a bit player. Not even a second player. You will feel like the top elf in Santa's workshop. Because that's how it makes you feel. A little help goes a long way.

~Linda A. Lohman

Chapter 5

Volunteering & Giving Back

Giving Back

41

I Would Have Starved Without the Food Bank

*Not what we say about our blessings, but how we use them, is
the true measure of our thanksgiving.*
~W.T. Purkiser

I stood there shocked. It was the day after my roommates and I had thrown a huge party. I had just opened the cupboards and realized that we had no food left.

When I first moved out on my own there was a tremendous amount of adjustment time. I was young, foolish and kept bad company. To make matters worse, I didn't know how to budget, I had bills to pay, I had to finish my schooling, and I couldn't find a job better than a counter attendant/bakery assistant at a donut shop. I worked graveyard shifts for over a year at the wage of $6.10/hour and I did this while attending high school. How I did it, I really don't know. Those were not the best times in my life.

I remember moving from cupboard to cupboard and feeling completely overwhelmed by their emptiness. To make matters worse, we had no money. Nothing. Not a penny until our pay cheques, which were over a week and a half away. I knew I could eat one free meal at the donut shop every day but I had no idea what I was going to do for my other meals.

That was when I realized: We needed to go to the food bank.

I remember trying to think of an alternative. I believed that food banks were for homeless people, that I would be taking from someone needier than myself. However, I soon realized that if I didn't go, there would be repercussions. I needed food to keep my mind and body healthy.

I swallowed my pride and went.

I remember being so fearful, wondering if they would turn me away. My stomach was in knots, partially from the hunger and partially from the anxiety of knowing that my life had come to this.

The staff at the food bank was kind, understanding and gave us more than enough food to get us through two weeks.

Due to ongoing financial challenges, I ended up using the food bank for almost a year.

This is something I haven't told anyone in my life... until now. I was afraid of being judged. I was concerned that others would think I was weak because I had to rely on a social service for help. I was frightened that it would change the way my friends and family view me.

However, the reality is, we all have times of need. We all have moments when we need to reach out for help. At that time in my life, I was thankful for the food bank and the services they provided. Their services helped feed my mind and body so that I could continue with my education.

A couple of decades later, I find myself regularly donating food and volunteering at the food bank. I've even written a post on how to help your local food bank. The help that they extended to me in my time of need will never be forgotten.

~Jennifer Bly

42

The Mayor of Kirkland

I would maintain that thanks are the highest form of thought;
and that gratitude is happiness doubled by wonder.
~G.K. Chesterton

Last summer I moved to a new city to live with my fiancé, giving up being a lawyer and academic for a job as a writer. I had no contacts so looking for work was hard. I spent my days aimlessly wandering around my new neighborhood.

That's how I met Steve. I'd seen him plenty of times before — disheveled, with a scraggly gray beard, leaning on his cane and holding a battered cardboard sign at a busy intersection. His sign asked for help with food or rent — nothing fancy, and never for alcohol or drugs. I had a granola bar in my bag, so when I approached his corner, I opened the window and offered it to him.

He came over and smiled.

"Thanks, but I don't have any teeth, so I wouldn't be able to eat it. I appreciate the gesture though."

Then the lights changed and I drove away.

With this in mind, the next time I saw Steve, I offered to buy him a coffee. He hobbled along as we crossed the street to a small coffee shop. I was essentially having coffee with a stranger, but Steve's ready smile and friendliness made conversation easy.

Steve had lived in the area for about ten years and was well known to the locals. He told me about his friend the bus driver who didn't let him pay the bus fare when he traveled. He told me about a woman with a dog that barked to greet him when they drove by. He told me that the owners of a local café gave him their unsold pastries at the end of the day. He was a local icon. Even as we chatted, several people waved to him as they went by. I jokingly called him the Mayor of Kirkland, because it seemed like he knew everyone in the neighborhood. He laughed and said he hoped the name would stick. There was more he had to do before his term was up.

We met a few more times when I drove by his corner. I talked a little about myself, but Steve's stories were much more interesting than mine. In September, he told me he'd been homeless because he had an ongoing legal issue for the last thirty years and, as a result, his social security payment had been halved. The remaining amount wasn't enough to live on, so he was forced to spend his days trying to make up the difference.

By this time, Steve knew I had legal experience, so he asked me if I could help him with this matter. I recalled something my mother often told me: "You have a set of skills and you should use them for good, to help people." Something that might be easy for me — such as understanding a legal document or printing a form — would be much more difficult for someone without the right training or even access to a computer. What would take me a few minutes might take someone else hours.

I began by gathering information about Steve's case. He owed about $67,000 in taxes and had been charged interest on his outstanding amount for the past thirty years. He had about $700 per month deducted from his social security. Whatever small amounts he could pay back went to paying off the interest, which was accruing faster than he could repay. For him, this was a hopeless situation; the amount he had left was barely enough to live on. I made some phone inquiries. A court clerk directed me to a form requesting the court change his order, and once we had notified the court of our intent, the ball was rolling.

As the months passed, I threw more time and energy into Steve's case. I made phone calls on his behalf to collect materials, contacted his caseworker, printed out his forms and helped him complete them. When we met to discuss his case, it was as if a heavy weight was lifting off his back. Steve was already an upbeat guy, but I could still sense his growing optimism. He started describing me as his "little ray of sunshine" and telling his friends, so that the local bus driver would tell me what a great job I was doing, and the mailman would thank me for helping Steve. In early November we filed the forms with the court — all two hundred pages of them. After that, all we had to do was wait until the court date.

It was a blustery December morning when we met at the conference room I had reserved at the local library for us to use for the phone hearing. As I wasn't acting for Steve in any official capacity, he did all the talking during the hearing. He told the court that a payment reduction would help him pay for rent and groceries and that, in the future, he wanted to mentor homeless youth so they wouldn't have to go through the same thing as him.

After a quick consideration, the magistrate returned with her decision. The court forgave $57,000 of what Steve owed, and his payments were reduced from $700 per month to just $100 — which meant he would have enough money to get his life back on track. There were tears in Steve's eyes when he heard the decision.

As he grasped my hand and thanked me, I couldn't help but feel a little wistful. I was proud of what I had done, and happy that I used my time and effort to help him. But it would also mean that I wouldn't see him as often anymore. When I told Steve this, he grinned. "We're friends," he said, "and friends make time to see each other."

Then, with a wink, he added, "Besides, the mayor's still got to do his rounds."

~JC Lau

43

Full Circle

*As we express our gratitude, we must never forget that the
highest appreciation is not to utter words, but to live by them.*
~John F. Kennedy

A fellow volunteer and I were at a home visit for the Saint
Vincent de Paul Society, seated at a young mother's kitchen
table, reviewing her financial situation. "Thank you so
much for coming out to help," she said, with tears in her
eyes. "You have no idea what we're going through."

My heart went out to her; she had no idea how much I did know.

Only a few years before, I had been a struggling single mom.
When someone knocked at my front door one day, I secretly hoped
it was some wonderful surprise like flowers being delivered. But
it wasn't flowers. It was a man from the electric company coming
to shut off our power. I handed over our food money to avoid the
shutoff.

Things got worse. The child support stopped and I didn't have
enough money to cover our basic expenses. Our rent was overdue
and way too expensive for the income I earned.

Unfortunately, this wasn't the first time I'd been down and out.
Years before, I had sought help at the Women's Opportunity Center
in Mount Laurel, New Jersey when my marriage ended. I had been
laid off from my job and forced to sell our home. The Center had provided me with a mentor, food, scholarship information and business

suits. I returned to college and earned my bachelor's degree. It was a major victory when I landed a job in the nick of time — just as the unemployment ran out. Then I secured a loan to get a decent car. With child support and my new steady income, I covered the bills and provided for my daughters. I thought my financial problems were over.

Now the child support had stopped, and that made all the difference. I couldn't make the rent and pay bills on my small salary.

With one daughter still in college and my youngest daughter at home, I had to do something. I needed help right away. Then someone told me about Saint Vincent de Paul.

With a heavy heart, I called them. They set up an appointment for their volunteers to come over for a home visit. I was so embarrassed. What if I knew one of them? The doorbell rang. With shaking hands, I opened the door. I sighed in relief. I didn't know them.

The woman and the man introduced themselves as I led them to the kitchen table. They were gentle, compassionate and courteous. Soon they were reviewing my financial information.

"Do you need food?" the woman asked. I looked in my cabinets. There were only a couple of items left.

"Yes." I felt like a failure.

After they finished their assessment the man said, "We can tell you are trying hard to be financially responsible and this situation is only temporary." That made me feel a little bit better.

After our session I realized I was living way above my current means. We concluded that I should start to look for a more affordable place to live, and I was grateful to receive a phone call a few days later saying that their board had agreed to cover my rent for a month.

The first time I went to pick up food was so embarrassing. It was at my church, and again I was praying I wouldn't run into anyone I knew. But the volunteers at the center were so kind that my fears melted away. They gave me two large bags of food and told me to keep coming back until I didn't need help anymore.

Because of these kind volunteers, my girls and I made it through a very tough time. A few years later, my youngest daughter and I were doing much better, and the child support was consistent again. I was able to save a little money after paying our bills. Eventually I would be able to move out and buy a home.

Life was good, but something was lacking. I couldn't stop thinking of those volunteers who helped me when I was down and out. I needed to do the right thing and give something back. I picked up the telephone.

Soon I found myself volunteering once a week at the very same center that had helped me. The first thing I did was help pack bags in the food pantry. It was impressive how organized the volunteers were. Every item had its place and there were specific rules about what went into each bag. After filling bags for a while, I decided to help give bags of food to the people who lined up at the center.

I was amazed to see the staggering number of people who showed up for food. Many of them were seniors, struggling to get by on meager funds. Others were young families, with the moms apologizing for asking for help. There was a homeless man who could only carry one bag at a time. I was shocked by the huge number of people who desperately needed assistance.

It impressed me that there were so many generous people in our community donating their time to the food pantry. I saw Girl Scouts and Boy Scouts, school groups and caring individuals bringing food and helping out. People donated bread and even fresh vegetables to the families. Others gave money to purchase meat and stock the pantry.

I volunteered to go on home visits. I was the person sitting at the table this time, interviewing people about their financial struggles. It was so strange being at the other end listening patiently. I could totally empathize with what they were feeling and going through although I never told them why. And now, as I listened to the young mother's story and remembered what it was like to be in her shoes, I realized that I had come full circle.

Life can change in an instant. One minute you are in famine and the next you are feasting. You never know what challenges life will bring. Sometimes you are humbled and sometimes you are lifted up.

I've been in both places, and one thing I've learned is that volunteers are so important. If it weren't for the volunteers at Saint Vincent de Paul and the Women's Opportunity Center, my children and I might not have made it through our tough times.

Volunteers can be the difference between whether a family eats or not. They can bring hope when there is despair. When you think about it, volunteering is probably the most important thing you can do in this lifetime.

~L.A. Strucke

44

Road Kill Lady

*Move out of your comfort zone. You can only grow if you
are willing to feel awkward and uncomfortable when you try
something new.*
~Brian Tracy

"What's that lady doing?" I asked my babysitter
Audrey, pointing out the rain-soaked window on
our way to school one morning. There was an
elderly woman dressed in a bright orange vest
carrying a garbage bag and one of those trash claws. At the time I was
twelve years old and had just moved to Salem, Oregon. My parents
traveled for a living, so Audrey took care of me while they were away.

"Picking up road kill," Audrey answered flatly.

"Really?" I asked, eyebrows pulling together in disgust.

"No," Audrey laughed, "but that's what I like to call her: Road Kill
Lady. She just picks up trash around here for fun."

"Oh," I murmured. "Interesting..." Why would someone think
picking up trash looking like a construction worker was fun?

For six years I'd witness this mysterious Road Kill Lady — rain
or shine — on my way to school. In the beginning I thought she was
insane for picking up trash. However, eventually I smiled and waved
at her each time I saw her.

Later, when I moved to college, I'd see trash caught in the grass
or wedged in various bushes and feel really angry about it. I'd think,

"Why isn't anyone picking up this trash? People are so inconsiderate!" Shortly after, a light bulb went off in my head when I realized that (A) I'm a person and (B) I want to be a considerate one. Why did I think picking up the trash was someone else's problem?

Now I can't walk past litter without feeling guilt-ridden. While scuttling off to class or hiking with friends, I am constantly picking up pieces of trash and making sure the world is in better shape than I previously found it. I volunteer with SOLVE (Stop Oregon Litter and Vandalism), cleaning up trash off the Oregon Coast and the streets of Portland (where I now live). Last summer I volunteered for the Hood to Coast Race, where I specifically wanted to pick up and sort through trash and recycling. As weird as it may sound, picking up litter is kind of a thrill for me! In fact, I was so adamant about the whole trash-picking-up thing that for my twenty-second birthday my friends bought me my own trash claw and a bright yellow vest with my name on it.

During my first outing in my stylish gear, I was met by hostile looks from others. A married couple literally crossed to the opposite side of the street while others glared disapprovingly at me as if I were a criminal doing community service.

One night, I had an epiphany: "Oh my gosh... I'm the next Road Kill Lady!" The funny thing was that I hadn't thought about the woman in years, and now here I was acting just like her! It made me laugh out loud seeing how this story came full circle.

I'll be honest; some days it's overwhelming when I realize the amount of trash there is and how few people actually pick it up. Now I understand what Road Kill Lady must have experienced, but the thing that inspires me most about her was her determination. No matter the weather or how many weird looks Road Kill Lady received, she kept on picking up trash day after day, year after year, because it was the right thing to do. I suppose seeing her every morning doing her own thing somehow seeped into my subconscious and turned me into the compulsive trash cleaning person that I am today.

One day in Portland, while waiting for the streetcar to arrive, I stood in a group of strangers and noticed the large amount of trash that lay at our feet — cups and bags from McDonald's mostly. My fingers twitched with irritation, but still, there remained a part of me that didn't want to pick up the trash because I assumed it would be weird. Then I thought: *What would Road Kill Lady do?* So, as you can probably imagine, I began cleaning up the space and something amazing happened — the strangers around me helped out too! It made me wonder what would have happened if I hadn't gone first? And even though the little girl to the left of me looked at all of us like we were weird, she might be the next initiator years from now. I don't think people are careless; they just need reminders now and again.

So thank you, Road Kill Lady, for being my constant reminder and inspiration. One person can and should strive to make a difference. I don't know your name but you have made a significant difference in my life and deserve a huge thanks.

~Amanda Claire Yancey

Making a Difference

When life kicks you, let it kick you forward.
~Kay Yow

"Breast cancer scares me," said the oncologist. "You can have the best prognosis and be dead in a year, or have the worst prognosis and live for twenty."

The first time I heard those words I was still getting used to my cancer diagnosis and could hardly say the word without tearing up.

The young doctor needed training in giving newly diagnosed cancer patients some much-needed hope. Didn't they teach them in medical school how words could make a difference?

While the oncologist was delivering his speech on statistics and survival rates, I was searching for the nearest exit so I could take a deep breath (and then cry!).

Working in health information management, I dealt mostly with patients on paper—not in person. But I realized there was a need for a special human touch, especially with a cancer diagnosis.

Later I spoke with Dr. Bieber—the head of the practice where I worked—and he shared with me that he would like to develop a course on cancer patient protocols for his residents at Hershey Medical Center. I told him that I thought "survivor" would be a better word to use than "patient" and he agreed.

Because I was undergoing radiation treatment for six weeks,

I used my time in the waiting room to observe and take notes on the interaction between medical personnel and patients. Since the radiation center was not directly connected to the oncology unit, some of the patients came by ambulance from the hospital to receive treatment.

Many of the patients were terminally ill and radiation was palliative (pain relieving). It upset me terribly, so I charged up to the receptionist and asked, "Do you think it would be possible to have a 'well' waiting room for the rest of us cancer patients?"

The receptionist rolled her eyes, shook her head, and slowly turned away. I realized that day that I was no different — we all had cancer — and we were in different stages of dying. I just wasn't ready to give up!

Over the next few weeks and months I developed a seminar on "What to Say and How to Help When Someone You Know Has Cancer." I made several booklets and called my local library and asked if I could give a presentation to the community. The receptionist said she would have to speak with the head librarian and get back to me.

I didn't know what to expect, but the phone rang five minutes later. "Hello, may I speak to Connie Pombo? I'm Nancy from the Milanof-Schock Library and we would be pleased to have you present your topic to the community."

As soon as I got off the phone, I made a list of all the people who might benefit from the presentation: neighbors, friends, co-workers, family members, and my breast cancer support group.

As the day approached, I got nervous. What if no one showed up and all the preparation and work was for nothing?

The evening of the presentation I set up my PowerPoint and had multiple booklets available for those in attendance. It was mentioned in the daily newspaper, so I had no idea how many would attend.

At 6:45 p.m. on a Tuesday evening people started walking through the doors. Dr. Bieber was first in line, followed by more people until the room was full… and more chairs had to be added.

When Nancy introduced me I didn't feel nervous, but rather empowered, because I knew that I was going to make a difference in other people's lives. The lights dimmed slightly as I started my presentation and introduced myself as a breast cancer survivor. I explained the first words the oncologist said to me and I saw tears and heads nodding in agreement as I spoke. At the end of the presentation, everyone clapped.

Afterward people came up to me and said I should write a book and do more lecturing. I smiled politely. Little did they know, I had just finished treatment and still felt weak and tired. But somehow giving the talk helped me stop being a patient and start acting like a survivor.

That was eighteen years ago, and during that time I have given countless presentations to medical centers, universities and cancer hospitals. In 2008, I was awarded the "Eileen Stein Jacoby Celebration of Life Award" for my service by the Fox Chase Cancer Center.

After seven years, I left the medical field to speak and write full-time and volunteer my time at the Stowe Weekend of Hope for Cancer Survivors in Stowe, Vermont. I've had the privilege of speaking on behalf of cancer survivors across the country with the same message of empowerment that comes from knowing that when we can't change our circumstances, we can certainly change how we react to them.

And that makes all the difference!

~Connie K. Pombo

A Sort of Shelter

The challenge of history is to recover the past and introduce it to the present.
~David Thelen

checked my e-mail again. Still no answer from the local women's shelter I had contacted about making a book donation. I stared at the box of Stephen King novels on the floor. I had volunteered to be a World Book Night giver, and tonight was the night. I wondered if the shelter's lack of response was due to the fact that the book I offered happened to be a horror novel. I didn't think that should matter. A literary escape was a literary escape, after all. As it happened, this very story had been my own sort of shelter once upon a time.

It was a young volunteer at a Huntsville, Texas women's shelter who had given me my first copy, years ago. My mother and I, homeless and terrified — she of her schizophrenia demons; me of her, and what would happen to us if she didn't find some place for us to call home again soon — had stayed at several shelters over the previous couple of years. We had disappeared off the map; none of our family or friends knew where we were as we attempted to escape the illusory "them" my mother was so obsessed with. Of all the places we had stayed, the shelter in Huntsville was by far the most comfortable and homey.

This was our summer "on the run," and I was fifteen.

Allie, a young twenty-something from the local college, volunteered at SAAFE House in Hunstville to gain experience and volunteer credits toward her college degree, but I also think she did it for the connection. She loved the women, broken and timid and strong as we were, and she always brought a sense of "everything's going to be all right" with her when she was there. She was smart, warm and funny, and I took to her instantly.

"Have you read *The Stand*?" she asked me one sunny afternoon as we sat listening to the local college radio station. Allie let me hang out with her in the office while she did paperwork sometimes. There weren't any other kids my age in the shelter at the time, and even though my stay was to be only a few short weeks, she treated me like a kid sister.

"Not yet. I want to. My boyfriend back in North Dakota said it was good." A weighted response, but I tried not to let her see just how heavy. He had been my first love, and I'd had to say goodbye on a Burger King payphone, so "they" couldn't trace the call. I hadn't even been able to call my best friend. I'd had to rely on my confused and heartbroken boyfriend to do that for me. North Dakota represented all the love and hope and stability I had left behind.

Allie nodded knowingly. Always intuitive but never intrusive. That was Allie.

"You'll love it. It's long, but really good. There's a lot in this."

She handed me a fat, well-worn paperback. I held it in my hands like a sacred tome.

"Good books make real life more bearable," she told me.

I laughed, knowing that was true, but not really understanding why.

"Even horror stories?" I said, holding up her gift.

Allie smiled, nodded again, and said, "Especially horror stories."

I started reading it that very day, and by the time I was halfway through, Mom and I were back in the car, heading to who-knew-where. But I had my book—this brave tale about good standing against evil, about love and truth and loyalty. And I was just a girl reading a novel, like thousands of other high school girls. That book, and many others after, would carry me through some very dark nights. I wished my momentary friend and benefactor, Allie, a silent farewell and hoped she wouldn't worry too much.

Suddenly inspired by my memories, I called our local Youth Services chapter that helps and houses homeless teens.

"Of course, we'd love the books!" said the chipper twenty-something on the phone. That young voice reminded me of Allie. I wondered what she did with her life, and if she still, after all these years, worked with women at the most vulnerable times of their lives.

I hung up and saw I had a Facebook message. A friend wondered if I had a few copies I could throw her way as she had a small group of "regulars" at her soup kitchen who would be thrilled to receive them. They had formed an informal book club. Her regulars didn't have homes, but whenever they could get them, they read and shared books with each other. I understood. It is during our most desperate times, when we must struggle for the very basics of life — where we'll sleep, how we'll find shelter, when we'll next eat — that we need stories, art and songs the most. Humans require a well-fed soul to inspire us to keep our bodies moving, to have the will to live.

I loaded up my box of paperbacks, tearful yet elated. I had found my recipients. I could share not just any story, but this story. Maybe it would make a difference. Maybe it could be for them what it had been for me — a sort of mental nightlight to keep away the shadows and silence the internal, fearful chatter.

Someone's going to need this, I thought, as I drove to hand out touchstones to the homeless, beacons to the lost and courage to the scared. It was my way of telling people I didn't even know, "you are not alone; you are not forgotten."

~A. K. Francis

Filling the Well

If you want to touch the past, touch a rock. If you want to touch the present, touch a flower. If you want to touch the future, touch a life.
~Author Unknown

My path to volunteerism was non-linear. Ten years ago my son Neil was hit by a drunk driver. That crash killed his girlfriend and left him with a serious traumatic brain injury. For years, it was all I could do to put one foot in front of the other, arranging physical therapy and mental health appointments, monitoring medications, and advocating for academic modifications. But somewhere along the line I began to ask myself questions about our situation. Why us? Did I really get to grieve for my son's losses when the fact was he was still alive? Shouldn't I just be grateful? Could I ever forgive the drunk driver for what he did?

To answer these questions, I turned to writing. For years I kept a journal, venting on the page about our horrific experiences. The great memoirist Joan Didion once said, "I write entirely to find out what I'm thinking, what I'm looking at, what I see and what it means." I found myself agreeing with her. This private habit of daily reflection finally helped me come to grips with our fate and the fallout from the crash.

Eventually, I wanted to share my experience with others. I wrote articles for disability journals about our experience coping with the accident's after-effects. I published essays in medical journals for other doctors who, like myself, may be grappling with whether and how to share our families' experiences with patients. I wrote essays for literary anthologies on journaling through sorrow. Eventually, I wrote a memoir called *Crash: A Mother, A Son, and the Journey from Grief to Gratitude*.

With the publication of that book came many volunteer opportunities. I was invited to become an ambassador for the Brain Injury Association of Massachusetts. The ambassador program is designed to put a human face on the tragedy that is traumatic brain injury. In this role, I give talks to high school juniors and seniors during prom season about making appropriate decisions behind the wheel. I discuss the adverse effects of underage drinking and drunk driving with college freshmen during Alcohol Awareness Week. I speak to civic and business organizations, raising awareness about the subtle, long-term effects of traumatic brain injury.

Recently I was able to merge my passions for writing and for the topic of brain injury into another volunteer project. The Krempels Center in Portsmouth, New Hampshire is a non-profit organization that offers a wide range of outpatient services and enrichment programs to local TBI survivors and their families. I now lead a once-a-month writing group there called "Express Yourself." A surprisingly large number of survivors were committed writers before their injuries and have missed the joy of putting their thoughts down on paper. We start each session with an icebreaker, introducing ourselves, sharing our connection to brain injury and explaining what we hope to gain from the group. We then delve into a particular aspect of writing.

One time we talked about description. I passed around a colorful feathery butterfly and we took turns describing it using all five senses. "Vibrant." "Silent." "Light."

Last week we learned about metaphors and similes. I asked them to finish the sentence "Brain injury is…" Their answers were as varied and complex as their injuries. "Brain injury is an unstable roller coaster." "Brain injury is like living in a foreign country." "Brain injury is a pain in the butt." Their strength, resilience, humor, willingness to help each other and sense of community are inspiring. As happens so often in volunteering, I always leave these sessions feeling guilty — like I'm getting more out of them than they are.

My life now feels like a perfect balance of purpose and prose. I still work part-time in my pediatric practice. That has its own rewards. But as satisfying as it is, it's my volunteer life that fills up the well. I embrace it as a way to give back. I can tell our story — of accident, aftermath and acceptance — and by doing so, take something unexpected and tragic and turn it into something meaningful and just.

~Carolyn Roy-Bornstein

Editor's note: Dr. Carolyn Roy-Bornstein is the coauthor of *Chicken Soup for the Soul: Recovering from Traumatic Brain Injuries*.

The Cycle of Hope

*You give but little when you give of your possessions. It is when
you give of yourself that you truly give.*
~Kahlil Gibran, The Prophet

know what it's like to sleep under a bridge. For the majority of
my adult life, I was homeless. Sometimes it's hard for people to
understand how and why someone ends up in that situation, and
it's natural to make assumptions. The reality is that homelessness
is a cycle that's difficult to escape, and every individual circumstance
has different contributing factors. My personal struggle began when
my divorce, economic downfall and the housing market crash all
collided.

When I was homeless, I spent most days just trying to find the
next meal and a safe place to sleep. Some nights, sleeping behind a
Dumpster was my best option, and sometimes I simply stayed awake
because it was safer.

After years of this pattern, I was ready to give up. I had lost hope
that life could get better. But what happened next was that instead of
me finding hope, it found me — and its name was Jay.

Jay was part of a homeless outreach program at Catholic Charities
Fort Worth (CCFW) called SOS. I truly don't know where I'd be if
CCFW hadn't reached out to me. For the first time in years, I knew
that someone had my back. CCFW stayed with me every step of the
way, and because of the help I received from SOS and other local

organizations, I was able to get on my feet and move into my own apartment.

For me, volunteering and giving back to the community that helped me is a natural fit because I know the difference these programs can make in the lives of others. One of the most rewarding ways I have been able to give back is right in my backyard — a soccer field for my refugee neighbors.

My apartment complex is also the home to many refugees, another group CCFW serves. Getting to know my refugee neighbors has truly been a humbling and meaningful experience. Interacting with people who have been through such traumatic experiences, yet remain so positive, has blessed my life in countless ways. When I had the opportunity to help build a soccer field for the refugee children, I was happy to volunteer. The children's joy as they play on their new field is a beautiful example of what's possible when strangers come together for a common goal.

In less than two years, I've gone from having nowhere to lay my head down at night to being able to serve and help others. And as grateful as I am to have a home, it's not the reason I give back or even the most valuable asset I've been given. The most profound and life-altering gift I received was hope, and the true value of hope is hard to fully grasp until you know what it's like to lose it.

Working with people and hearing their stories reminds me that we're all connected in ways we'd never imagine. I've experienced the power of compassion and have firsthand knowledge that acts of service can change lives. I used to be trapped in a cycle of homelessness that left me empty, but now I'm part of a cycle of hope that fulfills me beyond measure.

~Dominique Smith

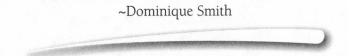

Do You Want to Talk?

*There is no exercise better for the heart than reaching down and
lifting people up.*
~John Holmes

"Do you want to talk?" She shook her head from side to side as her long, dark hair caught her tears. Her task was to draw how she felt since her loved ones had died. She continued to push a black crayon back and forth. I tried to make out any images, but all I saw was one big, black blob.

We were sitting on a concrete floor at Camp Kenan in Barker, New York, where Niagara Hospice annually holds Camp Hope, a free weekend event for grieving children.

Eleven-year-old Alyssa was a former student of mine. She was there because she had lost both her grandmother and mother within a few short months.

"Alyssa," I spoke softly. She raised her eyebrows. I caught a quick glance of her dark brown eyes, which seemed to be focusing on an unknown spot. "Let me tell you what I remember about your grandma." Her coloring slowed. "She's the person who encouraged you to tell me the truth when we had that incident in school and you couldn't sleep. Remember?"

She nodded. "Your mom," I paused. "Well, I never told you, Alyssa, but when I had a workshop for parents to teach them how to help their children…" I paused again because I needed her full attention. I wanted her to hear the magnitude of my next words. "Your grandma and mom were the only people who showed up."

She dropped her crayon. "Really?" She looked at me uncertainly.

"Really," I said with conviction.

"I didn't know that."

I spoke very gently. "You didn't need to then, but now you do."

I continued. "Your mom and grandma loved you so much." I had to steady myself as I silently prayed for the ability to continue. My heart was beating fast.

"I know there were problems. Everyone has them, including me. But one thing I'm one hundred percent certain of is that your grandma and mom loved you very much. Know what your mom said to me?"

"No," she looked at me quizzically. Her whale earrings bobbed up and down as if gasping for air. She brushed aside her long bangs. I could see her brown eyes. They shifted right to left as if expecting someone. Eventually we made eye contact.

"Your mom said, 'Mrs. Torreano, please help me teach Alyssa how to read better. I want her to become whatever she wants in life. I want her to have a better life than I do.'"

Alyssa smiled. She cautiously put her arms around me. Our tears blended together.

I have been an adult volunteer at Camp Hope every year since 2006. The first year, I went for myself. I had just experienced the death of my father. His passing was gradual, a result of congestive heart failure. I craved tranquility. I wondered if the camp would help me with the grieving process. It did.

Now, as I quietly listened to the voices of the children around me speak to volunteers about their loss, I realized my memories are the glue that keep my father alive.

Pointing to the black blob on Alyssa's paper, I said, "Tell me something you remember about your grandma." I paused. I placed my hand as much as I could over the black. "Something good, Alyssa."

Alyssa suddenly giggled. "She made me eat my vegetables or no dessert," she said with a hint of indignation.

"Peas?" I asked.

"Yes," she replied.

"Me too, Alyssa. I hated those green things."

Finally, communication.

"What about your mom, Alyssa?"

She scooted away from me. She put her head in her hands and cried.

Barely above a whisper, she said, "Grandma raised me. I don't remember much."

"I do remember." I spoke my words carefully. I reminded her what I told her before. "Your mom was the only mom who came to my workshop." I paused while she processed that. Ever so slowly she moved her hands away from her teary eyes. She focused on me. I put my arm on her shoulder.

"Your mom loved you." Her body shook as I placed my other arm around her.

A year later, I received a phone call from her dad.

"Mrs. Torreano, Alyssa wants to go back to Camp Hope. It really helped her."

There were a few seconds of silence. I could sense him choking up.

I thought back to the cold concrete floor where I sat with Alyssa.

He continued, "She wants to help other kids like you helped her."

~Joanna Montagna Torreano

Soap Kitchen

Your present circumstances don't determine where you can go;
they merely determine where you start.
~Nido Qubein

or years my husband worked a very good job that allowed me to stay home with our two girls and gave me plenty of time to volunteer at our local food pantry. Every other Monday I would go and help in whatever capacity they needed me. Sometimes it was stocking shelves. Sometimes it was carrying food out for older folks. Sometimes it was working the registration table.

Over time I got to know many of the regulars, but I never got to know their stories. I had no idea what led to them needing this kind of help. I also got to know the other volunteers and was very discouraged when I would hear them snickering in the back workroom about the people who were coming in for help. They would complain about their body odor, make fun of the way they were dressed, roll their eyes at the ones using a cell phone, and make many other snide comments. I too wondered why so many had not taken the time to bathe or shower. Why would they come in wearing clothes that looked like rags? Had they given up on life to the point where they did not care?

Then, I found myself on the other side. My husband lost his job and since I had not worked in over ten years we quickly went through what little savings we had. Now I was the one seeking help. The food pantry would give us what they saw as a month's worth of food, but in reality it only lasted about two and a half weeks.

After two months of job searching we ended up getting government assistance to buy food. Prior to having the food card I never purchased soft drinks or certain snacks. Now we were eating things we never could have afforded on our own budget. We felt like we had hit the lottery.

However, I also quickly learned that keeping ourselves, our clothes, and our home clean was a challenge. No one offered us a way to get laundry soap. We ran out of toothpaste and I searched the Internet for ways to make our own with baking soda and peroxide. My husband did his best to shave with a dull razor, but over time gave up on that for fear of hurting himself. I will spare you the details of what it is like to have three women in the house with very few feminine hygiene products.

That was when I realized that the others at the food pantry had not given up on life; life had given up on them. It is hard to go for a job interview when you no longer have the means of properly showering. When the laundry soap ran out I did my best to hang the clothes outside to air out any body odors. It was discouraging. How were we to get ahead and find a good job when we barely felt human anymore?

We were a middle class family in America, and while we were fed well, we could not take care of our personal hygiene needs. I went to the directors of the food pantry and explained to them that the need for soaps, tissues, toilet paper and other personal items was as great, if not greater, than the need for food. One gentleman joked that they were a food pantry, not a "soap kitchen." I couldn't hide my emotions and the tears welled up in my eyes.

A nun who served on the board noticed and put her arm around me. Then I told them my story and how not being able to properly clean myself was hindering my job search. It is very difficult to face a potential boss when you have not showered in three days. You do not know embarrassment until you can no longer find a dress shirt that has no stains or wrinkles. It is hard to feel presentable while wearing way too much perfume or cologne to cover up your own scent.

The food pantry directors listened intently to my story and began making a plan. It took a few weeks, but they began collecting liquid hand soap, razors and Laundromat-sized boxes of detergent, as well as toilet paper and facial tissues. They were ready to begin handing them out at Christmas.

In the meantime, I had taken two part-time jobs and my husband had found another job and we were at least able to keep the lights on and the roof over our heads. But it also meant I no longer had the time to volunteer at the pantry. On the day they began giving out the soap and hygiene products I made it a point to be there.

When I handed an elderly lady her bag she saw the bar of soap and the roll of toilet paper and she gasped, grabbed my hand, and cried, "Thank you! Oh, thank you!" It was as if I had handed her a million dollars. "You have no idea how much this means to me!" she cried. With tears streaming down my own cheeks I smiled and told her that I did know what it meant to her. I would never look at someone in need the same way again.

~Janice VanHorne-Lane

A Commitment to Life

It's not how much we give but how much love we put into giving.
~Mother Teresa

To be perfectly honest, I was proud of myself. The snow was falling and the roads had become treacherous. The schools were having early dismissal, but much to my surprise my appointment wasn't canceled. And so I went, feeling especially heroic. After all, as far as I could see, I was risking my life to keep my word. Snow or no snow, I would be on time for my scheduled donation at the local blood center.

When I got there, I discovered I wasn't alone. Four more "hero-types" were already lying back in donor chairs with lines attached to their veins, and machines quietly pumping away to collect their lifesaving gifts. At least two were donating whole blood while another might have been donating plasma and platelets — just as I was there to do.

Seeing my fellow donors in the process of honoring their own commitments gently reminded me that while I was proud to be there, I wasn't a hero. And it wasn't about me or, for that matter, about them either. Inclement weather doesn't negate the need for what we were doing, so any previously held silly heroic thoughts quickly disappeared as I lay back in my own contoured donor chair, my ear buds in place and the music lulling me to sleep as I began my one-and-a-half-hour donation procedure. I was ready to make a difference in the life of someone I'd never meet — while the swirling snow continued to blow outside the center's windows and cover everything it touched.

My wife Karen is a donor too. And more importantly, she has been on the bone marrow list for fifteen years, ever since she signed up to provide bone marrow to a kindergartner with leukemia. That little girl died before Karen's bone marrow could help her, but Karen was called again recently. Her test results were still on file, and it turned out she was a potential match for someone else. The caller came right to the point and asked Karen if she would still be willing to become a bone marrow donor. "Yes," she said and then immediately began answering questions in preparation for the pages of paperwork to follow — all of which would give way to further testing and hopefully the chance to save a life. It was a race against time.

I wish I could say that this race was won. It wasn't. The caller later thanked Karen for her participation and asked a few follow-up questions — including whether or not she'd remain on the donor list. "Of course," Karen answered, but I already knew she would. That's just who she is.

I'd never really thought about why I donate, or why Karen does. We just do. But a few months ago I learned that particular components that were to be harvested during one of my regular donations were earmarked specifically for a cancer patient and for somebody's newborn baby boy — both patients needing what I had to give in order to live. I've viewed our visits to the blood center differently ever since.

Last week Karen gave blood and next week I'll be eligible to make my usual donation. I'll clear an afternoon from my schedule and call for an appointment. Whether they need plasma and platelets, whole blood or red cells, I'll gladly give because each are so desperately needed. And I don't know whose life my donation may affect, but it really doesn't matter. On any given day the person needing a blood product could be you or me or maybe a loved one, but most likely it will be a stranger. And sadly, while so few among us actually take the time to donate, Karen and I always will.

It may not be snowing right now, and while I'm still not a hero, I really do feel proud every time I donate. And to be perfectly honest, I like the feeling.

~Stephen Rusiniak

The Privilege of Service

Then join hand in hand, brave Americans all! By uniting we stand, by dividing we fall.
~John Dickinson

The lights are on inside the Red Cross building. The emergency response vehicle and the van sit out front with their rear doors open. Guys are loading the boxes of comfort kits and snack bags we're taking to the soldiers. It's a few minutes before 6 a.m. and I'm on my way to a drive-through for breakfast biscuits. The city is gradually coming alive.

With a bag of fresh-baked sausage biscuits in hand, I pull into the Red Cross parking lot a few minutes later. The doors to the vehicles are closed now, but they're both running, warming up for the ninety-minute drive to north Alabama on this chilly morning. Paul opens the front door of the building for me. Scotty, another volunteer, sits on the couch in the waiting area.

Larry hasn't shown up yet. We eat our biscuits while we wait. As we start out the door, Larry pulls up. Scotty and Larry get into the ERV, Paul and I into the van.

Paul adjusts the heater and tests the radio, talking with Scotty in the ERV. He sets the portable global positioning system on the dash. As we pull out of the parking lot, the GPS indicates the anticipated time of arrival is 8:03 a.m. The deployment ceremony starts at 9, so we'll have plenty of time to unload and set up inside the armory.

Approximately 163 Alabama National Guard soldiers from Winfield's 166th Engineering Battalion are deploying to Afghanistan for the next year. Their families and friends will be with them today as they receive their orders. We're carrying about two hundred comfort kits filled with toiletries and other personal items that we put into camouflage nylon bags a couple of weeks earlier. We also have two hundred snack bags for the soldiers to take on their long bus ride.

Looking at the snack bags in the back of the van, I flash back to the Friday afternoon when six of us assembled them. As I placed each item in the bag, I hoped the soldier opening it would appreciate the choices we made for them.

Paul hands me a folder of papers. I find the directions where we're supposed to go upon arrival at the armory in Winfield and read them to him. The short speech he's prepared is also there if I'm interested. He says he wasn't sure what to say to these soldiers, knowing that some might not make it home. I'm feeling emotional; my stomach churns and my lips tremble slightly.

I tell Paul about the latest fallen warrior I wrote about for *The Tuscaloosa News*. I'm thinking if I can continue week after week for all these years (it's been at least three now) to write these stories and talk to grieving families, surely I can make it through a deployment ceremony intact. But I'm having doubts.

At the armory, a young soldier directs us to the appropriate place to unload. It's still early, but a number of soldiers are milling about, getting ready for the day. Several offer to help us. Inside the staging area, young children run around with mommies and grandparents following them. Soldiers greet each other as they arrive. Families and friends of all ages and colors walk around wishing the soldiers a safe trip. Others sit quietly waiting for the ceremony to begin.

More volunteers arrive. We put on the Red Cross aprons so we're easily recognizable and listen to Paul's instructions on how the morning will proceed. We will distribute the kits and snack bags at the end of the ceremony but before the soldiers break formation. With twelve of us, we don't expect it to take too long.

I'm seeing the soldiers through my own filters. This is someone's son or daughter. It's also someone's husband or wife or sweetheart and someone's best friend. My heart aches. A strong sense of pride to be part of this day swells from deep within me. I realize similar events happen around the country all the time. And often the units are much larger, affecting even more people.

The armory fills up. No chairs remain, so people stand along the wall, many holding squirming toddlers or infants.

The emcee announces that a young musician will perform a song he wrote for his brother, one of the deploying soldiers. As he sings, I find I can hardly believe the enormity of what's happening.

I fight tears. I envision my son, revisiting the terror I felt the day we entered Iraq six years ago — with him among the first troops going in — and all the weeks that followed until he came safely home. I survived that; surely, I can make it through this. The national anthem plays. The soldiers salute and the rest of us place our hands over our hearts. I'll just have to cry; there's no point resisting now. That only makes it worse. I breathe deeply and let a few tears roll down my cheeks. We're all moved. I'm not alone in this. I can see it in the faces all around me.

The dignitaries and officers weave through the rows of soldiers, shaking hands with each one. Some even walk along our row of volunteers, thanking us for our support. Paul goes to the podium. He's nervous. He doesn't like public speaking. He and the head of the Jasper Red Cross chapter each say a few words. We line up and start to deliver the bags. We quickly distribute them, moving even faster than we thought. I express Godspeed and thanks to each person I hand bags to and shake some hands. One guy reaches out and hugs me. "I prefer hugs," he says. That's fine with me.

We finish and the soldiers are dismissed. They won't actually be leaving until early the next morning, but they're now officially launched. Many come to thank us as they break rank. Their families and friends thank us, too.

We walk past one soldier holding a small infant in her arms, not more than a couple of weeks old. I ask if it's hers. "Yes, this is little Joshua," she says. Oh goodness, I think. This baby will be walking the next time he sees his mom.

The empty boxes are loaded back into the vehicles and we're ready to return to Tuscaloosa. We say farewell to the other volunteers. Many of the soldiers are already enjoying the snack bags, sharing them with children and friends. There may not be much left by the time they board the bus, but they got the message.

On the way back, Paul and I debrief. Neither of us had known what to expect, but we're pleased. I am grateful for the opportunity to contribute to the soldiers and their families on this poignant occasion. I love being part of an organization committed to making such a difference for people. I thank Paul for the profound privilege of serving today and being served in return. He slowly nods his understanding.

~Jane Self

Volunteering
& Giving Back

No Strangers Here

The Great Ice Storm

Never believe that a few caring people can't change the world.
For, indeed, that's all who ever have.
~Margaret Mead

The Great North American Ice Storm of 1998 affected the lives of millions of people in eastern Canada and the northern United States. The culprit was a stalled low-pressure system that took its sweet time moving out of the area. When the storm hit I was living in Ottawa and I was able to see its devastating effects firsthand.

Things were very difficult in the city, with power outages and shortages of basic essentials. Stores and supermarkets were taken by surprise by the extent of the power cuts. On the positive side, it was an opportunity for the community's spirit to be exhibited. People were checking in on neighbours to make sure they were able to keep warm and fed. Everyone shared their resources. The hospitals and essential services were given priority in having their power restored. Despite the prolonged outages, everyone seemed to wait patiently.

Ontario and Quebec Hydro employees were working full out for days on end to restore power. It would only be a matter of time before they were overcome with exhaustion, given the massive task facing them. After a few days of trying to deal with it locally the call went out to unaffected areas of the two countries for help. In response, electric utilities from all over North America sent workers and equipment to help with the cleanup. The mild temperatures at the root of the weather phenomenon did not last as long as the power outage and, as the weather began to turn colder, other problems began to develop in an icy world without electricity.

At the time of the storm I was working in a paper mill as an electrical technician. The mill was an enormous complex straddling the border between Ottawa and Hull, located on a group of islands in the middle of the Ottawa River. Our whole installation was self-sufficient in electrical power as we had six generators dependent only on the flow of the river. Throughout the storm we remained able to generate enough hydro to supply our papermaking needs. As days passed and the after-effects of the storm worsened, the company made the decision to shut down production and to send our self-generated hydro into the system feeding the city of Hull. This went a long way toward alleviating some of the dire conditions that were developing in the area.

Without much to do at the mill, five friends and I decided to volunteer with the City of Ottawa. Regional administrators had activated a rescue plan and were slowly and steadily coming to the aid of people living in outlying areas, but it was an enormous task. We knew that the people living in the city were having a difficult time, but nothing had prepared us for how bad things were in the countryside. Hydro poles and transmission cables lay in ditches. Abandoned cars and trucks littered side roads and many routes were completely blocked by huge ice-covered tree limbs. Smaller trees were so laden with ice that their topmost branches had bent far enough over to touch the ground and become frozen there. Roads that were clear of debris resembled ice rinks and there was very little salting and sanding. Everything had an ice covering.

Had it not been for the seriousness of the situation I would have described it as visually stunning. Light sparkled like glass decorations from the trees and bushes. Houses and cars were coated with thick ice coverings and huge icicles hung everywhere.

With our toolboxes in the back of the city-loaned trucks, we made up work teams comprising a millwright and an electrician. We headed out into the countryside with a list of the places in direst need.

The main issue we were dealing with was the repair and maintenance of faulty generators. City authorities had managed to get their hands on hundreds of generators — some new and working well and others that needed a lot of TLC to get them into working order. In many cases there had been no time to properly evaluate the units before they were sent out, so it fell to our little teams to catch up with on-site maintenance and repairs.

The sights that met us were often heartbreaking. Many farmers had been doing their best with what they had available, but you can imagine trying to keep a fully automated farm running when the power goes out and the standby generators do not work. Often, as we approached up the farm driveway, the farmers would come down the road to meet us and direct us to the generator site in an effort to minimize time before we got to work. Of course, when the units were back in service the farmer would want to show his gratitude by inviting us in for lunch or tea. Being practical individuals they understood when we pointed out that we needed to continue on to help the next farmer down the road. We had to stay on track and get through the dozens of calls for help. The farmers' gratitude was nevertheless appreciated, and inevitably their wives sent us on our way with bags full of sandwiches and soft drinks.

I have to say that I have never worked so hard in my life. Certainly I have never been so cold, so dirty, and yet so happy. We were on the road from sunrise to well beyond sunset. As time passed and the crisis continued, the circumstances for some farmers and their animals became even worse. It was not uncommon to arrive at a farm and to find the farmer reduced to tears after he had tried everything he could think of to save his animals. We were the last hope for many.

Being able to bring some relief to people in these extreme conditions was the best reward I could ever have hoped for. Volunteering during the crisis had immediate and long-lasting effects on the lives of my fellow volunteers and myself. It started me out on a life of working to help others who are in difficult circumstances beyond their control. I have an indelible memory of a big, gruff-looking farmer who, lost for words, took me in his arms and hugged me tightly when we managed to put his generator back into service. To him it meant the difference between life and death for his animals. We were just happy we could be of service.

~James A. Gemmell

54

A Call a Day Keeps the Loneliness at Bay

We cannot direct the wind but we can adjust the sails.
~Author Unknown

For much of my childhood, my mother filled the evening hours doing something for someone else. Sometimes she knitted hats for preemies, and at other times she cooked chicken soup for sick neighbors. Therefore, I wasn't surprised when one evening my mother announced she'd undertaken a new project.

"I'm going to telephone seniors," said my mother.

"Every night? But you don't even know these people."

"Doesn't matter," she said. "What's important is that I listen."

I was sixteen years old and couldn't fathom why my mother was willing to spend her evenings talking to strangers. She had friends and my two older sisters to call if she felt lonely. "They'll talk your ear off," I said.

My skepticism didn't diminish my mother's enthusiasm for the project. That evening, after washing up the dishes from supper, she settled on the sofa with the heavy rotary phone in her lap and dialed.

For a while, I listened as she asked the woman on the other line about her day, inquired what she had eaten for dinner, and asked if she had noticed that the daffodils in a neighboring park had begun to bloom. When she finished the call I said, "What do you care whether she had Jell-O or rice pudding for dessert?"

My mother grasped one of my hands and gave it a slight squeeze. "I'm the only person she talked to today."

It took me close to thirty years to fully understand the significance of that statement. Now, as my mother is nearing eighty, I find myself thinking about those nightly calls she used to make.

I am often the only person who telephones my mother, and sometimes I'm the only person she speaks to all day. I ask her what she cooked for dinner, but mostly I just listen as she recounts a walk she took, or how her dog Lucky stole a bunch of Brussels sprouts from the refrigerator.

I realize now that my mother's calls were lifelines that ensured housebound seniors remained connected to the world. Without her, their world would have been eerily empty. Somehow, she managed to juggle working full-time and raising a family while improving the lives of others. That kind of service requires commitment and superior organizational skills — traits and skills I do not possess. While she lifted the shroud of loneliness from the lives of five seniors, I struggle to call just one — my mother.

~Alicia Rosen

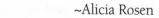

55

Eighty-Year-Old Volunteer

*I am only one, but I am one. I cannot do everything, but I can
do something. And I will not let what I cannot do interfere with
what I can do.*
~Edward Everett Hale

My mother is eighty years old, and every Wednesday for the past fifteen years — except for a couple of months after she had her hip replaced and several weeks after a subsequent knee replacement — she has driven twenty minutes to volunteer at the "old folks home" where she spent many years employed as a healthcare aide.

She was forced to retire when the Ontario government decided to make retirement at age sixty-five mandatory. She swears she would still be working at the nursing home if they hadn't made her quit. The government saw the error in their ways and a few years later mandatory retirement was revoked, but it was too late for my mother. Though she had loved the job and the old people who lived at the nursing home, she was already retired. So she started her stint as a volunteer.

Every Wednesday, even though she is now older than many of the nursing home residents, she volunteers her time to help "the dear old souls" just as she did when she was an employee and being paid for her services.

Mom was, and is, old school. When she worked, she really

worked. No sitting around and shirking responsibilities for her. No letting someone else do what needed to be done. As a farmer's wife she raised five children, kept house, helped with the farm work, and canned and preserved the yield from a huge garden that she planted and tended annually. When she got the full-time job at the nursing home she added night school to her many responsibilities and graduated as a healthcare aide in her middle age.

She worked hard during her career. She helped residents with their meals, helped them in and out of bed and the bathtub, even cleaned up the messes resulting from incontinence. One of her favourite stories is how an older woman, totally embarrassed because she had messed herself, couldn't believe that Mom was singing as she calmly and cheerfully cleaned things up.

"You can sing while you do that?" the old lady, who was known for not saying much of anything, said as Mom worked away. After having so many children and looking after her mother-in-law during the final years of her life, it wasn't a big deal to her. She had changed lots of diapers and cleaned up lots of messes in her lifetime.

A second favourite story is how a supervisor remarked on Mom's "handy-bag" of knitting projects, which she always had with her when she arrived for overnight shifts. While many of the overnight staff took catnaps once the residents were safely in their beds, Mom would work on her projects, ever alert and vigilant in case the residents needed her help — or just a reassuring voice after a bad dream. Night terrors aren't strictly for the young.

Nowadays Mom isn't responsible for the same work she did as a member of the paid staff. In her volunteer role she mainly visits with the residents. Most of the ones who lived at the home when she was employed there, including her own father, have passed away. But she makes new friends each week. She gets to know the new residents, many her age or younger, and is quick with a smile or a pat on the back. She has the time to listen to their life stories and reminisce with those who, like her, grew up in the community. There are lots of stories to tell when someone has the time to listen.

She has taken it upon herself, during her Wednesday afternoon volunteer stints, to make sure people aren't sitting alone in their rooms feeling sorry for themselves or pining for company. It is her personal mission to talk each and every one of the residents into taking part in church services and musical entertainment programs in the common area.

"A lot of them would just sit in their rooms being lonely," she says. "I don't give them a choice. I just tell them that there's a lovely program going on and they should attend and before they can say no, there we are."

Some she walks with arm in arm, others she helps into their wheelchairs and then pushes to their destination. She is proud the Wednesday afternoon events, when she's volunteering, have the largest attendance of any of the special events held at the nursing home.

Mom is there over the lunch hour and often helps those who need assistance eating their meals, coercing some without appetites to have just one more bite, the same as she did with her children when they were little. She has helped residents with knitting projects, taught some the nearly forgotten art of tatting, which she herself learned from her mother, and taught others how to play euchre, crazy eights, solitaire and other card games. There's very little Mom likes better than a good game of cards.

"Solitaire is wonderful for someone who is alone," she says. "It keeps them occupied and it's great for the brain. Anything to keep a person thinking."

Up until a couple of years ago Mom hosted a barbecue for the residents who were mobile enough to visit the home she shares with my dad. She would supply the lemonade and her famous homemade butter tarts and everyone would sit on the front lawn, in the shade of the stately old trees, reminiscing about their lives before "the home."

Also until just a few years ago, she would drive carloads of residents to neighbouring towns for shopping expeditions or lunch out at a local restaurant. When she turned eighty she took a Wednesday afternoon off from her volunteer duties and took the mandatory training course to have her driver's license renewed. Now, though, she usually gets a ride with a younger volunteer or takes the bus when excursions are planned during her Wednesday volunteer time.

Mom swears that she is going to live at the nursing home "when she gets old." We tease her and remind her that she is older than a lot of residents living there now and that if she lives as long as her father, who was at the nursing home for a brief period of time before his death at age ninety-eight, she still has a lot of volunteer years left.

Mom transitioned from hardworking farm wife and mother of five to healthcare aide to hard-working volunteer. She will continue to think of herself that way, and when she moves in she will surely help the staff members with the other residents. That's just the kind of inspirational woman she is.

~Lynne Turner

One Hundred Smiles

Those who bring sunshine to the lives of others cannot keep it from themselves.
~James Matthew Barrie

As I sat in my car in the Target parking lot, killing time before my next appointment, it came to me like a vision. My hands were shaking as I picked up my cell phone to tell my husband how I would use what we had been through to help others. He agreed, and just like that, in a matter of minutes, a new purpose was born from our pain.

After several years in the trenches of autism, my daughter Lizzie was finally doing better and I could breathe again. She was in school all day now, so I had some free time. More importantly, her recent progress had freed up my mind to think about something other than the daily needs of our family.

I had joined the local National Autism Association board a few months earlier in hopes to volunteer wherever I was needed, but it wasn't until that day in the parking lot that I really knew why I was a part of that group.

When Lizzie was first diagnosed, life was really rough. On weekdays we had thirty hours a week of behavioral, occupational and speech therapy. At night, I spent hours on the Internet researching the latest and greatest treatments that could help give her a chance at a normal life.

No Strangers Here | 203

Days turned into weeks, weeks into months, and months into years. Our finances were drained, and although Lizzie was progressing well, I soon realized that I was exhausted physically, mentally and emotionally. Even when I was not with my daughter, I was thinking about strategies to help her speak better and learn how to socialize with her peers. At one point I realized that I hadn't had a conversation with another adult that didn't involve autism in over five years!

I never took time for myself, and even when I found myself with a few free minutes, I couldn't relax. Autism owned me. What I would have given during that hard time for an event that pulled me out of my daily responsibilities and allowed me to be carefree… even if it was just for a day.

So… that was my idea! I was going to use my time and newly freed-up mental energy to make life just a little more bearable for moms deep in the trenches with autism.

The finances were secured and the NAA was on board! We were going to treat moms of kids with autism to a relaxing day that would rejuvenate them emotionally, spiritually and physically.

The big day arrived and one hundred amazing, strong, hardworking moms walked through the doors of an exclusive local country club. I recognized their tired eyes and crushed spirits and prayed that what we had planned for them today would change that.

First, they were given a fun shirt and twenty raffle tickets they could use to try to win the more than one hundred prizes that had been donated. They could put all their raffle tickets down on one prize they really wanted, or spread them out across a variety of prizes. Next, they could relax with a massage, participate in a yoga class or simply lounge by the pool, all while listening to live music from a decade that would bring them back to a time when their responsibilities were not so heavy.

At noon, they gathered inside the beautifully decorated ballroom to enjoy a gourmet lunch and listen to an inspirational speaker, who challenged them to find peace in their tough circumstances. There was laughter and tears. At one point, I looked around the room and each and every mom had a smile on her face! One hundred beautiful glowing smiles! I had known some of these women for years and never seen them smile.

As the clock struck two, the women slowly filed out the door with their bags of goodies and new friendships. Many seemed a little lighter, as if a burden had been lifted, even if only temporarily.

When life's circumstances are so difficult, sometimes it is important to take a break from reality and just relax. I was so grateful that I was able to spearhead this event and see each of these women leave with a renewed spirit of hope and determination. The "Autism Moms' Day Out" was so popular that it has become an annual event.

~Julie Hornok

57

Hope in Orange

Whenever you read a good book, somewhere in the world a
door opens to allow in more light.
~Vera Nazarian

Once a month, every month, I'm surrounded by orange: orange shirts, orange pants, even an orange sunset. But never fresh oranges; the officers tell me the inmates make the fruit into prison hooch.

They mix pieces of stale bread with slices of oranges and water in plastic bags. Then they tie the bags beneath their ill-fitting orange clothes. Days later, when the hooch begins to smell like yeast and rotten fruit, the mixture is ready. For an hour, drunkenness dulls the color orange and the reality of barbed wire.

I understand their need to escape. I have nightmares about prison and I'm only a volunteer.

Perryville Prison is located on the outskirts of Phoenix, Arizona. Surrounded by desolation — desert and mountains of dirt — the prison could be hell, except people don't leave hell, whereas they do leave Perryville. And often return.

I don't believe in ghosts, but I do believe Perryville Prison is haunted by the women themselves. The ghosts of the past surround their heads like teased hair, and I see reflections of loved ones in the edges of their eyes.

My dear friend Sue Ellen Allen harassed me (in a good way) for a year before I finally agreed to volunteer at Perryville. Sue Ellen, an ex-con herself, started a book club during her lengthy tenure at Perryville, and what better place for a writer than a book club?

Why the initial hesitation? Was it because my father was once a parole officer? No, although he wasn't thrilled at the prospect of his daughter working with ex-cons. Was it because I don't like to volunteer? No. The main reason I didn't want to volunteer at Perryville Prison was because I was scared.

I had visions of prison movies like *Con Air*. I just knew I would end up running from some Steve Buscemi freak show. Or maybe end up murdered. Or kidnapped. Something. Because to an outsider, that's what prison is — a dark, scary place filled with hardened criminals who know how to turn a toothbrush into a lethal weapon. Was I wrong? Of course.

Getting into Perryville the first time wasn't fun. There were intimidating security guards and metal detectors that went off because of my underwire bra. Once inside, it was obvious I was in prison, what with the barbed wire, heavy locked doors and orange uniforms. Then I met the inmates, and they didn't look much like hardened criminals to me. They looked like waitresses, lawyers, mothers and aunts — normal people in abnormal and unfortunate circumstances.

Many women who end up in Perryville are there because of drinking and driving. One of the saddest stories I've heard is that of Jessica Robinson, whose mother Jeanne first introduced me to the world of Perryville Prison's book club. Jessica was in radiography school, on her way to a successful career, when her life changed forever. On September 5, 2008, she went out with friends, had a couple of drinks, stayed up late and fell asleep at the wheel on her way home. Her car accident killed someone, and she received a seven-year sentence to Perryville.

I've been a Perryville volunteer for two years. I now run the book club. During each visit we discuss books like *The Secret Life of Bees* and *Memoirs of a Geisha* — novels that beg to be discussed, especially by women. Every month, I have the chance to meet spectacularly intelligent women trapped in unfortunate self-made circumstances.

Yes, they feel guilt over what they did. Some nights turn into full-on therapy sessions as we discuss forgiveness and how these women worry that their children will never love them again because of the mistakes they've made. Then, later, we laugh together, because women like to laugh, even in prison.

Has my life been altered by my experiences at Perryville? Yes. Do I still have visions of *Con Air*? No, because I've come to see these women for what they are: human beings who made horrible mistakes.

I believe in the inspirational, healing power of books, which is why I'm glad to host the monthly book club. I believe in second chances, which is why educational activities are necessary at Perryville. How can we expect inmates to be rehabilitated if they do nothing but rot in a cell for seven years? They need to be reminded that there is hope, because someday the women I've worked with will be free. They will need forgiveness and support, so why not give them both while behind bars in order to make the transition easier?

I'm a proud volunteer at Perryville Prison — once hesitant, now empowered. I do it because I've made bad mistakes, too, and I want the women in orange to realize their lives aren't over. When they are free, they will be given new lives. It won't be easy for them, but I hope in some small way I've helped by teaching them the beauty of books and the beauty of sisterhood, even in the most dire of circumstances.

I walked into Perryville two years ago as a stranger. Now my girls give me hugs. They call to me from across the yard. We have inside jokes. We might be surrounded by orange, but for at least an hour a month, we transcend color and become light. For an hour, we are free.

~Sara Dobie Bauer

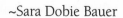

58

The Vigil

To everything there is a season, a time for every purpose under heaven. A time to be born and a time to die...
~Ecclesiastes 3:1

She lay in the hospital bed, head to one side, staring toward the dark window with unblinking eyes. Her chest heaved with every breath. The death rattle gurgled in her throat.

I knew her name but nothing more.

She looked very old.

A wedding band encircled her ring finger. Was her husband still living, or had he passed on and now waited for her to join him?

Her hand twitched, then became still.

I studied the frail form under the bedcovers. In my mind's eye I saw a little girl wearing black patent-leather shoes and white ankle socks trimmed in lace. She giggled and twirled in her Sunday-best dress, which was gathered at the waist and buttoned down the back.

Did she make chocolate chip cookies with her mommy and lick the bowl clean? Did her grandmothers shower her with hugs and kisses?

How quickly life passes by.

Did she become a mother? Was she blessed with grandchildren to love? I would never know. Our lives only intersected during my two-hour watch in the wee hours that morning.

I was on a vigil for No One Dies Alone. I'm a NODA volunteer, one of over forty such volunteers at our local hospital.

I became interested in the program while listening to a talk given by our hospital's volunteer coordinator. In her talk, the coordinator explained why an ICU nurse began NODA.

This nurse, while checking on her critical care patients at the Sacred Heart Medical Center in Eugene, Oregon, prepared to leave the room of an elderly man. In a weak voice he begged her to stay with him.

Although her heart filled with compassion for the gentleman, she had to continue her rounds. However, she promised to come back as soon as she could. But when she returned to the man's room, he had already passed on... alone.

This story about the elderly man deeply affected me. I decided to take the training and become one of our hospital's NODA volunteers.

The call for a NODA vigil comes when a patient appears to have less than seventy-two hours to live and family members are unavailable.

Upon entering the patient's room, I introduce myself, whether or not the person is responsive. During my two-hour shift I read poems, play calming CDs, hold the patient's hand, sit quietly by the bedside, or do whatever seems to console the person. I'm there only as a comforting presence.

Every NODA vigil is different. On one occasion I entered the hospital room to find two family members sitting around the gentleman's bed. Had a mistake been made? Why was I here? Our NODA training instructs us to leave the patient's room when family arrives.

After introducing myself to the women, I turned to leave. "I'll be down the hall in the little lounge area if you need me."

The older of the two ladies shook her head. "Oh no, please stay. We want your company." She introduced herself as the gentleman's wife and then gestured toward the other, younger lady. "This is his daughter."

I listened as they reminisced about the man's fondness for trucks and his love for the grandkids. They talked about their pleasant memories of him as a husband and father. All the while the man's breathing grew shallower, with longer gaps between breaths.

My two-hour vigil ended. The ladies hugged me goodbye when the next NODA volunteer arrived. As I prepared to leave the room, I noticed the man's breathing had stopped and he lay very still. The daughter had noticed it, too. She bent over her father and placed a hand on his chest.

He was gone.

Sitting with patients who have only a short time to live has made me face my own mortality. Although I have a strong faith, death itself is an unknown. Stepping into any unknown is always a bit scary. I don't want to pass from this life into the next without someone by my side, nor do I want anyone else to begin that journey while alone.

Being a NODA volunteer is bittersweet. I cannot stop anyone's final farewell. However, there is a deep satisfaction in simply being a comforting presence to a patient. Most important, on a NODA vigil, no one will pass from this life into the next all alone.

~Kathie Mitchell

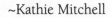

59

The Heart of a Home

It takes hands to build a house, but only hearts can build a home.
~Author Unknown

My best friend's mother was a social worker in the mid-nineties in Detroit, Michigan. Because of that, my friend Victoria and I were introduced early to the world of volunteering. We did plenty of charity work, loading non-perishables into boxes, setting out place settings for hungry children, organizing coat drives. We always had a good time, and picking up the habit young, we continued to volunteer whenever we had time, often even when we didn't. It became second nature. Hairstyles came and went, and so did boyfriends, but Victoria and I found places to donate our time because that's how we were raised.

One particular morning we had signed up for "Paint The Town," an organization in Detroit to help low-income homeowners spruce up their properties. We were assigned a dilapidated house in one of the worst areas of the city. I was afraid as we approached the front door, not knowing who we would find on the other side. We knocked three times quickly and stepped back, waiting to be let in.

When the door opened, my mouth did, too. Standing there was a little old lady with wisps of white hair and a dainty purple apron tied around her midsection.

"Hello," she said, "I'm Amelia. Please come in and I will show you where to start." Her smile shone brightly. "I was just baking some cookies for you to eat when you've finished with your work."

As she led us to the parts of her house that needed painting, my heart softened. Here was one of the scariest-looking houses in the city, but behind its doors was a sweet old lady with a cane and a big smile.

Here we were coming to help her, and instead she was doing something for us — baking homemade cookies and serving us tea!

There was no age barrier that day as we worked on Amelia's house. She stayed close by, talking to us as we painted, telling us about her native Ireland and how she came to Detroit.

I felt so sad for her then, living in such a poor part of the neighborhood with no one to keep her company. When I told her so she scoffed at me.

"Nonsense!" she scolded. "I love it here. This is my home... even if it is falling down around me. I feel blessed that you girls came to help me fix it up, but I'm happy here. I've watched the neighborhood change, seen people come and go, but I always stay. You would be amazed at the camaraderie this little city has. We may all be different on the outside, but on the inside, we are all just after the same thing... community. It's a beautiful thing you girls are doing. Keep it up. Nothing will make you happier than giving to other people, and just when you least expect it, I promise you, good will come your way — and just when you need it."

Amelia looked into my eyes and touched my heart. What she said to me that day stayed with me always, and replayed itself as I took on new volunteer work in different parts of town.

I am sure Amelia has passed away and I am uncertain as to whether her sweet little house is still standing, but what she taught me that day has stayed with me.

As you volunteer, take what you can out of every scenario. Find the positive everywhere. And never ever stop volunteering. As you make it a routine, it will become second nature, and all of the lives you touch will be forever grateful. Or maybe it will be you who is grateful, just like I was, from all I learned spending time with the little old lady with the broken-down home that was so full of love.

~Kate White

Learning Life's Language

*Always walk through life as if you have something new to learn
and you will.*

~Vernon Howard

was twenty-five years old when my first relationship ended. I
was young enough to feel like I would never get over the heartache, yet old enough to realize that I must keep busy and not
sit around moping. So I boarded an uptown subway train and
headed to midtown after work one evening.

A few days earlier, I had seen a flyer in the subway calling for
volunteer literacy tutors. I vaguely thought about helping others, but
mostly the posting intrigued me because the weekly stint was held in
the cafeteria of Colgate-Palmolive in a landmark modernist building
on Park Avenue.

That location was worlds apart from my work with graphic
designers and illustrators in a crumbling Tribeca loft that was stifling
in the summers and barely heated in the winters. And what I needed
during my time of transition was something new.

On that first night, I figured we first-time volunteer tutors would
just hear a presentation and maybe fill out some paperwork. Instead,
the volunteer coordinator ushered me to a "student" table filled with
men and women who looked twice my age. I recognized one guy
from my subway ride.

I was struck by the fact that none of the students were from other countries. They all spoke English with heavy New York accents like mine. I excused myself from the table and pulled the coordinator aside.

"Excuse me but I thought these people needed to learn English," I whispered.

"They do," he said, "but not as a second language." He could see I was perplexed so he pointed to the workbook he had given me. "This is a literacy class. These are all native English speakers who haven't learned to read or write at an adult level."

"How could that be?" I gestured back over to the table. The students were all reasonably well-dressed individuals. One woman had a cardigan sweater buttoned over her fast-food restaurant uniform. A physically fit man wore a jacket that identified him as a youth swim coach at the Y.

I pointed at one man who was browsing the scores in the sports section of *The New York Post*. "Surely they went to school."

The coordinator sighed with exasperation and led me by the arm back to the student table. In a loud voice he said, "Your past circumstances do not matter. All that matters is that you are here now — to learn from each other."

He added that last part more for my benefit than theirs. But I got it. This wasn't an "English as a Second Language" class for foreigners.

I took my seat and we began by introducing ourselves. None of the adults were indigent or homeless. They all had jobs. Most had families. One person even owned his house in Queens.

One woman cleaned offices; another woman repaired watches at a jewelry store. One guy was a bike messenger (which was a bustling occupation in the pre-Internet days of the 1990s), and another man was applying for medallion insurance for a taxicab.

We opened the workbook and it was heartbreaking to watch each, in turn, struggle to read at a fifth-grade level. For whatever reasons, they had never mastered reading and writing in school, even though they were highly articulate individuals. But being New Yorkers, they had a grasp of money and arithmetic at an Ivy League level!

These were intelligent and successful people. Yet if I didn't know them and had just encountered them briefly in my daily life, I probably would have labeled them as "stupid" because they couldn't read. I was embarrassed to realize that despite my college education, I was the stupid one.

A fire lit within me.

My life's journey has taken me far from that modernist cafeteria in New York City. But in the ensuing twenty years, I have never once stopped being a volunteer literacy tutor. I am that passionate about it. And to this day, I begin every tutoring session by saying: "Your past circumstances do not matter. All that matters is that we are here now — to learn from each other."

~Yvonne Pesquera

Finding My Future

*Life is like a game of cards. The hand you are dealt is
determinism; the way you play it is free will.*
~Jawaharlal Nehru

Books have always been some of my best friends. "When you were little," my mother always said, "you would sit in your playpen for hours reading your books. And you didn't like anyone to bother you, either!"

Like most suburban households of the sixties, ours had a steady supply of magazines and so, even as a young child, I'd avidly flip through the pages of *National Geographic*. I was raised on *Wild Kingdom* and loved to look at the colorful photos of African animals, dreaming of one day traveling to exotic places where I'd help people solve their problems. Just exactly what I'd help them with, I didn't really know. Still, I guess it came as no surprise that as soon as I graduated from college, I volunteered for the Peace Corps.

My assignment was to Jamaica, where I was one of forty-two volunteers in Group 42. For the first two months of our service, we had training every day in Kingston, the capital. Each of us lived with a Jamaican host family in hot, dirty Spanish Town, which we called Punish Town. Most volunteers were housed in one neighborhood, but because our group was so large, some of us were sent to live on the other side of town. Every morning we walked to the local bus park to catch a half-hour ride to Kingston, and every morning the neighborhood dogs attacked us. I never walked alone.

One of my neighbors was Andy and, because of the dogs, we walked many miles together, gaining a greater appreciation for each other with each step.

Andy was from the town next to Newport, Oregon, and I was from the town next to Newport, Rhode Island. One day we were sitting at the dining room table in my host family's home playing a game of Hearts with some of our fellow volunteers. Glancing up from my cards, my blue eyes met Andy's green ones above his dimpled smile. My stomach flip-flopped and my breath stuck in my throat as I swallowed a surprised "Oh!" before snapping my gaze back to the cards in my hand. I already had a boyfriend back home, so I didn't return Andy's affection. At first.

When our training was over, I ended up working in Kingston. I lived with three other volunteers who spent their weekends at embassy parties or sailing. I hailed from the sailing capital of the world and if I'd wanted to sail and party, I would have stayed home. I'd broken up with my boyfriend by this time so going home to my old life wasn't an easy option. Still, I grew despondent and was ready to resign, when one day Andy came to town. Our house served as the local flophouse for volunteers coming in from the country, and Andy was one of them. He lived in Christiana and worked with yam farmers in a town called Wait-A-Bit. "I think I'm going to quit," I told him.

"What?" he said, "don't do that. I know another volunteer who needs help. She teaches environmental education and I'll put you in touch with her." And he did.

I made arrangements to visit and talk with her about working with the Jamaica Junior Naturalists. "You can stay with me," Andy said. So one evening I stepped off the bus in Christiana, where Andy lived in a two-bedroom apartment with only one double bed. As the night wore on, he smiled that familiar dimpled grin and proposed, "You can sleep in my bed with me or on the floor with the cockroaches."

I hate cockroaches. The rest is history.

I believe you won't miss what you've never known, and I spent the next two years teaching Jamaican children to know and love some of the many beautiful animals of their island. Together, we learned about sea turtles, manatees and crocodiles, and we explored coral reefs and mangrove swamps. I helped to establish the first marine sanctuary in Jamaica, and I hope I instilled a newfound appreciation for the natural world in the hearts and minds of its youth.

When their service is concluded, most Peace Corps volunteers will readily admit that in spite of their efforts, they feel like they received more than they gave. I returned home with my future. I didn't join the Peace Corps to meet my mate, but Andy and I have been married for twenty-seven years now.

The Peace Corps' motto is "The Toughest Job You'll Ever Love" and it's the first job I ever held that could be defined as such. We have five children, and being a parent is definitely my second job that fits that description. We don't subscribe to *National Geographic*, but we do raise our children to be citizens of the world. And from the day they're born, we teach them that their purpose in life is to make the world a better place.

~Kelly Kittel

Giving Kids the World

When someone tells you that you can't do something, perhaps
you should consider that they are only telling you what they
can't do.

~Sheldon Cahoon

"What would you wish for if you could have any wish in the whole wide world?" I asked, in what I hoped was an ethereal and magical voice. The child I was interviewing didn't care about the tone of my voice — she already knew exactly what she wanted.

"To visit the Mickey Mouse Clubhouse!"

I'm not a regular viewer of the Disney Junior channel, but I knew enough to know that Mickey's colorful clubhouse existed only in the cartoon world.

"How about a trip to the Walt Disney World Resort?" I enthused. "At Disney you can explore Mickey Mouse's house! And Minnie's house too!"

The little girl batted her eyelashes and looked up at me expectantly. "No. The Mickey Mouse Clubhouse, the one on TV. I really want to go there. To the real one on TV."

"Right. Silly me." How was I going to make this happen?

I am a volunteer Wish Grantor with Make-A-Wish® British Columbia and Yukon — a non-profit organization that grants the wishes of children with life-threatening medical conditions to enrich the human experience with hope, strength and joy.

This means that as a Wish Grantor I am often required to get creative to find ways to fulfill the unique wishes of children.

We joke amongst ourselves that the only limitation to a wish is the limits of a child's imagination — which we all know can be endless!

I sometimes say that I'm a "jaded" Wish Grantor after so many years, but I still tear up at those magical moments that can't help but restore my faith in humanity.

Like when firefighters or police officers take time out to deliver a laptop to a child in the hospital. Or when an entire restaurant staff decorates a booth, buys gifts, and dresses up in costume in anticipation of a wish kid's visit. Or the time I took a family out to a pricey dinner to celebrate their child's wish and when the time came to ask for the bill, we were told an anonymous stranger had already paid it. Or when a celebrity learned that the teenaged boy who wished to meet him was too sick to travel and called him at home, only to be told "No way. I'm still coming. I'm hanging in there."

We get to see inspiring stories play out regularly, and I think all of us volunteers are better people because of it. We get to see the good in the world, every day.

In *Chicken Soup for the Soul: The Cancer Book* (2009) I shared a story about a significant experience that helped shape my life — volunteering as a camp counsellor at a pediatric oncology camp in British Columbia, Canada, called Camp Goodtimes. That experience touched my soul so much, but I don't think I could fully relate to what those kids were going through until years later, when my nine-year-old cousin was diagnosed with a malignant brain tumor and we were told she might not survive the night.

When things seemed at their most hopeless, a fairy godmother from Make-A-Wish entered our lives. The timing was perfect because Paige was already physically, mentally, and emotionally drained from the first part of her treatment. Her wish — for a baby grand piano — gave her the strength she needed to push through the second half.

In her words, "Playing my piano took me to a world of my own.

A world that held no pain; a world that held only beauty; a world that was filled with hope; a world that brought me comfort: a world that gave me strength."

Shortly after seeing how this experience changed her life, I contacted Make-A-Wish to find out how I could get involved in this incredible organization. The first wish I was assigned was a celebrity escort — accompanying a wish child onto a movie set to meet her favorite star. I was stoked to say the least.

Visions of hunky heartthrobs danced through my head, so I was naturally surprised to learn that the celebrity guest we'd be meeting wasn't exactly a conventional human movie star. A five-year-old girl from North Dakota had wished her most heartfelt wish — to meet the canine stars of the *Air Buddies* movies — an adorable quintet of Golden Retriever puppies who always seemed to find themselves on unique adventures.

When Ellen's limo rolled up on set, we were immediately escorted to a trailer where the Buddies were eagerly waiting to meet her. I can't even begin to describe the adorably cute chaos that followed but it involved lots of puppy hugs and squeals of glee from a spunky little girl dressed in head-to-toe pink who defined the phrase Bald Is Beautiful. We spent a full day on set. Ellen got to play with the puppies, watch them film stunts, and sit in her own pint-sized director's chair with her favorite puppy — Rosebud — curled up in her lap. When the film wrapped, we were all stunned when the producer decided to put Rosebud on a plane and send her to live with Ellen in North Dakota!

Years later, I still get e-mailed updates from Ellen's family with photos of Ellen and Rosebud growing up together. Rosebud even helps give back to Ellen's cause — people donate to cancer fundraisers to get their photo taken with Rosebud the celebrity dog! Ellen's story, my first wish-granting experience, resonates with me to this day.

Since then, I have granted dozens of wishes — Disney parks, cruises, celebrity-meet-and-greets, shopping sprees and even a gym membership. Sure I've met some of the "heartthrob celebrities" I'd signed on hoping to meet, but in every case they were overshadowed by the true star — the joyful child whose dream was coming true.

My full circle moment was when I recently granted the wish of a little girl named Paige — just like my cousin — who also had a malignant brain tumor. Instead of a piano, this Paige wished to spend time on the beach stomping sand castles with her grandma, so we whisked her off to Mexico to stomp to her heart's content.

Some people mistakenly refer to these special joyful moments, like stomping sand castles, as "final dying wishes," but in most cases I have witnessed, they are instead actually life-affirming wishes that give sick children the strength to continue to fight and survive.

It shows them that miracles can happen and that many people are wishing them well. Out of dozens of wishes, two wish kids have sadly passed away, one almost immediately following his wish to visit a popular television show. But I feel so fortunate to have gotten to know him, and truly believe he held on an extra month and a half and created so many more priceless memories with his family until his wish could come true.

I have heard similar stories of other kids — whose doctors advised they might be too sick to travel — who suddenly perked up as soon as they arrived at their destination and enjoyed a carefree week with family before returning to the realities of their lives.

Call it karma, or just plain luck, but a few years ago I received a phone call from the Orlando Tourism Bureau, informing me I had won a trip to Orlando! I was stoked to visit Disney and Universal Studios, but I was most looking forward to the opportunity to visit a very special place called Give Kids The World Village® where so many wish kids had visited.

It's a magical fairytale seventy-acre resort that accommodates kids (and their families) who wish to visit theme parks in the Orlando area. I spent an afternoon there as a "Volunteer Angel" where I had the opportunity to meet wish kids from around the world and hear their inspirational stories.

The most inspirational story I heard that day though, was about how this magical village came to be. The founder, a man named

Henri Landwirth, did not spend his childhood in a fairytale village.

He grew up, instead, as a prisoner of Auschwitz concentration camp, and lost both his parents before the war ended. Henri worked his way to America on a ship with only twenty dollars in his pocket, but through hard work and perseverance, eventually became a hotel manager.

Henri heard about a little girl named Amy with leukemia who sadly passed away before the arrangements could be made to organize her dream trip to Orlando, and Henri was determined that other kids have the opportunity to fulfill their wishes in time. He felt his own childhood had been ripped away from him too soon, and he didn't want that to happen to any other child.

Through his efforts, an astonishing 138,000 wish families have stayed at Give Kids The World Village since it opened in 1989 and have enjoyed all-inclusive experiences while making day trips to ride roller coasters and meet Mickey Mouse.

My volunteer work with children with life-threatening medical conditions has truly opened the world to me, helped me uncover my passions, and helped mold me into the person of purpose I am today. I feel so fortunate that these brave kids have invited me into their lives and into their imaginations and I have learned to live life to the fullest and fulfill my own dreams, by asking myself regularly: "What would you wish for if you could have any wish in the whole wide world? Then attempting to make it a reality.

~Cassie Silva

One Little Human

Unless someone like you cares a whole awful lot, nothing is going to get better. It's not.
~Dr. Seuss

One little human
Falling away from the pack
Can restore hope to the world
Bring humanity back

One little human
Stepping away from the crowd
Can feel the anguish of the multitudes
And voice it out loud

One little human
Scarred and nearly broken
Can take faith, hope and love
Where it's never been spoken

One little human
Abiding by love's creed
Can heal the whole planet
Let's wish it Godspeed

One little human
It may very well be you
Can teach all other humans
What they are able to do.

~Jen Ward

Volunteering & Giving Back

A Calling

64

Carving Out a Future

*A dream doesn't become reality through magic; it takes sweat,
determination and hard work.*
~Colin Powell

don't actually remember the accident. I had some pretty massive
injuries, like a broken back and shattered pelvis, and a big shard
of steel went right through my leg. I was told that I probably went
through the windshield on the car's second rollover and bled out.
I died and had to be resuscitated three times in the ambulance. And
that wasn't even the worst of it. I had a fractured skull, which caused a
traumatic brain injury. But all of that news came later. All I knew when I
woke up was that I didn't remember anything that had happened to me
since I was thirteen years old. I had lost half my life's memories. Despite
all the missing memories, there is one thing I remember from the night
of my accident. I remember lying in the road, all broken and bloody,
trying to drag myself out of the wreckage. I remember feeling like I was
floating up and out of my body, looking at the whole scene below me.
And then, all of a sudden, I was in a much different place.

When I was a kid, my family used to go to Rifle Falls, a really
beautiful, peaceful spot in Little Box Canyon. During my out-of-body
experience, I went there and found my mother waiting for me in the
sunlight, sitting at a table covered with all the food we used to take
on those picnics. She said to me, "You know, it's alright if you want
to stay. But you have more to do." I didn't know what she meant, so

I asked her what it was I had to do. She said, "I can't tell you that, but it will find you. And you will find it." Her message was a mystery.

I was born in Pueblo, Colorado, and at the age of three, my family moved to Glenwood Springs, where I grew up with two older brothers and a sister. Everyone in the family is really creative and talented. I loved drawing and painting and music, and I was constantly building things, too. I had a happy, normal childhood until I was thirteen and my mom died of esophageal cancer. I don't remember what happened after that, because it was all wiped out in the accident, but my family and friends told me that I really changed. I stopped trying at school. I was playing guitar and joined a band, which I guess gave me some direction, but I also got overwhelmed and depressed at times. I was going nowhere and doing nothing. They tell me I even tried to end my own life.

The memories I lost seemed to be all the ones after my mom died. After her death, the next memory I have is of the aftermath of the accident.

When the doctors took out the pins holding my leg together, MRSA, a staph infection, developed in my femur. Heavy-duty antibiotics were started which affected my hearing. I found myself in the unfortunate position of having to choose between saving my hearing or my leg. I decided to choose my hearing but then the decision was made for me, anyway. The infection blew up, entered my bloodstream and was about to take my life, so they performed an emergency surgery to remove my right leg.

What I didn't know was that I would experience something called Reflexive Sympathetic Dystrophy Syndrome, from separating my spine from my pelvis. The nerves in my lower body, due to the damage, continue to send pain signals even though everything is as healed up as it is going to be. This causes me to burn from the waist down. I do experience "phantom pain" as well and I had another surgery to control both of these, a laminectomy. A device was implanted in my back that has wires that go up into my spinal cord to override my motor neurons. It's remote controlled, so when I turn it on, I can interrupt the signal between my lower body and my brain to help me sleep at night. I have to turn it off during the day and just deal with the pain, because it affects my ability to walk.

Some months after the accident, I was fortunate enough to meet a wonderful woman named Kelly, who would become my soul mate. We were married only four months after meeting and have been together going on eighteen years now. She has the heart and patience of an angel and without her by my side I would have never been able to chase these dreams. She made the years of recovery seem to go by quickly and was not afraid to stick it out through hard times. She is the love of my life.

After years in physical therapy and rehabilitation, I was desperately searching for meaning to my life. As fate had it, an old friend from high school, Nick, not that I remembered him from those years, came to me with some alabaster stones from a local quarry and reminded me that I was an artist. He left me with the stones and a file.

When Nick came back a few weeks later, I had carved one of the stones into a bear, reigniting the artist within. The owner of the quarry was so impressed he invited me to carve in a small corner of an old coal chute. When I started to carve that first little hunk of rock it felt natural, like it was what I should be doing. I wasn't truly convinced until I was halfway through "An Eagle's Dream," my first commission. I realized that I had potential, as did the owner of the quarry. He invited me to tour the quarry and showed me a wall of alabaster 176 feet long and 12 feet tall. He asked me what I could do with it.

That's when I understood my mom's message. I had found the eagle and it had found me, 100 feet inside a mountain.

I decided to dedicate the eagle to America's soldiers — all of the men and women who fight and sacrifice and die to protect our freedom. I can't really explain it; I was just so proud of my friends and everyone who has served our country as soldiers. I guess I felt left behind or somehow cheated out of the opportunity to serve in a similar fashion. It was very important for me to find a way to serve, even if I couldn't serve as a soldier. I knew I could serve my country by thanking and honoring our soldiers, and I could raise awareness of the cost of our freedom. I call the monument "Freedom's Eagle." Some people eventually hit a wall in their life; I guess when I hit mine I decided to carve it.

The amazing thing about carving this monument is that there's something about the work itself that takes me totally out of my body. I don't know if it's the deep concentration or because I'm so passionate about it, but when I'm there and I only have twelve inches of visibility from all the dust, those twelve inches are my universe. While I'm carving, that's what matters, not my pain or my past. Everything is focused right there.

I had a lot of support the first couple of years I was carving. I founded the Cost of Freedom Eagle Foundation and was able to help out some local high school students with college arts scholarships. I also used the eagle as a platform to raise funds for prosthetics research and development for veterans. One naval officer was so touched after seeing the project that he offered me his service coin; I've been extremely humbled and honored by the overwhelming support of all branches of the military that have become aware of this project. And then, a tragedy: After receiving approvals to work on my project, government bureaucrats caused the mine to shut down and the Freedom's Eagle project was grounded. The quarry shut down, and I lost the freedom to continue working and all of my hopes and dreams were gone in a moment. I continued to sculpt smaller pieces, but my heart and soul were trapped inside a 13,000-foot Colorado mountain. My life reached a low point and at times I had given up all hope. Unexpectedly, after a decade of persistence, the doors for the quarry and my project were opened.

I have a personal belief that guides me: "Adversity is the spice of life." Even though I lost so much in that accident, in an ironic way I gained something better. I awoke with a new appreciation for life. I wanted to work hard and do everything I could to really live. I've recovered enough to hold a full-time job, too, almost two decades after my life nearly ended. I can't be a soldier, so I do what I can to honor and show how proud I am of the American Armed Forces.

I have learned a lot of lessons in my life. One is that people with disabilities can accomplish whatever they set their minds to. Another is to never give up on your dreams. But the greatest lesson the Cost of Freedom Eagle project taught me is this: Get out of yourself and do something good for someone else. Make a difference. That's what has saved me after all these years. That's what it's all about.

~Jeremy Russell

For more about Jeremy and the Cost of Freedom Eagle, go to: www.thevalleyinsider.com/location/carving-freedoms-eagle/ or www.thevalleyinsider.com/videos/jeremy-russell-sculptor/ or www.thefreedomeagle.com.

65

My Hero

*I believe that what we become depends on what our fathers
teach us at odd moments, when they aren't trying to teach us.
We are formed by little scraps of wisdom.*
~Umberto Eco, Foucault's Pendulum

I stared at the black box sitting in the bathroom. "I must have heard wrong. Certainly. Please, Lord." I waited, frozen. The sticky May air, combined with the hot curlers in my hair, was causing me to sweat. My heart beat wildly as I watched the box, hoping, praying that it would be silent.

"There's a man on the water tower! He's got a gun, and he's shooting at people!" The distressed voice of a police officer shattered the air. "We've got to block off the streets!"

"This isn't happening," I tried to convince myself. "This is NOT happening!"

I ran to the phone and called my mother. "What is going on?" I practically yelled into the phone.

"I'm not sure. Your dad is on his way to find out." By the sound of her voice, I knew that she, too, was trying hard not to panic. As the principal of our school, graduation day was already hectic for her. That, coupled with the fact that my father, who had just been released from the hospital, was on his way to a possibly life-threatening crime scene, and I, her last child, would be graduating that night, could only have made the panic of the situation more pronounced.

I looked at the radio again, reminding myself that bad things like this just don't happen in our small town of approximately 1,200 people. Gunmen on water towers were only for the movies and big cities.

The large box radio was actually my dad's connection to his volunteer job with the fire department and ambulance service in our city. Before we had moved to the small town, my dad had been a full-time firefighter on the large Kansas City force. In a change of pace from the big city, our move had brought volunteer-only opportunities on the rural department.

My father's life had always been about helping others. After graduating from high school not knowing how to read, he worked hard to overcome the odds against him and began a life of service. He taught himself to read, became a firefighter, received his certificate in emergency medicine, founded and pastored a church, and founded a volunteer-staffed school with the vision of providing an affordable education for children who were like he had been. He also went on to become the chief of police of a larger town near us. His hospital trip resulted from a scaffold falling on him while he was helping me decorate for my graduation. My mother always joked that if there had been a volunteer trash department, my father would have been in it.

A screaming voice jerked me from my thoughts. "Unit 18! Somebody get unit 18!"

They were calling for my father. I stared at the big red numbers on my clock — 6:00 p.m. One hour left before I was going to graduate from high school. One hour. Why now? Why MY father? Get someone else! My mind was racing. People were on their way for MY graduation. What was supposed to be a memory-filled night had the potential to turn out tragic.

My dad was in no condition to be climbing a water tower, but I knew that was exactly what he was going to do.

I called our school secretary as my mind raced with worst-case scenarios. "He knows what he is doing," she reminded me. This hadn't been his first time climbing a tower to rescue someone.

"He's going up!"

I looked in horror at the radio.

"Unit 18 is going up!"

"Why do you always have to be the hero?" I cried to no one in particular.

I waited in silence for what seemed like an eternity. Tears came as I pictured a graduation without him. Minutes ticked by like years as I waited for something. Anything.

"They are coming down." I exhaled for the first time in thirty minutes, and I suddenly realized that life was moving again. Thanking God, I dressed quickly for graduation.

Graduation began late, but the day's events made us even more thankful that we could all be together—happy, healthy and safe. A few minutes didn't seem to matter after such an unbelievable day.

As I rose to give my speech, I thanked those who had played a significant role in my life. I looked at my father, with his broad shoulders, bruised face and tear-filled eyes. My admiration for the man overwhelmed me.

"Tonight you were the town's hero," I said through my tears. "But you will always be mine."

~Corrie Lopez

What If It Had Been Me?

*Give freely to the world these gifts of love and compassion. Do
not concern yourself with how much you receive in return, just
know in your heart it will be returned.*

~Steve Maraboli, Life, the Truth, and Being Free

Sitting alone in my office on a late December evening in 2013,
I was too tired to do any more work, yet also too tired to face
the hour-long commute home. Scrolling aimlessly through
Facebook, I came across a news story about two children in
Atlanta, Georgia and the one wish they had for Christmas. It wasn't
a wish for the latest video game, or smart phone — it was a wish for
a kidney. Not a kidney for either one of them, but for their beloved
grandmother. After learning that no family or close friends were a
match, and with the help of their mother, they set up a Facebook
page called "A Kidney for Gran." They were asking everyone, anyone,
to help.

I was struck by these kids' selfless nature, but I was also deeply
moved by their decision to reach out to a world full of strangers, hoping for a miracle. What if I needed a kidney and no one I knew was
a match? How hard would I pray every night that someone would
not only be a match, but also agree to share a vital organ with a total
stranger? How full of fear would the people closest to me be wondering how much longer we had together? What kind of person would
willingly endure travel, months of testing and major surgery — to

help a stranger live?

That kind of person turned out to be me. An average forty-eight-year-old divorcée from California with four kids, a full-time job in high tech and a belief that we should do unto others as we would have them do for us.

Sharing a blood type with the grandmother in need was the first sign that I should throw my hat in the ring. The next sign was simply a quiet voice inside me that said, "You know of the need and you can meet it. You'll be fine."

I picked up my cell phone and dialed the Piedmont Transplant Center in Atlanta. I left my contact information. Within a week I was contacted by a transplant coordinator, a kind woman with a warm Southern drawl. She asked questions; I answered them. After going over my answers with one of the transplant doctors it was decided that I was a viable candidate, and thus began my eight months of multiple blood tests, urine tests, travel to Stanford Hospital for a nuclear "glofil" kidney clearance test, and travel to Atlanta the next May for a full physical, mental and social evaluation.

From a treadmill stress test and a CT scan of my vascular system to a psychological exam and a review with a social worker of every personal facet of my life, no stone was left unturned.

I was not a direct match for the grandmother, who I now knew as Beverly, but I agreed to enter into the paired donation program, where another team who is not a direct match for each other would essentially "trade" kidneys with us. What this meant was that I went from volunteering to save one life to being a part of a trade that would save two lives.

During the eight months of testing I had plenty of time to think, and I received input from friends, family and strangers. Most were encouraging, some not, but only out of fear for my safety. Through it all, I never felt like I needed to turn back or rescind my offer. As simple as it sounds, it was the right thing to do. And I was never afraid. I imagined myself in Beverly's shoes. What if it had been me?

Once the testing was complete, we were entered into a database of other potential donor/recipient teams. We had an immediate match, but the recipient had too many antibodies against me. The second match came just as quickly and after a bit more testing it was confirmed: The transplant surgery would be on August 26th, 2014.

With my twenty-three-year-old in tow, I flew to Atlanta and back to the Southern hospitality of Beverly's family and the Piedmont Transplant Center on August 24th. Our families now inextricably bonded, my son waited with Beverly's family while my kidney was removed and flown to New Jersey, and a new kidney was flown to Atlanta and transplanted into Beverly. Bev's new kidney started to work immediately as did mine for the recipient in Jersey. The surgeries were a total success.

After a week of recovery I flew back to California and back to my life. Beverly is healthy and active again with her family and friends. Another person is healthy again as well, having given a new home to my kidney. I wish him or her the very best.

I came away from the experience knowing it was I who received the blessing. How often in life are we called to do the heroic, to set aside our fears and selfish natures to voluntarily help another person live? I don't feel like a hero. I feel like I paid forward a life debt and I would gladly do it all over again. During the psychological evaluation, the psychiatrist, with his measured Southern tone, asked, "What in the world would possess you to donate a kidney to a person you do not know?" My answer was simple, "What if it had been me? What if I needed one and my only hope was a stranger? I would hope someone would step up."

What if it had been me, indeed.

~Leslie Calderoni

Treasures Ransomed from the Trash

We are each of us angels with only one wing, and we can only
fly by embracing one another.
~Luciano de Crescenzo

Sitting on the playroom floor, I held a beautiful little boy named Joshua. His infectious smile seemed to fill the room. Gazing into his eyes, there was little sign of his horrific beginning. My eyes blurred with tears. This precious boy was one of many thousands of abandoned infants in Uganda, left on the streets to die of starvation by parents suffering from severe poverty or disease.

Joshua was one of the fortunate few. The police discovered him just before he would have died of exposure. Starving wild dogs wandering the streets and alleys commonly devour such babies. Little Josh faced another challenge; he inherited the deadly AIDS virus. As soon as he arrived and was tested at our baby home, he began receiving regular doses of life-saving medicines, nutritious food, and loving care from our staff of Ugandan "mothers." What a radiant, energetic boy he was now, giggling and squirming in my lap. Three other rescued babies crawled over my legs and reached out to be held. Each one was adorable.

I had come to Uganda to see the miracles being worked there, and a fountain of tears erupted again as I pondered the fact that Joshua's hopeless state, as well as those of all the darling children clamoring around me, had been forever changed by a divine encounter I had just a few years earlier.

I had been speaking at a women's conference in England when I met a beautiful Ugandan woman. During the luncheon, I felt drawn to go over and talk with her. Her name was Agnes, and she was dressed in a beautiful golden-colored African-print gown. We chatted, and I learned about her life and ministry in Uganda, where she and her husband founded a church and a school for orphaned kids. She remarked that the talk I had just given at the conference, entitled, "You Are Treasure, Not Trash," had the kind of message desperately needed by the struggling women of Uganda. She was taking it back to uplift them. Her own story was compelling. Her parents died of AIDS, and she and her siblings survived by selling popcorn on the streets. I knew immediately that meeting her was a direct answer to my prayers about investing my life more into helping orphans around the world.

I shared about our own beloved daughter, who we adopted from China, who also was abandoned as an infant, and my desire to help more like her. Agnes divulged some unforgettable and cruel facts. "Many women are hopeless and desperate in my country… often they cast their newborn babies into the trash and latrines." Her eyes filled with tears as she continued in a low, compassionate voice. "Recently in my own neighborhood, children were screaming hysterically as they witnessed a wild dog devouring a dead baby." At this point, we were both gulping back sobs.

"Your present school is wonderfully assisting kids older than five," I commented, "but what about the abandoned babies? What could we do together to rescue these babies from being put in the trash?"

She replied candidly that in Uganda, "There are no government funds to rescue children or support homes for them—none. The future of these babies rests solely in the hands of those whose hearts and hands are moved to help."

"Well, I guess that would be me," I said. I didn't have the money personally, but I knew I could be a voice for these kids in America. I took that first scary step with which every important journey begins. I knew in my heart that we had to build a home for them. I had just enough faith to take my own first baby steps for the sake of Uganda's babies.

After returning home to Colorado, the excitement in my heart began to spread through my social circles. Like a seed planted and watered in the soil of caring hearts, I felt encouraged as my vision began to grow. In a way, it reminded me of a long row of dominoes falling one upon another and creating momentum. Children, family members, close friends, teenagers, teachers, moms, dads and grandparents began to respond to the call for help. Friends told friends who told other friends. Benefit concerts, ladies' teas, garage sales, spaghetti dinners, hand-knit baby blankets and baked goods sales spontaneously multiplied, the message of hope for these needy newborns amplified.

The elementary school where I taught adopted the project as part of the school's outreach program. The school brilliantly gave each student one dollar as a fundraising "seed." They encouraged each girl and boy to "think outside the box" and multiply that dollar to support the baby home.

The children's ideas were as multifaceted as a rainbow: Some made and sold friendship bracelets or brownies; those with musical talent gave open-air concerts in malls with a donation bucket at their feet; others shoveled snow from sidewalks, scrubbed floors or walked people's dogs for a small donation.

The kindergarten families organized their own garage sale at school and invited the older grades to shop... all for the love of the babies in Africa. Then, during a designated chapel, the children brought in their profits with laughter and celebration. One boy dumped his entire savings for a new bicycle (more than one hundred dollars) into the offering basket. "I'd rather give this to the kids who need bikes in Uganda," he said, glowing with the happiness that accompanies such sacrificial giving.

During that year, many others were moved by these babies' stories and joined in the unfolding miracle. The result? Land was purchased and the new baby home transitioned from "faith to fact." It now houses twenty-five priceless human beings ransomed from the trash.

Since we opened our doors, over fifty children have been rescued, with eighteen of them placed in loving forever families. Boys and girls who arrived with marks of abuse, parasites, and malnutrition are now healing inside and out, being nurtured body and soul. Tragic beginnings are being reversed. Their fragile lives now include loving caretakers, bikes to ride and swings to swing on, good food and safe shelter. They have "brothers and sisters" to play with and a safe oasis in which to bloom and be children.

After a tearful goodbye and many, many hugs, the time came for me to return home. Sitting on the airplane high over the ocean, I realized I left a huge part of my heart in Africa. The joyous images of these rescued little ones, these "treasures ransomed from the trash," will forever be imprinted in my heart and soul. I am continually amazed at how the Lord can plant a seed in the heart of just one person, and multiply it to so many. The work goes on month to month to meet the needs of these little ones. What the world so easily throws away as trash, God treasures, and so must we.

~Claudia Porter

The Work of Our Hearts

When you walk in purpose, you collide with destiny.
~Ralph Buchanan

woke up in the middle of the night with the answer I'd been seeking: I would self-publish the book of essays I had written about my journey through my mother's Alzheimer's and I would donate all the monies from the book to Alzheimer's research and programs.

It was the summer of 2006, and for weeks I'd been wrestling with a question: Should I seek a traditional publisher or independently produce the book? Both seemed daunting; in the past, I had primarily written books for and with other people and publication wasn't my problem. But this book, *Love in the Land of Dementia: Finding Hope in the Caregiver's Journey*, was the work of my heart, born out of my desire to stay connected with my mother and find the joys and blessings in her experiences with Alzheimer's. I wanted to share my stories of hope so they might help other caregivers.

"What about donating a portion of the proceeds?" my partner Ron asked. I was already making a marginal living; Ron's suggestion was practical but I shook my head.

"I think I'm supposed to donate it all," I told him. "That way, instead of selling a book, I'll be raising money for a cause I'm passionate about."

I talked through the details, consulting knowledgeable friends, an attorney and our local Alzheimer's Association. My mission: to use the book as a catalyst to raise $50,000 for Alzheimer's. There was one glitch; I estimated the cost of designing and printing could be in the thousands. Where would I get the money? But even though I was often worried about funds, this hurdle didn't bother me. My intuition was strong. I was supposed to do this and would raid my savings if needed. Ron was excited about the project and pledged to work with me and help me make it happen.

"We will also help you," my friends Rex and Jane said. They had shepherded several books through production and were extremely savvy. Plus, they wanted to be part of my mission.

Over the next months, Ron and I spent hours with Rex and Jane, working on design, cover, production and print details. Endlessly patient, they were dedicated to creating the book I envisioned. And they kept their fees to a minimum.

When the finished product arrived months later, I felt a sense of pride and completion. The beautiful cover featured one of my mother's paintings, the type was easy to read, the interior design inviting.

Ron and I had often performed my stories together, and we began speaking and sharing stories from the book with Alzheimer's associations, healthcare professionals, caregivers' groups and others. When we traveled, we reached out to Alzheimer's groups to set up speaking engagements. We were always moved and inspired by the people we met.

"The person with Alzheimer's is the pupil in God's eye," the priest in an eleventh-century church in Florence, Italy told us.

"Your story is my story," a man in Istanbul, Turkey said.

"I've been caring for my mother for ten years," a woman from Brooklyn, New York said. "It has been the most meaningful experience in my life."

"When I learned Mama had dementia, I quit my job in Houston and moved back home," a woman in St. Thomas, Virgin Islands said. "I wanted my children to know their grandmother in all the stages of her life and I wanted to be here to care for her."

Sometimes we spoke in front of hundreds of people; other times we talked to groups of ten. When possible, we brought books and people often donated more than the suggested fifteen-dollar price, knowing that all the proceeds went to Alzheimer's research and programs.

By 2011 we had done it! We had raised $50,000 for Alzheimer's. But we kept going; we were still learning and growing. The work was healing for both of us and we loved connecting with other caregivers.

In 2012 I was ready to give the book a wider distribution and reached out to Central Recovery Press. They published an enhanced edition in 2013. Today, our fundraising journey continues as we donate a portion of our proceeds to this important cause.

The self-published version of *Love in the Land of Dementia* served as a catalyst for raising more than $80,000 for Alzheimer's programs and research. My stories of looking for the blessings in the journey reached thousands of people, fulfilling my goal of making a contribution to the world. And the bonus was that both Ron and I had changed. By following our intuition and doing the work of our hearts, we became more compassionate, understanding and trusting.

~Deborah Shouse

An Honor to Be an Honor Guard

No duty is more urgent than that of returning thanks.
~James Allen

f George Brown can do it, then so can I. George is Captain of the all-volunteer Honor Guard for the Gloucester County Veterans Memorial Cemetery in southern New Jersey. George is ninety years old.

After retirement, I was anxious to do volunteer work. As a military veteran myself, I was drawn to serve with the twenty-member Honor Guard, which pays tribute to our deceased veterans as they go to their final resting place. Seven years ago, I joined the group. After receiving a uniform, George said, "I'll call you when the next funeral is scheduled." I learned the procedure by doing.

Everyone knows how fulfilling volunteer work can be. But serving at the cemetery has been especially rewarding for me. It is a sad time for the families of the deceased, but they are genuinely grateful for the honor and dignity of our ceremony. We see the comfort on their faces when they arrive at the cemetery and find us already in formation. As the American flag-draped casket or an urn with a folded flag is carried from the hearse, we remain in formation.

We then present arms. The casket or urn is placed at the gravesite. The flag is removed from the casket or unfolded for those with an urn. Then we fire three volleys from our rifles. We present arms while "Taps" is played. The soulful notes from the bugle often echo across the vast fields of gravesites. We then stand at parade rest as two members of the military branch of the deceased perform the flag folding and presentation to the surviving spouse or family member. Once again, we present arms, and then march off the field.

We leave the field feeling certain that we have brought a well-deserved honor to the deceased and, hopefully, a sense of healing to his or her loved ones.

Whenever I'm called for a funeral, I accept whatever role I am given that day. I've been the bugler, a member of the flag brigade, and most often one of the firing squad (the peaceful kind). The Honor Guard ceremony is truly a team effort. Each role is equally important to our veterans' families.

Our veteran's cemetery was carved out of a farm field. The first interment was in 2004. To date, more than 1,800 military veterans are buried in a grave or inurned in a columbarium wall on the cemetery's grounds.

Throughout the year, the cemetery is a peaceful, solemn place for families to visit their departed loved one. However, special ceremonies take place a few times a year. The Honor Guard is present for each one.

Memorial Day ceremonies bring out local dignitaries, television crews, newspaper reporters, and relatives and friends of deceased veterans. The Honor Guard marches out with a flag brigade and a firing squad to commemorate our fallen military veterans' service to our country.

Christmastime finds the cemetery graced with winter wreaths of fresh evergreens and large red velvet bows. The organization People for People Foundation of Gloucester County spends many months preparing for the Wreaths for Remembrance ceremony when holiday wreaths are placed on each grave marker.

The organization coordinates a huge undertaking to collect donations for the wreaths and a call-out for volunteers. For me, it is a family affair. My daughter and son-in-law are members of that organization.

Many hundreds of volunteers answer the call each year for the laying of wreaths. Before formal ceremonies begin, volunteers visit every one of the 1,800 graves. As they place a wreath, they say, "Thank you for your service" to each deceased veteran.

The Honor Guard stands in formation during the formal ceremony. Then we fire three volleys and play "Taps."

On that day, the usually quiet cemetery becomes a field filled with love, honor and holiday spirit. It is both a day for those who kneel in front of the grave markers to reflect upon their loss, as well as a reminder to all of the patriotism of those who served in the military.

Each year, I am honored once again to be part of the ceremony.

Our Honor Guard shares the U.S. Postal Service's adage, "Neither rain nor snow nor heat nor gloom..." We are out there whenever duty calls — be it a hot July afternoon or a bitter, wind-blown January morning. And yes, George, at age ninety, is always there, so I have no excuse for not showing up. Not that I'd need one.

~Christian Harch

Kindness Matters

*Too often we underestimate the power of a touch, a smile,
a kind word, a listening ear, an honest compliment, or the
smallest act of caring, all of which have the potential to turn a
life around.*
~Leo Buscaglia

V olunteers always seem to step up to do the hardest jobs, and it's hard to imagine a more difficult job than sitting at the bedside of a suicidal patient. But that's exactly what folks do at a rural medical center in northwest Colorado.

For five years I worked as a tech in the emergency room in a small, friendly regional hospital that serves thousands of people in rural northwest Colorado. For some reason, which researchers still don't understand, the Rocky Mountains have the highest rate of suicide in the country. Those living in the region — which stretches from Montana through New Mexico and includes over one hundred ranges — suffer more acutely from depression that leads to suicide than any place in the country. I had my own untested theory about such sadness in places of immense beauty. Maybe people came to the mountains to "be happy" and found that sadness followed. Maybe living at a high altitude really affects the brain in ways we don't understand. Or maybe the culture of the West — guns and independence — fosters feelings of inadequacy. Whatever it was, when I saw suicidal patients my heart would break.

Depression runs in my family. There is a history of men in my family suffering from a darkness that seems insurmountable. I had too much experience with very sad and depressed people in my life, and so when a patient arrived mired in hopelessness it triggered the same in me.

Statistics suggest that seventy-five percent of people who commit suicide seek help from a healthcare provider within the two weeks prior to the act. This means doctors' offices and emergency rooms are often the last places a deeply depressed person will call for help. Yet our system seems unable to either diagnose or treat this illness well. The protocol in many ERs for suicidal patients is as follows:

(1) Make them safe: clear out the room completely; patients have been known to try to kill themselves in hospitals with anything around, from monitor cords to rubber gloves.

(2) If appropriate, medicate them. This is very often the case.

(3) Call a social service designated to screen these patients for placement, though often there is no place to put them.

(4) Isolate them with a "one-on-one" hospital employee responsible for keeping eyes on their patients at all times. Often this is a security guard who is generally not supposed to talk to the patient.

Isolated, medicated, left alone with a stranger. Wow. What could be worse for someone in the throes of such deep suffering?

Our town actually had the dubious distinction of the highest per capita suicide rate in Colorado, and we had a strong advocate who was devoting herself to the cause. Rhonda had lost her own son to suicide when he was in his thirties, and she decided that she would do everything in her power to prevent suicide in our community. She hosted a mental health outreach event I attended and we connected. It seems Rhonda had been trying to find "a way in" to the emergency room system, knowing how many people ended up there. I was her way in.

We collaborated to design a simple and effective program for our small emergency room: a cadre of well-trained volunteers, available 24/7 to come to the ER and be the "hospital sitters." These were the people designated to "watch" the patient, only they could do more than stare. They would accompany the patient on his or her journey in a way no one else might be able: listening deeply, talking, sharing and providing resources. The volunteer was there to do everything possible to make sure the patient wouldn't leave the ER and kill himself or herself within the next two weeks, as the dire statistics indicated.

Rhonda and I set about making a plan. She was certified to train volunteers in this kind of crisis management and, in fact, her group consisted mostly of people who had themselves been suicidal or had suffered a loss or "near miss" by suicide. Each of the volunteers had a personal story, so each one knew exactly what a patient could feel (or not feel) when in such a desperate condition. Too often we create an unspoken patronizing distance between those we "help" and ourselves, as if the former are somehow the less fortunate and therefore more needy. There would be no such hierarchy in this program, as these volunteers understood suicide way too well, from the inside out. They would walk with the patient, side by side.

As Rhonda prepared the volunteer corps, I went through all the appropriate channels at the hospital to get the program up and running. Health care is perhaps the most complicated, problematic system in this country. Though generally highly regulated and convoluted, my hospital was small enough—and caring enough—to support the program in a way that made it easy in comparison to huge hospitals with complex processes.

It took time and effort, a committee, policies, procedures and training, but we did it. Starting with a roster of about ten trained volunteers, we created an on-call schedule for 24/7 ER coverage. We then rolled the program out to the staff, who were frankly surprised and confused, as if they were thinking, "You're providing us with a volunteer to help these patients?" It was so unusual that at first they didn't use the service, unable to truly comprehend the kindness of people at this depth. But once they got the hang of it, they started calling the volunteer as soon as the suicidal patient came to triage. We called ourselves Suicide Prevention Advocates (SPAs) and it was music to my ears when I was working the desk to hear a doctor or nurse say, "Call the SPA volunteer."

Generally within twenty to thirty minutes of a call from the ER, a volunteer would arrive and — having been trained in ER protocol — communicate with the nurse, go to the patient's bedside and generally say something like "My name is Jean and I'm a hospital volunteer, here to be with you as long as you need me." They would often help make a plan for the patient's discharge to a safe environment. Because the patients talked plenty to the volunteers, they were able to provide valuable information to the staff, and when the patient left, the volunteer would give him or her or the family a packet of resources. If the patient signed a release, the volunteer or Rhonda would follow up with a phone call or whatever was necessary within the next twenty-four to forty-eight hours.

I don't know the actual stats, but I can tell you the program was successful in amazing ways. I know our intervention helped desperate people to connect. Can you imagine a more fulfilling volunteer "job" than helping someone stay alive just by being present and available and kind? I moved from Colorado last year, but I'm so happy I was able to leave my mark in a way that will continue to help hopeless people reaching out for help. True kindness saves lives.

~Phyllis Coletta

Blankets of Love

It is the greatest of all mistakes to do nothing because you can
only do little — do what you can.
~Sydney Smith

A sick child in a bed that dwarfs her. A soft, cuddly blanket, purple, her favorite color. Clearly not hospital-issue. She smiles when I give it to her, though she doesn't know me. She tells me about her dog, Moose, and how she can't wait to get home and play with him.

I used to see stories on TV or in the newspaper about people who fed starving children, clothed the needy or took care of the elderly, and I always felt a twinge of guilt. I wanted to be like that, helping others. But I was busy raising two kids and working a stressful job. I never got enough sleep and by the time I fed my family supper, my energy gauge would be hovering on empty. There was no extra time.

So I settled for contributing to good causes and delivering canned goods and old coats for local drives, along with the occasional present for a needy person selected from a Christmas tree at the mall. I thought this would set a good example for my kids. Then I read a magazine article about a different type of organization.

Project Linus is comprised of volunteers who provide new, handmade blankets for children who have traumatic illnesses or injuries. The article touched me, and I knew this was something I could do. I might not have a lot of money, but I could sew and I could crochet. I searched online for a local chapter.

My heart sank. There was no local chapter in the Tennessee area where I live. The nearest one was in Atlanta, about 120 miles away.

I could not stop thinking about these children. Over the next few weeks I reread the article and looked at the pictures of children wrapped in brightly colored blankets. In the midst of their pain, they smiled. Their sweet faces tugged at my heart and I knew I had to find a way to help them. But I am shy by nature and I couldn't step out on my own. My wish to volunteer seemed hopeless.

I decided to call the chapter in Atlanta. Perhaps they had a hub closer to me or another way I could send blankets to them.

"Why don't you start your own chapter?" the lady on the line asked.

I couldn't do that! Just the thought of reaching out to strangers frightened me. But the lady in Atlanta was encouraging and I spent the next day or two mulling it over. I reviewed Project Linus's website several times and read how to apply to be a Chapter Coordinator.

I could just make a few blankets myself and not involve anyone else.

Encouraged by the thought, I sent in my application. A week later a package arrived, and I was as excited as a child on Christmas morning. I spread the contents out on my table and read all the instructions and suggestions. I had done it! I was now a Project Linus Chapter Coordinator.

Once my application was approved, Project Linus added my Chapter to its website. In a matter of days I had received several phone calls from other people in my community who were interested in making blankets. I quickly realized I would not have to do this alone.

It began small. I contacted the oncology department at our local children's hospital and the nurse who answered said they would love to receive blankets for the children. Encouraged, I made blankets and picked up blankets, sewed on Project Linus tags, and delivered them.

A local television reporter spoke with his neighbor who had a child in the hospital. The neighbor told the reporter about the quilted blanket his daughter had received in the hospital and how she carried it with her everywhere. The reporter called me and asked to do a story about Project Linus for their weekly "Friday's Hero" segment. I was flabbergasted!

Since then, our chapter has grown to the point it can now provide hundreds of blankets to several local hospitals.

You would think bringing a moment or two of happiness to a sick child would be reward enough, but the satisfaction volunteers derive goes so much deeper. In addition to nursing home residents, some of the ladies and men who make blankets are homebound or bedridden after surgery and have a need to feel useful.

I thought volunteer work was about giving, but now I see it is a two-way street. Those who make blankets become part of something greater than themselves. They find a new circle of like-minded people. A Project Linus volunteer discovers joy in knowing that a blanket made by his or her own hands can make a seriously ill child smile.

Giving enlarges our hearts and fills us with a sense of purpose and a reason for being. There is no greater joy.

~Linda L. Peters

No Strings Attached

Believe you can and you're halfway there.
~Theodore Roosevelt

I sat at my desk and stared at the pink slip in my hand. Like many other non-tenured personnel in my school district, I would now spend my summer updating my résumé and looking for a job. We would have to purchase health insurance out of pocket and pay a much higher premium until the end of the year. This also made it much more challenging paying college expenses for my son and daughter.

There was additional fallout — a part of my job had been to create service projects for students in the community. Six months previously, I had planned and organized a major community fundraising dinner to benefit our community food bank, Cullman Caring for Kids. The concept for an "empty bowls" fundraiser was not new, though it was new to our community. This fundraiser provided much-needed revenue for the food bank and involved students of all ages, businesses, churches, artists and musicians in our community. The plan consisted of local potters and students making keepsake clay bowls to serve soup and chili to the people attending the dinner. Afterward, the bowls would be a daily reminder of the hungry people in our community.

This was the perfect service project for our community, whose food bank frequently had to close its doors because the number of people financially struggling increased while the funding and donations decreased. The first event had been held the previous November, after a mere two months of planning. We had expected to serve about two hundred people and raise about $2,000. However, the response from the community was far greater than we anticipated, with more than six hundred people attending and $5,400 raised for the food bank. In fact, we ran out of homemade chili and clay bowls. Ultimately, we had to send high school students all over town to buy every can of chili they could find in order to continue serving people.

Our community loved the event, and everyone was excited about it — from the potters making the bowls and the students making placemats and busing tables, to the musicians, the people serving and working in the kitchen and the people donating the food and the facility. Literally, the whole community worked to make it possible, and it was a tremendous blessing to all involved. The financial contributions enabled the food bank to stock its shelves for several months. Everyone wanted to make it an annual event and our small committee was already hard at work planning the following year's dinner.

I thought of Bobby, the man who prepared our food, and his passion for helping the hungry people of our community. On his own, he raised the money needed to purchase the food for the event and spent long hours in the kitchen preparing chili and making sandwiches. I thought of Sandra, the college art instructor who, in her excitement, had made hundreds of bowls and recruited others to do the same. I also thought of the hundreds of other people in our community who wanted to help their neighbors through the fundraising project.

What would happen to it now? Because my job was being downsized, I was not sure if anyone else would continue to plan and coordinate the event, and if anyone did, would he or she do it with the passion that only the author of it would feel? Could I take the chance? After much thought, I knew that I had to do the right thing. It would be selfish of me to let my wounded ego and the lack of a paycheck be the end of this wonderful event. So, I checked with my former employer for approval to continue the project independently. They said yes, and were in fact grateful that the project would continue.

Therefore, my small committee and I decided to step out, independent of any large organization, to continue the project on our own.

Over the years, our small planning committee — Bobby, Sandra, Jane, Lynn, TJ, and several others — and I have faced many challenges. However, we can truly say that the blessings have far outweighed the work and its obstacles. I personally have learned a lot about leadership and responsibility in ways that I probably would never have learned otherwise. I have learned that some of life's greatest disappointments ultimately give us the opportunity to grow in confidence and stand a little taller.

In February 2016, we will celebrate our thirteenth anniversary. To date, we have raised over $110,000 for our community food bank and we are eagerly looking forward to reaching the $200,000 mark. We have even written and illustrated a children's book, *The Story of Empty Bowls in Our Town*, and later a song was written. The book chronicles the story of how people in our community use their unique gifts and talents to help others and make this special night possible. Each year we eagerly look forward to a wonderful night of music and fellowship that warms the soul and chili that warms the body on a winter's night. It's like a family reunion when everyone gathers to celebrate. Friendships are renewed and spirits lifted as together we raise money for those in need.

Sometimes I think of what I would have missed if I had given up, and am so thankful that God gave me the grace and courage to step out in faith. Looking back, I truly believe that everything turned out just the way He intended it to. I also have learned that the greatest things that we can do are done out of love without any thought of a paycheck.

~Tanya Shearer

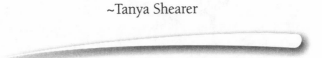

Because Someone Else Gave

Silent gratitude isn't much use to anyone.
~G.B. Stern

A young woman named Tann checked me and went over my health history. As she prepped my arm for the needle stick — the worst part of the whole thing if you ask me — she asked if I was expecting anyone to stand by my side. Tann remembered me from previous blood drives and how one of my children was always present to support me.

She remembered why I give blood.

Two years ago, my son Nathan was recovering from what we believed were symptoms of a concussion that he received from a hard hit in a football game. Everything seemed to indicate textbook concussion symptoms — light-headedness, headaches, difficulty concentrating, and tiring easily. The only real concern seemed to be that it was taking so long to see improvement in any of these symptoms. Instead of getting better, his symptoms seemed to get worse. It wasn't until almost a month later that we would find out why.

Nathan was just fifteen at the time, and had a restless night of sleep. I had gone downstairs to his room to wake him for school. He slowly stood up and started to get ready for his day. I was still there when his eyes went blank and he fell. I caught him enough to cushion his fall on the way down. One of Nathan's sisters called 911 and he was quickly taken by ambulance to the emergency room.

I told the doctors everything that had transpired. They still seemed to be looking for complications of a concussion, but it was his low red blood cell counts that earned him admittance into the hospital for more testing.

The doctors observed Nathan overnight and continued with more extensive tests. The next morning, as he was being wheeled out of his room for another test, our family doctor stayed behind to talk to me. He explained that Nathan's red blood cell counts were even lower than the day before. There did not seem to be a reasonable explanation for this that they could identify in their hospital. He explained that Nathan was being prepped for an immediate blood transfusion and he needed to be transferred to the university hospital. For some reason, Nathan was not producing his own red blood cells. He would undergo a bone marrow biopsy to test for leukemia.

It is a strange and bizarre feeling to be near your child but be completely helpless at the same time. That is how I felt as I held Nathan's hand while he received a life-saving blood transfusion in transit to the new hospital. And that is how I felt as I later watched a pediatric oncologist extract bone marrow from his hip.

As it turned out, Nathan did not have leukemia. Further testing revealed that a rare virus had attacked his red blood cells in a way that mimicked leukemia. We also learned some other things. For one, Nathan needed that blood transfusion to survive. He has the rare blood type of O-negative. His particular blood type can be donated to anyone; but those with O-negative blood can only receive the same blood type in a transfusion. There is a genuine need for donations of O-negative blood.

I do not have this blood type, so my blood could not be used to save my son. But someone else's donation did. I wish I could thank this person, who probably volunteered at a blood drive just like the ones I go to, but I know it is impossible to do so. The only way I know to show my appreciation is to donate my own blood.

That was why I was there about to have my blood drawn. I know, firsthand, that donating matters. And that is why Tann, the blood drive worker, remembered me and how my son took his turn to stand by my side at the last donation drive.

She remembered that I give because someone else gave.

~Robin Hakanson-Grunder

Chapter
8

Volunteering & Giving Back

With My Own Hands

74

Approaching the Throne

Great opportunities to help others seldom come, but small ones surround us every day.
~Sally Koch

Sunlight streamed through Bible Truth Ministries' multicolored windows. I relaxed on the blue padded pew, ran my fingertips across the glossy wood back of the pew in front of me, and enjoyed the fresh scent wafting through the air. This friendly church already felt like home.

My husband Jake and I sat with other new members in an orientation meeting led by a congenial deep-voiced elder. As the session drew to a close he said, "Should you feel a call to serve, we have many options available."

I squeezed Jake's hand and smiled. We enjoyed helping others. Surely there'd be a place we could be useful.

The elder read the list of service opportunities in his James Earl Jones voice.

Grounds crew: Jake perked up. He already helped many of our neighbors with their mowing and snow shoveling. I knew he'd found his niche.

Food teams: I thought of my nonexistent culinary skills and pictured black smoke billowing from the church kitchen. I knew to steer clear of that one.

Choir: No need to inflict my voice on our new church family.

Youth ministry: I'd taught children's church for years. I thought, "This is it, right Lord?"

Silence. No Holy Spirit nudge. No divine light bulb shining overhead.

I slumped back and listened to the rest of the list. Ushers. Safety Patrol. Technical services. Then the elder paused and proclaimed in a voice of doom, "Church cleaning team."

I felt a nudge in my spirit. I scanned the gleaming sanctuary and mentally calculated the hours it might take to clean the large space. I decided I wasn't hearing God after all.

God prodded again.

I adopted a "Get thee behind me, Cleaning!" posture. "Lord, surely you don't expect me to clean the church?"

But he did.

I signed up for a cleaning slot.

The next Friday evening I joined a team of church members. Five women, ages ranging from young to grandma, plus one forty-some-thing man, extended a cheerful welcome.

"Do we meet every week?" I asked, trying to hide my apprehension.

Our team leader had the grace to look appalled. "Mercy, no! Each team cleans once a month."

I silently congratulated God. I could handle once a month… maybe.

The team leader explained the division of tasks: dusting, vacuuming, window washing and so on. The lone man on our team pointed to a mop and said, "I always clean the throne room."

Throne room?

The Bible talked about God being on his heavenly throne, but I'd never heard of anyone taking a mop to it. "Um, I'm not familiar with that theological reference," I said.

Good-natured laughter erupted. A lady put her arm around my shoulder. "'Throne' is slang for toilet."

Another woman patted my arm, still giggling. "Girl, you're a hoot."

I smiled weakly and took the backpack-sized portable vacuum

she handed me. I strapped the shell-shaped appliance to my back and, like a middle-aged mutant cleaning turtle, sucked crud from the pew crevices as instructed. The rest of the team sprang into action.

With Bellevue, Nebraska's Strategic Air Command close by, Air Force members and veterans comprised the majority of the church. This group demonstrated military precision in their search and destroy mission against Enemy Dirt. Dust bunnies quailed before their feather-duster onslaught.

Most surprising to me, no one complained or grumbled. Between vacuum bouts I heard snatches of laughter and song.

The ensuing months brought a myriad of new "opportunities," like pew polishing and carpet cleaning. One evening, washing windows beside a cheerful mite of a woman, I asked, "Do you enjoy cleaning?"

She laughed. "None of us like cleaning. We do it to serve God and serve others."

Her words rose to mind soon after, the day our regular bathroom volunteer went Missing In Action. Our team grandma asked, "Jeanie, would you mind cleaning the throne room?"

Unwilling to show my apprehension before this hard-working woman, I gulped and squeaked, "No problem."

Shouldering the arsenal of bathroom cleaning weapons, I headed off to do battle in the throne room.

I pulled on two pairs of rubber gloves and gingerly entered the first of four bathrooms. The churchmen may be aiming for Godliness, but they sure weren't aiming for the thrones. I backpedaled and sent up a King James–type plea. "Oh Lord, surely thou canst deliver thy servant from the evil before me."

No answer from the heavenly throne, so I set to work on the one in front of me, anointing it with copious quantities of Pine-Sol. After completing the fourth bathroom I sprayed myself with enough Lysol to open a new ozone hole in the atmosphere.

Although I never grew to love cleaning, I did grow to love my teammates, and learned their true mission—prayer. After every cleaning session we gathered together, clasped hands, and approached

God's heavenly throne, seeking his help for people and situations around the world.

Each time we prayed, their dedication struck me afresh. Their love for God overflowed, evidenced by their faithful service to Him and others.

Time passed and I volunteered for other church activities, like holiday productions and the praise dance team. My kitchen stints remained limited to non-cooking areas for the health and safety of all involved.

Through it all, I stayed on the cleaning team. Ironically, I became our regular bathroom cleaner, the "Throne Room Queen" wielding a toilet brush in place of a scepter.

One day someone will settle into the pew I'd occupied years before. Sunlight will stream through the clean windows. She'll run her fingertips over the glossy wood pew. Her children will play nearby on the spotless carpet. She'll think, "I want to join the cleaning team." My replacement will join the ranks.

In the meantime, God's on his throne, and I still have one to clean.

~Jeanie Jacobson

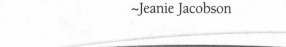

75

Hooked on Crocheting

*Kindness in words creates confidence. Kindness in thinking
creates profoundness. Kindness in giving creates love.*
~Lao Tzu

Over the years I have put my passion for crocheting to good use. Though some may refer to my hobby as an obsession, it serves as great therapy for my busy, sometimes hectic life.

In my yarn-spinning lifetime I have made scarves and blankets for everyone I know. Soon after family and friends were all wrapped in the warmth of my wooly creations I came up with an idea. I went to Walmart and bought out their stock of red, white and blue yarn. I decided I would make lap blankets for veterans at the VA hospital. Now, it didn't matter to me that I did not know any veterans and couldn't even tell you where a VA hospital was located. I would make them first and figure out the details later.

I continued with my crochet-a-thon until I had made fifty blankets. My husband asked what I was planning to do with all these flag blankets now that they were made. Good question.

A couple of months later an older cousin and I reunited after many years. She called one day and asked if she could stop by for a visit. I couldn't wait to see her. Catching up on all those years gone by takes a lot of time, and sharing family stories brought many laughs and ah-ha moments for both of us.

When she was getting ready to leave she mentioned that she had to stop at the hospital on her way home. I asked if anyone was sick. Thankfully, no family members were ill. She was doing a favor for her retired Navy husband. She was going to the VA hospital in their area to visit her husband's friend.

Could the timing be any more perfect? I asked her to wait a minute while I ran to the garage.

Her eyes were wide as saucers as I returned with three heavy-duty garbage bags filled with those American flag lap blankets.

Somewhere in a VA hospital in Illinois there are beds decorated with American flags, bringing a little warmth to men and women who deserve to be acknowledged for their service. Just the thought warms my heart.

My next project became scarves for our troops overseas. After all, it does get bone-chillingly cold in the desert at night. Quite a few boxes of neck warmers were sent to Iraq and Afghanistan.

Thankfully, my passion—some might say addiction—has taken me in different directions, so I am rarely bored when I pick up my crochet hook.

A few years ago I was introduced to a woman whose ministry is to make tiny blankets for preemies. Her group meets once a week at our church. Though I was unable to make the scheduled meeting time, I did make blankets for her, leaving bags of tiny pink and blue blankets on her front porch.

Now that my daughter is a nurse working on the maternity floor of our local hospital, I have found a way to bring joy in a different way. I send my daughter to work with a variety of flowered headbands for the newborn baby girls. The feedback is so positive; the nurses and the new mommies love them! As I make them I find myself saying prayers for the little ones who will be wearing them.

I got the opportunity to see my labor of love in person when my grandson was born. Peering into the nursery, I saw a variety of colorful flowers dotting the tiny heads of baby girls. It was a joyful sight.

The spare bedroom in our home has become a holding area for all my yarn. Totes, hampers and bins line the wall with a multitude of yarn colors and styles. In the corner is a shopping bag filled with headbands ready and waiting to go.

Everyone can volunteer in some way, no matter what your schedule. You don't necessarily have to join a group or club to be a volunteer.

You can volunteer your talent, whatever that may be. Do what you love; share what you love. With crochet hook in hand I'm stitching my way toward bringing a little joy to others while, in turn, I'm filling up with joy.

~Kathy Whirity

76

Perfect Purple Nails

Some people, no matter how old they get, never lose their
beauty—they merely move it from their faces into their hearts.
~Martin Buxbaum

"Mom, I've made the best nail kit ever," my ten-year-old daughter Brooke exclaimed. "I think the ladies at the nursing home will really love my new nail polish colors, don't you?"

My eyes grew wide as I viewed the hot pink, tomato red and neon purple bottles of polish. Not wanting to squelch Brooke's joy, I said, "I am so proud of you for caring about the residents and taking the time to make your wonderful kit."

Brooke beamed with pride and ran to get her sweater before we left for church. My husband was minister of children and youth at our church, and he had chosen the local nursing home as the mission project for the year. Our group of kids chose to read, sing and do nails for the residents that chose to participate.

Brooke always looked forward to her visits with "her" ladies, and they never minded if the nail job was less than perfect. She ended every visit with a big hug and a short prayer.

At the church we gathered hymnals and got everyone settled in the van for the short ride to the nursing home. I held on to the residents' much-anticipated chocolate cupcakes and the juice we were taking to the facility as treats.

The nurses' aide for our wing met us at the door and ushered us toward the large activities room. The halls were lined with men and women in wheelchairs and the distinct smell of disinfectant hung heavy in the air. My heart broke as I saw the distant stares in some of the residents' eyes. Many of them had the soft lap robes we had given them the month before folded over their legs.

Wheelchairs and walkers were pulled up to the tables in the activity room. The residents jokingly called it "the wheelchair train." Some of our boys had brought fishing and sports magazines to read to the men. By far, the most anticipated moment was Brooke's nail polishing event.

Millie, eighty-eight years young, was always first in line. The aide had told us she did not have family or friends come to visit and this was the highlight of her month.

Brooke greeted Millie with a hug and sat her polishes out for Millie to choose a color. I saw her shock at Brooke's color choices quickly cross her face.

"Why, Brooke, I think I will pick that purple shade for my nails," she said kindly.

I gave Millie a secret look of thanks and watched as Brooke carefully painted each nail.

"Yep," Millie said, "I have perfect purple nails."

Brooke painted each of the ladies' nails with the same enthusiasm.

That was twenty-four years ago, and now Brooke was at home under hospice care with end-stage breast cancer. I was Brooke's primary caregiver along with her husband and the hospice nurses.

Volunteers came and sang to Brooke, something that soothed her and seemed to help lessen her pain. One day I answered a knock at the door and there stood a mother and young girl. The mother introduced herself saying she was a nail technician and explained that her daughter loved to accompany her on her visits.

The young girl, Allison, asked Brooke if she would like her nails painted. Brooke nodded yes, I am sure more for Allison's sake than hers. To our amazement, Allison pulled out a bright shade of metallic purple polish.

Things had come full circle. Brooke's loving acts of volunteerism had come back to bless her.

After Brooke's nails were done, she and I smiled, sharing a precious memory.

I choose to believe angels welcomed Brooke to heaven, perhaps smiling when they spotted her perfect purple nails.

~Dee Dee Parker

77

The Musical Mom

Inaction breeds doubt and fear. Action breeds confidence and courage. If you want to conquer fear, do not sit home and think about it. Go out and get busy.
~Dale Carnegie

t was the second Sunday that the teen pianist for my daughter Michelle's children's choir hadn't shown up. I watched as their leader Bill accompanied the children on his guitar. "I wonder what happened to Greg?" I thought, sitting in a row toward the back of the church.

After the service, Michelle came running up to me.

"Mom, I told Bill that you would take Greg's place."

My mouth dropped. "What?"

"I volunteered you."

"Me?" I was in shock.

"Yes."

"But…"

"He's waiting up there to hear you play."

I looked toward the front of the church where Bill waited patiently.

"But I haven't played in front of anyone in years."

"Mom, you play fine. We really need you. There's no one else."

"But, I'm just… a mom." I was the full-time mother of four children, ages fourteen, twelve, eleven and six, and I hadn't played the piano in front of anyone besides my children since before they were born. I wrote songs at home, where nobody but my family and two cats heard them, and tried sending out some demos to publishers that never published them. I entered songwriting contests that I never won. The best I ever did was win a couple of Honorable Mentions. Since I'd become a full-time mom, I never had the courage to play in front of anyone except my family.

Bill was still waiting for me.

Michelle led me to the piano in front of the church. I felt awkward and embarrassed.

"I don't know what to play," I said.

"Play anything you want," said Bill.

I started performing something by Beethoven, so nervous my hands were trembling on the keys.

When I finished, Bill smiled. "That's great," he said. "Welcome to the choir."

I had no idea what I was in for. Frequent rehearsals took me away from home to learn new music. The rehearsals were fun for everyone, and I grew more confident.

Yet, the first time I played for an actual service I found myself frozen in my seat, staring out at a sea of faces. It was an entirely different world sitting at the front of the church instead of my safe anonymous pew. I was convinced that my mind would go blank and I would forget the music. But with Bill standing beside me directing us, I felt safe. After a couple of weeks, I thought maybe I could handle it. Little did I know what was in store.

"You're on your own next Sunday," Bill said. "I'm going on vacation."

My mouth dropped open.

"You'll be fine," he said, as he left me with detailed instructions.

I wasn't even used to playing in front of people yet, and now he was asking me to do it alone. I wanted to run away and hide. Michelle encouraged me. "It's no big deal, Mom, you can do it."

Every day I read Bill's instructions for the service. I practiced every song until I could play them in my sleep. Still I panicked, afraid my mind would blank and I would ruin the entire service. By the time Sunday arrived, I was a nervous wreck.

I trembled at the piano while frantically reviewing Bill's instructions. I hoped and prayed that I wouldn't mess up and let down the choir. The pressure mounted. Everyone was counting on me. The children stared at me with solemn faces. My nervous demeanor was negatively affecting them; you could feel the tension everywhere. My heart was pounding as we launched into the first song. The people rose from their seats and started singing along with the children. The first song went well. Michelle gave me an encouraging smile.

I had to wait for the priest to finish speaking before I played my parts during the service. My heart's hammering was almost drowning out their voices. Had the priest paused for the music? There was a deafening silence as I hesitated too long. To everyone's relief I played my part and the service went on. Despite my panic, we made it through without any more dramatic mistakes. I didn't relax until the last song was over and the congregation politely clapped for the choir.

Michelle was pleased. "See, Mom, that wasn't so bad. I knew you could do it."

Her confidence in me was wonderful, but I was still immensely relieved when Bill came back from vacation and took control of the group again. We played faithfully every Sunday and began composing songs together. As time went on, I calmed down and began to thrive in the ministry. My younger daughter Ann joined the choir and harmonized with Michelle.

Playing piano at church opened an entirely new world to me. My volunteer commitment led to many musical opportunities for my family. It gave me confidence and touched people's hearts in more ways than I could have ever imagined.

I discovered this five years later. The girls and I had returned after an absence to play a Sunday evening service. An elderly couple approached us after the service was over.

"We are so glad you're back," they said. "We've missed you so much. We're both afraid to fly and have been dreading a flight we're taking tomorrow to Florida. We prayed about it. When we came to the service tonight and saw you playing and singing again, we knew everything would be okay. We asked God for a sign, and you were the answer."

~L.A. Strucke

78

The Carpenter's Gift

He who works with his hands is a laborer. He who works with
his hands and his head is a craftsman. He who works with his
hands and his head and his heart is an artist.

~Louis Nizer

often wonder if people look down on me because I'm a construction worker. Sometimes, when I'm around white-collar professionals, I clench my rough, calloused hands and fold them into my side. In those moments I struggle with the question of who I am.

I didn't always think I'd be a carpenter. I can still hear my mom saying, when I was eighteen years old, "Now Scott, you really should be going to college like the other guys. You always said you wanted to be a doctor."

I'm not a doctor, but on a snowy Christmas Eve a few years back—at a children's hospital in Michigan—an encounter with a family reminded me that even though I never became a doctor, I know exactly who I am.

That Christmas Eve, I entered little Mia's ICU room. The ten-month-old girl had been born with a serious heart defect. Her family looked up. Wendy, Mia's mom, introduced me to Mia's grandma and grandpa.

"Is he the doctor?" said Grandpa from his wheelchair.

"No, Dad," said Wendy.

"Is he the nurse?" the white-bearded man asked.

"No," Wendy said.

The grandfather, throwing his hands up, said with a bit of senior citizen confidence, "Well then, surely he must be the respiratory therapist."

"No, Dad. He's the carpenter."

Without hesitation, the old guy looked up at me and said, "This hospital is great! They even have a carpenter working here." I nodded and then he asked, "Are you making something special for Mia, something to help her get better?"

Realizing he must have figured that I was making her a piece of medical equipment, I didn't know what to say. Before I could say a word, Wendy grabbed a shoebox-sized mahogany box from the windowsill. She walked over to her dad and placed it in his lap.

"Dad, Scott made this for Mia. It's a memory box."

Mia's memory box is just one of many that I've made for sick kids over the years since my son Evan passed away. When Evan was alive, our family spent many months at C.S. Mott Children's Hospital in Ann Arbor. Evan is the reason I now give back.

Sometimes I take the tools of my trade up to the floor and help young patients build things—a very cool experience. One of the terminally ill boys who I worked with died a couple of months back. His mom told me how much she cherishes the oak laptop desk her son created.

When I decided not to go to college and, instead, ride to work every day in my dad's rusting truck as a carpenter's apprentice, I never thought I would use my carpentry skills this way.

Mia's grandfather smiled as he opened the lid of the polished mahogany box and inspected its inner lining of silver cloth. He opened and closed the small sliding drawer. He looked up at me with a look I'll never forget and a smile on his face.

I smiled, too.

After leaving Mia's family, I went home, loving the gift they gave me: a clearer picture of who I am.

~Scott Newport

79

Fairy Godmothers

Just around the corner in every woman's mind—is a lovely dress, a wonderful suit, or entire costume which will make an enchanting new creature of her.
~Wilhela Cushman

Did you ever wish you could be a fairy godmother, wave a magic wand, and turn a sad girl into a princess? I got my wish when I started volunteering for the Cinderella Project of the Capital Region.

My daughter attended two proms a year while in high school, sometimes more. After she went off to college, the dresses remained in her closet, stored in plastic bags and gathering dust. Within a couple of months of graduating college and returning home, she found herself a much-in-demand bridesmaid. She was in eight weddings over the years, all requiring that she buy a gown. The formal gowns took up precious space in her closet. She could barely fit her work clothes in there.

When she got her own apartment, she took the work clothes but left the gowns. Worse still, even after she was out of the house, new bridesmaid's gowns found their way into the closet. I complained about the situation, but the dresses stayed put. One day she called and said she'd heard on the radio that someone was collecting prom gowns at the mall. The volunteers collecting the dresses were part of the Cinderella Project. They were recycling clean, "gently used" formals and giving them to underprivileged girls so they could attend their high school proms.

I was ecstatic. I was going to get my closet back! My jubilation, however, was premature. My daughter only wanted to get rid of six gowns. Then two years later we donated another five gowns. It was a win-win situation. The Cinderella Project got the dresses and I was slowly reclaiming my closet. I thought the program was a wonderful idea, but it never occurred to me that I might want to become one of their volunteers.

Formal gowns and accessories are collected at malls and businesses throughout our area and at various clubs and organizations. Some of the dresses are donated by local thrift shops and bridal salons. Various stores provide make-up, too. The non-profit also accepts cash donations to pay for cleaning, repairing and storing the dresses.

One day I received an e-mail from a women's club I belong to saying the Cinderella Project was in dire need of volunteers for their upcoming "boutique day." Though I wasn't sure exactly what a "boutique day" was, I happened to be free that Saturday, so I volunteered.

The event was to be held at a large college gym. I reported for duty at the appointed hour and was astounded when I walked in and found the room jammed with racks of beautiful dresses of every color, design, and description. They were arranged by size, from petite 0 to women's size 26. Changing rooms and full-length mirrors lined one wall. Next to them were tables piled high with jewelry, hair accessories, make-up, wraps… everything you'd need to attend a prom. The volunteers that day represented a variety of local clubs and service organizations, unions, colleges and businesses. Some manned tables. Others acted as "personal shoppers," helping girls choose dresses to try on; then assisting them in getting the gowns zipped, buttoned, laced or tied; offering advice as the girls picked out accessories to complement their outfits. Most amazing of all, everything was free.

That first year I took dresses from the return racks and rehung them. The work was tiring, but rewarding.

The Cinderella Project's slogan is "Once upon a time is now!" The girls who participate in the program must be referred by someone like a school counselor or teacher. When the girls first arrive they are often shy and uncertain, even sullen. They have no idea what to expect. Some appear hesitant, wondering what a free hand-me-down prom dress will look like. But their demeanor changes completely when they see how beautiful the dresses are and start trying them on. Every one of them smiles when she looks at her reflection in the mirror and sees a beautiful young woman. The gowns are a wish come true for these girls.

Two months after my first "boutique day," I donated the remaining five gowns to the organization. I was thrilled! My closet was finally empty, but that didn't end my association with the charity. The following year I volunteered again and was assigned to the repair and alterations table. Except for their first names, I didn't know the women I worked with, but we functioned like a well-oiled machine. Some brought their sewing machines. I lugged my heavy 1950s-style wooden sewing box filled with assorted pins and needles, multicolored threads, hooks and eyes, snaps, buttons of every hue, iridescent black sequins and opalescent white ones, and the clear crystal and jet black beads I've accumulated over the years.

The ladies with the sewing machines handle major alterations: hemming, replacing zippers, and taking in the dresses. Two other women and I do hand sewing. We adjust spaghetti straps, reattach buttons, repair beadwork and missing sequins, tack on bows and trim, mend small tears, adjust necklines, do minor hem repairs—everything and anything to make the dresses look like new.

It's fun to watch the girls, eyes big as saucers, zeroing in on the perfect dress. Who knew a dress could make such a difference in a young girl's life? But it does. Like Cinderella, every girl deserves to go to the ball and have a magical night to remember!

For a few hours every year my fellow volunteers and I become fairy godmothers. We might not be able to turn a pumpkin into a coach or mice into horses, but in our own small way, we make a difference!

~Mary Vigliante Szydlowski

The Garden

There can be no other occupation like gardening in which, if you were to creep up behind someone at their work, you would find them smiling.

~Mirabel Osler

A couple of years ago, my partner Paul and I were remodeling our kitchen. We had a garden full of produce that we weren't going to be able to use while our kitchen was under construction. I started contacting food pantries where we could donate our fresh vegetables. Surprisingly, the nearest food pantry was several blocks away at our neighborhood elementary school.

We were put in touch with Kelly, the coordinator of the school's BackPack Program. She told us about the twenty-four families at the school who were struggling. Hunger was an issue for them. The children from those families didn't always know where their next meal was coming from. School holidays, summer vacations and weekends were huge problems for these students; it meant these kids might not eat. This was mind-blowing to me. I thought hunger was an issue in developing countries, not in the U.S., and especially not in our neighborhood!

That season, we grew and donated more than seven hundred pounds of fresh produce for the pantry. We met with several organizations in town that help with hunger issues and began to realize how widespread this problem really is.

Paul and I loved that the produce from our garden was not going to waste. The next year, we dedicated our entire garden to grow food for the pantry. My goal was 1,000 pounds that year. As the season progressed, the weather was better suited for lettuces and greens, not the heavier squashes, tomatoes and pumpkins! I began to worry that we wouldn't meet our goal. As it turned out, we were able to donate 1,001 pounds!

We learned a lot about helping our community, a lot about hunger and a lot about the needs of our neighbors. We learned to follow your passion when helping... find what you love and use that to help others. Through our love of gardening, we helped others get involved with planting a row and donating a portion of produce from their own gardens. If your passion is writing, write letters to representatives; if your passion is fundraising, raise money; if your passion is education, teach... Find your passion and use that to help your neighbor.

~John Farnam

Freedom Hats

In the rhythm of the needles, there is music for the soul.
~Author Unknown

A few years ago my granddaughters took a class in knitting. They came home and told me, "Grandma, you need to learn."

I replied, "When I get old and sit around I will learn."

Then, right after Christmas, I watched as my friend knitted hats for her boys with this little gadget called the Knifty Knitter. As I watched her make a hat in only a couple of hours it sparked my interest.

I purchased the knitter and some yarn. First, of course, all my family members had to have matching hats and scarfs. Then I found that Save the Children needed hats for children in Africa. Before I knew it I was addicted! Whenever I was sitting down, in a meeting, watching TV, or wherever, I was knitting. It relaxed me and gave me purpose knowing I was helping someone somewhere. I worked with several other ladies and we filled a box with 140 hats to send off.

I tried to stop after that, but I could not do it! I had to continue. I have three baskets where the hats go as I finish them.

I am a burn survivor, and the next August I was preparing to go to our annual World Burn Congress. As I was getting my stuff together I looked over at the hats. Hey, I thought to myself, I can take the hats and sell them to burn survivors for a donation to the Phoenix Society.

After getting permission, the hats and I were off to New York City for our event. I quickly put them out on the Phoenix table with a sign asking for a $10 donation and went to my first session.

I don't remember how many hats there were, at least thirty, but when I checked later that night most of the hats were gone. At the end of the evening one of my longtime burn survivor friends came up to me with tears in her eyes. She held me close and said, "Thank you for the hat. I have not felt this free in a long time." As I looked at her pretty face I realized she was not wearing her wig. Instead she was wearing one of our pretty hats with a flower on it. For the next few days many women came up and thanked me for the hats. I never imagined that my addiction would make such a difference in so many lives.

Not long after I returned home I received an e-mail from a friend in South Carolina who runs a burn foundation. She reported that the "Freedom Hats" were a hit! Now the hats had a name!

Since then, many Freedom Hats have been delivered to burn centers. They are being used in Sacramento at the Shriners Hospital, given to children with tissue expanders on their little heads.

Not long ago I was visiting the hospital and there was a sweet little three-year-old girl crawling around me and my basket of hats. She was born without feet and was there for prostheses. I looked at her. "Would you like a hat for your pretty little head?" I asked. Her smile was as big as sunshine and she nodded her head. We found just the right hat and she crawled excitedly to her mom. My social worker friend called a few weeks later to report that the little girl and her mom came back for a checkup. The first thing they asked for was another hat! Apparently the little girl refused to take her hat off. She wore it day and night. Her mother just wanted to wash it. "Of course," my friend said, "she can have another hat." No problem.

As she picked another one out, her mom went on to explain that when she wore the hat, everyone noticed how pretty she looked and did not see she had no feet. What a difference a little hat made!

As long as there is a need I will continue to make Freedom Hats for burn survivors and others who need them. These hats are a token of my love.

~Susan Lugli

The 11th Hour

*Accept the things to which fate binds you and love the people
with whom fate brings you together, and do so with all your
heart.*

~Marcus Aurelius

I am a "patient volunteer" for a local hospice organization. Once a week I go to a hospice patient's home and offer something called Comfort Touch to the patient and/or the occasional family member. It's a mix of massage and acupressure techniques for shoulders, hands and feet. It's relaxing and offers a bit of physical touch to people who are near the end of their lives and don't get touched much anymore except for medical procedures.

A second hospice program I've joined is called "11th Hour." This is a relatively new program that only recently became an official one for which you receive volunteer training. I'm sure that it's been around for as long as hospice itself has, it just didn't have a name or formal structure. 11th Hour volunteers sit with someone during the last hours of his or her life. Medical staff may know a person is about to die, but they can't say exactly when. It might be in a few hours, it might be a few days. The volunteer is there so the patient doesn't have to die alone.

Even in nursing homes and hospitals with 24/7 staff, the dying patient doesn't always have someone right there with them. Families get tired and need to go home to rest. And it's not just the wee hours of the night; a morning or afternoon can be as lonely as any other time. Some hospice patients literally have no one: no family, no friends, and no caring human support left in their lives. I feel this time of imminent transition is a very sacred time. There is something special about it—holy even. With hospice care, the person is kept comfortable on every level. The hospice I volunteer for even takes in people who have no ability to pay.

A few days ago, I had such a patient. He had no children, no spouse, no relatives, no friends. He had gone to college. He had served in Vietnam. But he was in the last stages of acute alcoholism. He had come from a jail where he was serving time for DUI. The staff at the care center had asked for companion volunteers to be with him.

I walked into the quiet, pleasant room and stood for a minute next to the man's bedside. He was very thin. "Hi, my name is Chris," I said. "I'll be sitting here for a while to keep you company."

We volunteers introduce ourselves regardless of the condition of the patient. Hearing is the last sense to go, we are told. He was still except for his deep and regular breaths. His bed was spotless, his hair combed, the sheet pulled up and folded across his chest. I pulled the chair close to his bed so I could be near him. I put my hand on his arm and left it there, patting him every once in a while. Then I sat back and was left to my own thoughts.

My father-in-law had died of alcoholism, too. It's an insidious disease. It rips lives apart and wounds family members in ways that don't always show physically. I've known lots of people, in my family and others, who have struggled with addiction. The miracle is that anyone ever gets into recovery at all, and that millions of people have been able to pick their lives up and begin again.

I felt I understood this man a bit, as I watched him breathe, his skin stretched across the bones of his face, his mouth open against the pillowcase. What a contrast this place was versus where he had come from! The smell of freshly baked cookies wafted through the partially open door to his room. Caring and gentle staff came to check on him periodically. His pajamas were clean, his limbs arranged comfortably on the bed, under the sheet.

It was getting to be the end of my shift. I put my hand on the patient's arm. I mentally thanked him for his existence and his struggle. I hoped that at some point along the way he had known love and that his heart had known peace. I felt so grateful for the thoughts he had stirred in me, just by lying there in his hospital bed and breathing. "Thank you for letting me spend this time with you," I said out loud. "I am leaving now. Goodbye."

I hoped another person would come soon and fill that chair by his bedside. There was a blessing I was sure that, just like me, they needed to receive.

~Christine Cosse Gray

Chapter 9

Volunteering & Giving Back

Filling a Need

Innocence in Action

Truly wonderful the mind of a child is.
~Yoda, Star Wars

My husband and I were walking down State Street in Chicago on a hot summer night with our four kids in tow. We were on vacation, but my nine-year-old daughter Madison could not take her eyes off a homeless man sitting on a bus stop bench. Despite the warm temperature, he wore a heavy coat, looked unshaven and held a sign that said "Please Help. God Bless You!"

On our long walk back to the hotel, we saw a few more people asking for money, holding signs or cups. Madison kept slowing down to observe them, but the images didn't make sense to her young mind, especially in comparison to the other sights on State Street—from bustling tourists and an ice cream parlor to window shopping at the American Girl doll store.

Madison announced that she would bring her wallet and share her money when we returned the next day. It was a beautiful moment of innocence in action, and a real visceral reaction to address a human injustice.

I have to admit that in the craziness of getting four kids out the door the next day, I was impatient when Madison said she forgot something. Minutes later, she and my husband returned with her wallet, and she gave her first quarter to a homeless man just outside our hotel.

I told her in my most logical, professional, working-mom voice that she would be better off investing her money in a food bank or in an agency that helps more people. When she looked at me with her big brown eyes and asked what we could do right then, I started to explain how I approached my job. In my role leading the strategy for the ConAgra Foods Foundation, I had seen homelessness, disaster and hunger multiple times; accordingly, I had been professionally trained to focus on effective and efficient ways to make scaled social change. My husband gave me "the look" and I immediately understood: Get out of your professional work mode, be in the moment, and listen to your child who is truly demonstrating compassion.

Years later, I reminisced about this moment when I saw other young kids demonstrate empathy and kindness toward their peers after they learned that nearly one in every five kids in the United States live in households that are food insecure, meaning they don't have consistent access to food. Child Hunger is the signature cause at my company, and as part of our strategy we invest in youth, the leaders of tomorrow, to spark ideas, make change and ultimately have a ripple effect in their communities. In partnership with generationOn, the youth chapter of Points of Light—the world's largest organization dedicated to volunteer service—we launched the Make your Mark on Hunger campaign.

We provided grants to help youth bring ideas to life. As part of the campaign launch, my colleague released a powerful video of kids playfully talking about food — likes and dislikes — and then the tone changed when they learned about hunger. Their emotions ranged from alarmed silence and shock to tears and statements of "that is not fair;" and they turned those feelings into a list of ideas and actions for change. It was a raw, emotional reaction to what they saw as an inequity and injustice, followed by an impatient approach to solutions. The grant winners turned their personal experience and observations into acts of kindness, and here are some of their stories.

When Brittany, seventeen, was eight years old, her family was evicted from their home in Honolulu and she came face-to-face with hunger. Brittany's single mom relied on the Hawaii Food bank to feed her family. This motivated Brittany to do something that would help others, and she started a non-profit organization, The Future Isn't Hungry. Hawaii has the highest rates of homelessness per capita in the United States, and there are more than 47,000 children at risk of hunger just in Honolulu. This is something Brittany is passionate about changing.

The effects of hunger hit close to home for Malik, fifteen, from Norfolk, Virginia. When a nearby food market was shut down, so was the main source of food in his neighborhood. As a result, Malik's friends and neighbors without cars had to walk three or four miles to get groceries. Sometimes, this meant no food for families because the walk was too far. With the help of his grant, Malik helped organize a food drive in every Norfolk public middle school and high school with a goal to collect five hundred cans of food in April, National Service Month.

Riding in the back seat of his parents' car after a baseball game in Fort Worth, Will, a sixth-grader, saw a man standing on a street corner holding a sign that read "Need a meal." This sparked questions from Will, who learned that one out of four kids in his community in North Texas are at risk of being hungry, which is even higher than the national average. This motivated Will to gather his baseball teammates and friends from school to start his own nonprofit. Since then, Friends Reaching Our Goals (FROGs) has involved more than 1,000 kids in volunteer activities and served about 175,000 meals to people in need.

These young leaders were not inhibited by an obsession with logic models, evidence-based interventions, efficiency or measuring grant impacts. They weren't worried about metrics and scalability and all the other things we worry about as a business that is doing good, but is still a business with all the associated "grown-up" characteristics. The kids sprang into action, just like my little Madison that day in Chicago when she gave a man a quarter. Kids realize that every little bit counts. Admittedly, at times, they don't think too far ahead, but it is something I envy in them. I have a coveted job, one in which

I get to help potentially millions of people, and often I need to think two steps ahead before I act. Success on a large scale can get in the way of spontaneous action.

Now we have found a way to embrace the energy and enthusiasm of youth. The hope is that addressing hunger through the eyes of youth will engender a passion that will carry into their adult lives, and they will drive social change. I am amazed at the abilities of these young leaders to translate a challenge and/or curiosity into immediate action that helps others. My years of experience can be an asset, but when I watch the kids I see the splendor in simple goodness. In the words of Mark Twain, "Kindness is the language which the deaf can hear and the blind can see." These amazing youth remind me that sometimes it is more appropriate to be present and just do it. As a mom, and as a corporate leader, I keep reminding myself to embrace the innocence in action that I see in kids today. They are a potent force for change.

~Kori Reed

84

Delivering Love, Receiving Hope

One of the great ironies of life is this: He or she who serves
almost always benefits more than he or she who is served.
~Gordon B. Hinckley

fter my partner passed away from AIDS, I was deeply depressed. I didn't know what to do. It seemed that I had lost my purpose in life, despite being a social worker in homeless shelters. At a staff meeting, one of my colleagues mentioned God's Love We Deliver, a group of volunteers who were delivering meals to people living with HIV/AIDS during the height of the epidemic. I saw this as an opportunity to honor my partner's memory by helping others who were struggling in much the same way that he had struggled.

Inspired by this idea, I made my way to the Upper West Side to meet the founders of God's Love We Deliver — Ganga Stone and Jane Best—and to learn how I could get involved. That was twenty-eight years ago, and I've been a God's Love volunteer ever since.

Those early years were critical — people living with HIV/AIDS were suffering and desperately needed help. As a volunteer for God's Love, I would pick up donated meals from restaurants and deliver them to our clients in time for dinner. Sometimes a client would invite me in to sit and talk. I was always glad to spend time with them, knowing they were not only hungry, but lonely, too. In those moments, I'd be reminded of my partner, and I'd feel as if by helping others I was also helping him. So many family members, friends and strangers had been there for us when we were going through difficult times, and now I, too, was making a difference. Giving back was giving purpose to my life.

Ever since that day in 1987 when I began volunteering with God's Love, I have been blessed with the opportunity to help those in need. So many of their faces are imprinted on my memory—a young mother, nearly blind from AIDS, and her son standing in their small, meagerly furnished room as I delivered their meals. Christmas was approaching, and my heart broke as I listened to the little boy recite the list of toys he hoped to get from Santa. I suspected the toys would never materialize. Again, I was inspired by the chance to be there for this family. I submitted their letter to "Santa Claus," otherwise known as the generous New Yorkers of the Operation Santa Claus Project. A few weeks later the young mother and son received three shopping bags filled with toys. I was thrilled to help make their Christmas a little brighter.

I'll always remember the client in Staten Island who had no food or money. When I arrived at his home with a weekend's worth of food, I saw that he was severely ill. He asked me to stay, so I did, for four days. As I watched his health decline, I urged him to go to the hospital, but he refused out of fear. Finally, after I told him it was time for me to go home, he changed his mind and we rode together in an ambulance to the emergency room. At the hospital he learned that he had a blockage in his kidney, which was, thankfully, treatable. It has been an honor to be a point of contact through God's Love for so many people who are sick and don't have anyone else to assist them in getting the help they need.

Now, I am one of over 8,000 volunteers a year who support God's Love We Deliver and the clients they serve. The chefs and kitchen volunteers cook nutritious meals for people affected not only by HIV/AIDS, but by a variety of life-altering illnesses, who can't shop or cook for themselves. I have seen many changes at God's Love and in New York City over the past twenty-eight years, but one thing remains constant: the God's Love community has so much heart. The love we put into our work, and the love we put into the meals we deliver, always reaches the clients. It is an honor and a privilege to be a part of it, and I know I gain more from volunteering than I will ever be able to give.

~James Strickland

85

I Am Because You Are

Do your little bit of good where you are; it's those little bits of good put together that overwhelm the world.
~Desmond Tutu

Almost two decades ago I was a wide-eyed, wild-haired white boy from the U.S. who, after an inspiring conversation in an all-black South African township bar, ended up moving into the home of a teacher that I met that night. Now I'm a father of two and I lead an organization of seventy employees who are changing the lives of more than 2,000 children. Looking back, it's hard to imagine the road map from there to here. The most important parts of this journey were the most difficult decisions, the biggest mistakes and the people who taught me everything I know about overcoming hardship.

I didn't know anything about global development when I first went to the townships of Port Elizabeth, South Africa and not to Wall Street like my University of Pennsylvania peers. I started by having fun and taking chances—there really was no blueprint for what I was trying to do. In the township, every social event revolved around alcohol. At the time, as a twenty-one-year-old kid, I loved it. I was having the time of my life. Of course, I romanticized both the partying and the poverty. But I think my willingness to throw myself into these extreme social situations helped me become a part of township life. If I'd been more cautious, more sober (in both senses of the word), I wouldn't have been able to open myself up to this kind of life. I probably wouldn't have been in the township at all, to be honest.

I could have partied and left, but I got hooked by the things I saw and the people I met—especially the children. On one of my first morning walks in Zwide Township, I came across a group of kids pressing hot stones to their school uniforms to make them neat enough for school. They were that eager to go, to learn, to show how much they cared. I thought of my own life—good schools, proper healthcare, a warm home and more food than I could ever need. For me, that moment crystallized what Ubuntu is all about: the belief that all children everywhere deserve the same shot at making it.

Ubuntu is a Xhosa word that expresses the interconnectedness of all beings. Township kids, Banks—my co-founder who I met in the bar that night, me, the university I came back to so I could raise my first few thousand dollars... we are connected, and we are only powerful through each other. We are in it together and defined as human beings by the way we interact with one another—I am because you are.

I persisted in the crazy belief that poor African children deserve the same opportunities that I had. Banks and I started our non-profit in a broom closet. With unwavering support from a group we now call "The Ubuntu Family"—childhood friends, my own family, my wife, and various kindred spirits—Ubuntu has grown into something extraordinary. I can't count the number of mistakes we made, but through it all, we've remained true to our passions and our promises to the community. We are now a presence in our state-of-the-art headquarters in Zwide Township, and throughout the world, having been recognized as a best practice model by the World Economic Forum, the Aspen Institute and the Clinton Global Initiative. Today we successfully take the most vulnerable children we can find and help them build a pathway out of poverty from cradle to career.

It wasn't easy, and the reality didn't always match the vision. Even after persuading others to believe in us, we weren't always prepared for reality. At one point, one of our staff members was raped. We didn't have health insurance for our workers and we didn't know what to do. I was half a world away, and twenty-three years old, with no idea how to handle this kind of trauma. Banks would visit her and bring her soup and bread, but we didn't have any response in place: no funds, no counseling, no medical leave with pay we could give her. We did what we could, and what we thought was right, but we knew it wasn't enough. This led, eventually, to a human resources department that offers Ubuntu staff, most of whom are from the townships, a safety net and a work environment that supports them professionally and personally. It was part of our journey to the realization that to make real change in the real world, we had to take on our clients' lives in their entirety, to embrace all their complicated needs.

I feel lucky to have seen children who came to us as sick toddlers grow up, graduate from university, and enter the working world. I am lucky to be connected to people who represent greatness in the world—people like Archbishop Emeritus Desmond Tutu and Zethu, the little township girl who grew up to meet President Clinton not once, but twice.

I've learned so much about how charity works, and how it doesn't: A few months before we opened the first Ubuntu Library in 2000, *National Geographic* wrote a short piece about Ubuntu. A high school student in Seattle read it and decided to organize a book drive to help support a township school library. She worked very hard to gather as many books as possible so we could fill the shelves, but she clearly hadn't realized that she could—and should—reject some of the donations. When the shipping container arrived, it contained twenty-five copies of a Ph.D. dissertation on agriculture in Western Australia, encyclopedias so outdated they had entries on the Belgian Congo, and coloring books that had already been filled in.

Every one of these experiences taught us something. Most of all, the children at Ubuntu taught us. They taught us about hope and perseverance. They remind us every day that one's birthplace should not have to determine his or her future. It's hard work keeping it all going, raising the money oceans away, working out the best way to adapt to circumstances, making sure the community determines its own fate. It is a privilege to be part of such a grand social experiment. We have proven that if you invest in the world's most vulnerable children in the same way you invest in your own children and afford them the same dignity, you can truly change the trajectory of anybody's life.

~Jacob Lief

86

Chicken Soup for the Soul

Kindergarten Grandma

It takes a very long time to become young.
~Pablo Picasso

Helen entered my life after a parent approached me and asked if I would consider hosting a foster grandparent volunteer in my kindergarten class. My answer was an immediate yes.

As a teacher, I strove to make the classroom feel like a family. Many children did not have grandparents or had ones who lived far away, so I thought this was a wonderful opportunity for children to be nurtured by an older adult. I introduced her to the class by the name Grandma Helen.

I was not quite certain what to expect when Helen first came to us. I had envisioned a little old lady, possibly frail, who would read and spend time with the children. Little did I know that Helen would walk into the classroom with a spring in her step and a twinkle in her eye. She said she was available up to three days a week for about four hours. She was anxious to help in any way she could.

Helen's enthusiasm was contagious. Her energy level was so high I would joke that if we ran a race, she would win. She was agile getting up and down from those little kindergarten chairs even though "grown up" chairs were available.

The students gravitated to her right away. It turned out that she did not want to read to groups of students, but really enjoyed sitting at learning stations while students were working. There they would talk and she would make note of their questions and concerns. Not all students were able to focus and finish their work on time, so she helped the ones who needed a little extra guidance. She had endless patience helping a child learn to cut with scissors or tie shoelaces.

Wintertime always brought the battle of the coats and boots. The children had about twenty to thirty minutes of outside recess. Grandma Helen helped zip thousands of jackets. When the students came inside there were always a few stuck in their coats when the lining of their jackets got caught in their zippers. She would patiently lift the offending coats over their heads and work to loosen the zippers. This even happened to me, and I was grateful that I didn't have to wear my jacket until lunchtime!

Helen was only scheduled to work a few days a week, but that soon turned into every day. I looked forward to her cheerful presence and extra help. The students eagerly waved to her from their tables when she walked through the door. If she didn't arrive by snack time the students wanted to know where she was.

Her volunteer hours stretched into longer periods of time where I would find her standing at the sink washing paintbrushes, putting materials together or cutting the miles of laminated paper materials. Pitching in and doing these activities saved me so much time. Her work allowed me to leave school by 5:00 so I could spend more time with my family.

Grandma Helen loved coming to school. She was always disappointed when I called her on extremely cold and icy mornings and told her not to come. This lovely seventy-eight-year-old woman drove to our school from a town that was thirty minutes away. The school parking lot was situated a distance from the front doors and I was worried she would slip on the ice.

It was very exciting when the Department of Aging honored her and three other foster grandparents at a recognition dinner. Their families, teachers and principals were invited to join them. Grandma Helen remarked that she didn't understand why so many of her friends were content to stay home and be lonely instead of having meaningful activities to look forward to during the day.

She enjoyed attending class parties and delighted in the children's excited reactions when she gave them candy on Valentine's Day and books at the winter holiday party. She felt wonderful when she helped a child complete a craft. We were all grateful for the many times she cleaned up paint spills and kept papers from sticking together after an enthusiastic student used too much glue.

Grandma Helen became a special friend to me. I looked forward to her calming presence. I was filled with curiosity to see what she might pull out of her canvas bag on arrival: would it be hats and mittens, extra socks, maybe a snack for the class or even a teacher supply I needed?

She was supportive of me as a teacher and became a compassionate confidante. We shared stories and events about our lives and families as we became close over the years. We even met occasionally over the summer months.

Grandma Helen spent years in my classroom. Amazingly, I retired before she did. She graduated to second grade and continued to spread her kindness and generosity.

~Jean Ferratier

87

The Red Blanket Project

Help one another; there's no time like the present and no present like the time.

~James Durst

Last October, an extreme cold snap hit Denver for close to a week. It fell to well below zero for several nights. Driving to work early on one of those freezing mornings, I passed a teenager on the corner with just a sweatshirt and a cardboard sign with "ANYTHING HELPS" scratched on it. This young man was visibly shivering. My sister and I had recently closed up and sold my parents' house and moved them into a nursing facility. Remembering that there was an old red, wool blanket from their house in the trunk, I stopped in traffic and asked this kid if he needed a blanket. He nodded his head and I popped the trunk, handed him the blanket and slid back into my warm car with my heated driver's seat. As I drove off our eyes met and I will never forget the look of relief on this boy's face.

I went about my day but could not get that shivering boy out of my head. I wondered how many more homeless youth were struggling on the streets at that very moment. I also thought about that blanket and how many beds it had been on and all the individuals it had kept warm.

I grew up in a modest household, but my mother and father always taught us to give what we had. Mom was always making meals for the sick or knitting blankets, hats and scarves for others to stay warm.

In that moment The Red Blanket Project was born.

I visited my parents at the club where they spent their days at the retirement center and talked with the director about making blankets and scarves for the homeless. She loved the idea, and the seniors started making our no-sew blankets to give to their "adopted" group of inner-city homeless teens. These seniors wanted to help, make a difference and be involved with meaningful projects. They just needed a project that wasn't complicated and that they could easily complete.

The project grew and youth groups, senior groups, special-needs students, school groups and families all became involved making fleece scarves and blankets—cutting and knotting, but making each with love. It really was a win-win project as individuals and groups stepped up to help.

One day, I was looking at places to deliver our scarves and was talking to a teacher at the school on the campus of the hospital where I work. The school serves high-risk, medically fragile elementary students, many from very-low-income homes. I asked Sue if she thought the kids could use scarves. She answered, "Yes, but let's have them make some." The students would make a scarf to keep and make a blanket or scarf to give away. The older classes cut the fabric and the younger classes tied the knots. They worked in teams and made ninety-seven scarves and twenty blankets for a women's homeless shelter.

When the students presented me with their scarves and blankets, they were very proud of what they had produced and wanted to know exactly where their goods were going and whom they would help. In thanking them, I told them that every one can make a difference: It doesn't matter how old you are, how much money you make or how much education you have. No matter where you are in life, you can help others. The response was dozens of proud smiles on the faces of kids who knew they had helped keep someone a little warmer and made the world a little better.

~Paul Heitzenrater

88

Chicken Soup
for the Soul

Whether Web or Wand

*When we try to pick out anything by itself, we find it hitched to
everything else in the Universe.*
~John Muir

The e-mail attachment was a large photo of Vothy, a small, ema-
ciated girl in Cambodia. She was eleven years old and weighed
only thirteen pounds. Head slumped into a pillow, Vothy's big
dark eyes stared up weakly into mine. Ribs and elbows thinly
covered by tattered skin ended in scrawny fingers clutching emptiness over her heart. The pillow had a red-check pattern with cartoon
flowers, a bright rainbow and balloon letters spelling out: "California
Dreaming…"

The photo had been captured and e-mailed by Denisa and Martin,
a couple who had founded Magna, Cambodia's first rescue home for
HIV-positive orphans. Vothy had been brought to the rescue home
by a nurse from a local hospital that had refused to admit her. HIV-
positive orphans in Cambodia were routinely denied hospital admis-
sion, medical treatment, and even food and water because the official
position of the government was that there were no HIV-positive
children in Cambodia. Outraged by the sight of treatable babies cast
away to die horrendous deaths, Denisa and Martin had established
Magna to administer antiretroviral treatment to children like Vothy.

Vothy had been born into a well-to-do Cambodian family. Before
she was conceived, her father had contracted HIV and unknowingly

infected her mother. In the medical exam when Vothy's mother learned she was pregnant with her first baby she learned also that she was HIV-positive. For years after her arrival, Vothy's family cared for her and took her to the best doctors, but one day her father passed and eventually her mother did too. Vothy's medical care exhausted the savings of her remaining family. Without resources even for food, they finally abandoned her at the hospital.

At the rescue home, Denisa and Martin initiated intensive care and feeding through an IV, but Vothy's only response was to open her big eyes for a brief moment just in time for Martin to capture the photograph before she slipped into a coma. Frantically looking for a pediatrician to advise them on how to treat Vothy, Denisa and Martin e-mailed the photo in a note to a friend in New York, Helena, who had co-founded Sunflower Children, a small volunteer-run charity. Helena shared the e-mail with others who shared it with others who shared with others… Within the hour more than two hundred Sunflower volunteers ("Sunflowers") around the world were connected in a virtual Sunflower chain making calls, praying and taking whatever steps they could to help save Vothy.

Back in Cambodia, despite her coma, Denisa and Martin kept talking to Vothy, telling her about the rescue home, about the other children and about the new life that awaited her. They begged her not to give up because there were two hundred members of her new family that wanted her to stay. At that moment, Vothy's eyes opened… and stayed open. She began to drink weakly, yet steadily and then stably.

Denisa and Martin shared the news and Helena e-mailed the Sunflowers: "WE DID IT! WE SAVED A LIFE!!!" For that moment, two hundred of us were connected through a feeling of awe that we had changed the course of a forgotten child's life.

A year later, while visiting Cambodia, at the gates of the rescue home, Helena was greeted by an energetic young lady bouncing into her arms: "You're here! Ma Helena, you're finally here!"

Denisa translated Vothy's Khmer words. Over the next few days, the Sunflowers received photos and videos sharing Vothy's boundless energy in dance class, playing games with her new sisters and brothers and being scolded for her incessant chatter during math class (where she was the number one student). Vothy told Denisa and Martin that she clearly remembered the moment she heard them tell her about her new family and how that story made her choose to stay because she wanted to meet them.

The experience of those people inspired to action through the Web motivated me to become volunteer CEO of Sunflower Children and co-found Sunflower Children's U.S. organization. Sunflower Children grew to sponsor 11,000 at-risk children in eight countries around the world with more than 1,000 volunteers and only one paid employee. I am blessed to have experienced firsthand the Web grow from a work tool and a play toy into a lever for personal, social and geopolitical transformation.

Since then I have spent years studying the forces behind the phenomena of Web-linked crowds, which have toppled tyrants, elected the first African American president, and destroyed and created entire industries. Yet, when I think back on Vothy, and I think about the arc from the moment when Vothy first opened her eyes from her red-checked pillow, I often wonder about the deeper force which altered her path: Statistically, was it just coincidence that the effect of the IV kicked in just as she was hearing Denisa and Martin's story? Spiritually, did the prayers of a circle of two hundred people alter the judgment of a higher power? Scientifically, did we channel quantum physical energies through a virtual cyclotron that tipped some quarkian cue ball into a side pocket alternate universe where Vothy was fated to live?

Or might it be simpler still?

I've come to realize that the true magic behind Vothy's healing was hope, and that the wand that waved the magic was Story. Through Story, Denisa and Martin sparked Vothy's hope for life. I can't help but marvel at whether through cave paintings or YouTube views, Story does not merely narrate but actually creates our reality.

~James Colmenares

Devon's Story

*To learn to read is to light a fire; every syllable that is spelled
out is a spark.*
~Victor Hugo

t was a cold, snowy day in January when I first met Devon at a
local branch of the public library. Married with three children, he
was a large man, dressed in a scruffy duffle coat that was open at
the neck, exposing the ragged collar of his green flannel shirt. He
thrust his hand out to shake mine and smiled.

"Nice to meet you, Miss June," he said. "I'm fifty years old and
I never learned to read when I was a boy. But now I want to know
everything."

Devon's eagerness was infectious. We quickly got to work using
the library's literacy program materials. He could write his name and
knew some capital letters but wasn't able to recognize simple words,
such as "the" and "at."

We met for two hours each week, reviewing the alphabet with
flash cards and stringing letters together to form simple words. He
laughed at the passages about a bumbling man named Sam and his
no-nonsense wife Pat. He would take the stories home and study
them diligently.

When he got to the point where he could read these stories and
other more challenging texts, he confessed to me something he'd
wanted to do for a while.

"Do you think I could read to my three-year-old daughter now?"

We scoured the library for children's stories he could manage, such as *Good Night Moon* by Margaret Wise Brown and *The Very Hungry Caterpillar* by Eric Carle. He later told me that his daughter was so happy to spend time sitting on his lap and reading books before bed every night.

As well as literacy, we worked on numeracy—addition, subtraction, multiplication and division. He also wanted to learn how to tell time on a clock face.

"Miss June, what are the little dots between the numbers for?"

When I explained they represented minutes, his eyes lit up.

"Nobody never told me that before," he said, grinning.

Because Devon was the one responsible for the food shopping, he brought in grocery store flyers to figure out which items were on sale and which ones were bargains.

Devon noticed a single bottle of water cost seventy-five cents. "That is a good price," he said.

I pointed to a sale item. "What about this package of eight, same-size bottles of water for $4.00?"

"That's too much money."

"Is it? How much for each one?"

He did the calculation and figured out that the bottles cost fifty cents apiece. He looked up at me and said: "Them is tricky, eh?"

In the spring, the city was holding an election. On TV, Devon had been watching the candidates' debates and he told me he had a good feeling about one of the contenders.

"Devon, have you ever voted?"

"No, Miss June."

Together, we called to find out how he could register, where his polling station was located and what help was available. It turned out that an official could read out the candidates' names and instruct him where to mark his ballot. When his candidate won, he was thrilled.

As well as reading books, Devon loved reading lyrics to his favorite songs. That's when I learned that he was a musician and he wanted me to help him write down the lyrics to his reggae compositions.

Secretly he had always wanted to submit his music for copyright, which meant he had to write a letter and address the envelope. We walked to the mailbox and he dropped the envelope in.

"That feel good, Miss June. I never do that before!"

Devon grew bolder. He asked me to help him learn how to use an ATM. When he saw a printout of his account transactions, he was annoyed to see how his wife and teenage son spent money on frivolous charges, such as extra ATM fees and Internet games. A few weeks later, he told me he had taken them to task.

"I talked to my wife. She no like that I know. But now she know I no put up with that no more."

In December, almost one year to the day that we began our time together, Devon texted me: "Morning miss June. Have the flue so I cannot make it to day."

I wrote back to say I was sorry he wasn't feeling well. But I was far from sorry to see those beautiful words typed out on the screen.

~June Rogers Flahie

Weeding Baby Wendell

You can't live a perfect day without doing something for
someone who will never be able to repay you.
~John Wooden

I walk nearly every evening, rain or shine. Although the area where I live has sidewalks, ball fields and open spaces where most people do their walking, I prefer to walk in the cemetery across the street. It's nearly forty acres of rolling land full of mature trees and all manner of wildlife. It's filled too, with many graves. Toward a back corner, just a few feet from a rusted section of chain-link fence choked with honeysuckle, is Baby Wendell's grave.

On my daily walks I began to stop now and then to upright a vase, pull a weed or pick up trash. I don't always take the same route, so I never focused on any grave in particular. I just did what little thing needed to be done if I noticed, and kept walking. It was obvious when family or friends would tidy up around a grave, and it became clear that some graves never got attention other than the general maintenance by the cemetery staff. No one ever visited Baby Wendell. The little granite urn on his tombstone would fill with old leaves, grass clippings and spider webs. The day I noticed wiregrass smothering his tiny tombstone, I decided to make Wendell a routine stop.

My daily walks also meant that the many visitors who came regularly on Sunday afternoons or holidays would see me at one place or another on the grounds. I'd often be mistaken for an employee as they stopped to ask, for instance, where section L was, which gate exited where, or how to find the main office.

One Sunday evening, two elderly women who I later realized had seen me there many times, drove up as I was bent over picking a dead wasp out of Wendell's urn. Not wanting them to think I was up to no good, I stood and walked toward them to say hello. They were all smiles and I was surprised as they began to thank me.

"We see you out here real often. How long have you worked here?" the first woman asked as she adjusted the bouquet of artificial flowers she held in her hand.

The second woman added "Yes, and after that last storm you were the first one we saw out here picking up sticks. It's just so good that you work here."

I watched the first woman struggle with her bouquet and said, "Oh no, Ma'am. I don't work here. I just walk here."

As it turned out, they were sisters who had come to put flowers on their brother's grave. His is located just a few sites over from Baby Wendell, between a dogwood tree and a very old azalea.

"But you're here just about every time we come by," the first woman said, still fighting to get a grip on the bouquet in her hand, and looking puzzled that I didn't work there.

"And looks to me like every time we've seen you, you've been working," the sister added.

I explained to them how I might randomly pick up a stick now and then, or put some wind-blown trash back in the can, but that they only saw me so often because I had one day noticed the wiregrass that nearly covered the tiny tombstone near their brother's.

"I'm just weeding Baby Wendell," I said.

"Why? All that and you don't work here?" the first woman asked.

I'd never given it much thought. I walked there nearly every day and it was just part of my walk to upright a geranium now and then. I had occasionally remembered what Nannie, my grandmother, used to tell us kids: "If you see a need, fill it, and don't worry about who gets the credit."

"Well we can't thank you enough for all we've seen you do," the first woman said, as a little piece of her bouquet of flowers broke off.

"Oh, it's just wonderful that you would help for no reason," her sister added.

They both seemed about to tear up as they walked away. I never thought about needing or getting credit for any of the random things I only sporadically did as I walked, but these two women had noticed and they had thanked me. Those tiny efforts took so little on my part, but to them they meant a lot. They noticed and they appreciated.

I suppose we all do random nice things because we know it's right and it's kind. Baby Wendell could never thank me, and none of us imagine we'll ever be thanked for the tiny things we do, and we may not believe anyone even notices. But out there for each of us is the equivalent of those two old ladies, noticing and appreciating.

I reached down and picked up the tiny piece of bouquet the woman had dropped as she thanked me. I finished weeding Baby Wendell and put those flowers in his little urn.

"No need to thank me, Wendell. You're welcome."

~Stuart M. Perkins

Reading Lessons

It is the supreme art of the teacher to awaken joy in creative expression and knowledge.
~Albert Einstein

Years ago, my daughter Hope was in a fourth grade class with an eclectic assortment of children from all walks of life. Our small community centered on the paper mill that provided employment for the vast majority of its citizens, and most of the children in her class had at least one parent employed by the mill. Hope loved her class and often told me tales of various classmates, including a boy named Robert who was in trouble a lot, standing in a corner almost daily for some misdeed.

I was the classroom mom, meaning I brought snacks and planned parties and special outings for her class, even though I worked full-time as a social worker. I saw Robert standing in the corner one day and asked the teacher if he could join our Valentine's Day party. She refused, saying he needed to learn a lesson by missing the party. I wasn't sure what he had done to be placed in the corner, but I felt sad for him as we ate cupcakes and played games while he continued to face the corner. After the party, I asked Hope what he had done. "He talked back. He's always talking back like you said for me not to do. If you were his mother, I bet he wouldn't talk back."

I knew Robert's mother worked long hours at the mill. I knew she was a good woman who found it hard to care for her four children alone. She tried her best, but I was sure there were days she felt hopeless and unable to manage it all.

Hope said Robert got angry when he didn't know the answer to things or couldn't read as well as the other children. Hope's words struck me and made me ponder whether I could volunteer with Robert on a one-to-one basis.

His teacher allowed me to come two days a week during my lunch break and help Robert with reading. We read second grade–level books, the highest level he could master. Slowly but surely he began to master these books, almost enjoying them. His resistance to learning began to decrease as I introduced books about his favorite activity: baseball. Sometimes his teacher refused to allow him to have sessions with me because of his poor behavior, making both of us sad. I encouraged Robert to listen to his teacher and explain what he was feeling using words instead of anger.

I noticed him slowly becoming more engaged in his own learning. With each successful completion of a book, Robert began to show more pride in his schoolwork and more self-respect. His behavior improved and his attitude about school improved. It was not easy for me to get off work during lunch, but I carefully planned everything around my two hours per week of volunteering because I saw how valuable those two hours were—to him and to me.

One day, around Mother's Day, Hope came home with a beautiful card she had made me at school. She wrote a note inside her card that read: "Thanks for helping Robert. I'm glad you're my mom." That made me cry!

When Robert finished fourth grade, he was delighted to read his report card and see that he was promoted to fifth grade. His teacher gave him a certificate for the most improved reader during the end-of-school class party. His mother was there and cried as her son showed the certificate to her. Then, to my surprise, she handed me a cake she and Robert had made for me. "He read the recipe to me all by himself."

I think about Robert from time to time and wonder how the redheaded boy, now a grown man, is doing. I hope he remembers the value of reading and the sense of accomplishment he had after finishing each book. Volunteering became more than a few hours a week I donated, it became an investment in a child that hopefully has paid out dividends to him year after year. I can't think of any better way to spend my lunchtime than feeding a child hungry for worth through the power of knowledge.

~Malinda Dunlap Fillingim

92

Purposeful Waiting

In about the same degree as you are helpful, you will be happy.
~Karl Reiland

t had been two months since we got the news, and I was still trying to grasp the reality of what it all meant. My husband Greg was going to be deployed to Iraq for at least nine months.

For as long as I had known Greg, he was "just" a Navy Reservist, so I didn't fully comprehend what it meant to be a military wife, let alone how to endure a deployment. Yes, we were a military family one weekend a month when he had his drill weekends, but a deployment meant so much more. It meant he wouldn't come home each night; it meant he would be gone for months at a time; it meant we couldn't just call him on his cell phone whenever we wanted; and most importantly, it meant he was going to war. Worst of all, I knew the not knowing was going to be the hardest to endure—not knowing where he was or what he was doing, not knowing if he was safe, and not knowing when he would come home. I knew that I would have to keep myself busy while Greg was gone.

A short time after learning of his deployment, Greg asked if I would be interested in being the ombudsman for his unit. I had no idea what an ombudsman was, but the thought of doing anything for his unit was appealing.

Greg explained that it was a volunteer job taken on by the spouse of a military member. As ombudsman, I would be a point of contact for families back home—essentially a bridge between the Command, unit family members and the community resources. I was also there to be a sympathetic ear, someone who would understand the emotional journey the spouses were on because I was on it too. Ultimately, I would be the go-to person for the families because they couldn't go to their deployed spouse when they needed support.

My first task as ombudsman was to complete the required training for the position. It was almost like a volunteer boot camp. I learned so much, so quickly—but welcomed the new knowledge. For the first time since learning of my husband's deployment, I felt empowered. I had a focus and a direction to follow. My next task was to reach out to our families, introduce myself as their ombudsman and let them know what I could do for them during the deployment.

In July, my husband's deployment and my ombudsman position kicked into full gear. Officially, my main jobs were to keep resources handy so I could share them when requested, participate in conference calls with Command, relay all permitted information to our families, and pretty much be available 24/7 should any family need my support. However, over the course of the deployment, I found that it was the other unexpected volunteer opportunities I created that brought me the greatest sense of purpose.

The first unexpected opportunity arose as Halloween approached. I watched my children get excited about their costumes. My son was going to be a superhero—"just like Daddy." He would share this exciting fact with anyone willing to listen, and then get a little sad when he remembered that Greg wouldn't be there to see him in his costume or to take him trick-or-treating.

I realized that we had many holidays to live through without our military heroes, and I suggested that we support our troops by supporting their families. I was a teacher, so I turned to my middle school students and enlisted them to make holiday cards and gifts for the children of the deployed parents. We would eventually send care packages to the children in our group for Halloween, Thanksgiving, Christmas, New Year's, Valentine's Day, St. Patrick's Day and Easter.

With my students taking care of our families' children, I reached out to my fellow spouses. While I had a supportive network of family and friends who kept asking how they could help my kids and me, not all families had that. Therefore, I sent an e-mail to my family and friends telling them how they could extend their support to other military spouses. I was going to put together small care packages for the spouses—with a Starbucks card to let them know that people were thinking of them and their sacrifice at Christmas and to go "have a treat on us." My hope was to raise enough to give a $5 gift card to every spouse.

As expected, I began getting letters with money from my family and friends, and I was touched by how generous many of them were. Then, something truly awesome happened. I started receiving letters from people I didn't know. In their letters, they explained they had heard about what I was doing for the military spouses and that they wanted to donate, too. When all was said and done, I was able to send $15 gift cards to all forty-five spouses.

When I first learned of Greg's deployment I was afraid—worried about his safety, unsure of my ability to keep things together at home, and nervous about how our family would work when he returned. Being ombudsman made me feel like I was more than the wife waiting at home while her husband was at war. I had a job too, a purpose beyond myself. I wasn't in another country, I wasn't wearing camouflage, and I wasn't carrying weapons. But I was part of a team—a team of spouses who were fighting to keep it together while our loved ones were away.

It was truly the hardest and scariest time of my life, but at the same time, because of my opportunity to volunteer as ombudsman, it was also the most rewarding and enriching time. And even though my efforts were acknowledged after the deployment, I didn't sign up to be ombudsman for the recognition. Most people don't join the military for the recognition, either. They sign up because they want to serve and protect their fellow man. And through my volunteer experience I discovered that so did I.

~Andrea Bowen

Volunteering & Giving Back

Every Living Thing

93

On a Mission

A woman is like a tea bag; you never know how strong it is until
it's in hot water.
~Eleanor Roosevelt

D riving to a rural town in Illinois, I had an address, a full tank of gas and fifty dollars in my purse. I was on a rescue mission—one that I had volunteered for—and as I drove I rehearsed my tall tale.

Our rescue group had gotten a call from someone out of town: A Golden Retriever needed to be rescued. Chained up in a back yard day and night without any shade, without a constant supply of water, the dog was being neglected. It was late June. The summer had already started with a roar in the Midwest. Temperatures over 100 degrees were an everyday thing and rain was a distant memory. I knew I would have nightmares if something awful happened and we didn't try to save this dog.

"Could our group buy him?" I asked. I had already volunteered to drive the distance to get the dog.

"No, paying for a dog is against our bylaws," I was told. "But if you wanted to pay for the dog yourself, that'd be okay." Oh. I guessed I'd have to volunteer my car and my wallet for this adventure.

On the two-hour ride, I created the story I was going to tell. Normally we didn't concoct stories to rescue a dog in need. Most people called and asked us to take their dogs, so this was an unusual situation. Before I went to the address we had been given, I was going to knock on a few doors and tell a woe-filled tale about a beloved Golden I had lost.

I picked a string of houses about half a block from the home I was really interested in. Keeping my arms as close to my sides as possible—I was already perspiring with nervousness—I stepped up on the large wooden porch and knocked on the door. A white-haired lady opened her screen door. In all facets of my life I'm a scrupulously honest person, so in this situation I was worried I wouldn't be able to lie in a convincing way. When asked questions, I always tell the truth, but now, as a volunteer for our dog rescue group, I'd have to lie a little.

"Hi, I was at the gas station up the street, and somebody saw my Golden Retriever keychain while I was pumping my gas. I got to chatting, telling them about my Trixie, who just died, and they told me that somebody on this street has a Golden. I am so missing my dog, and just wanted to put my arms around a dog like Trixie and pet it. Do any of your neighbors have a Golden Retriever?"

Thankfully this sweet grandmotherly woman trusted me. We spoke for a few minutes, and then she pointed to the address I had already checked out. I thanked her and walked across the street to "the house."

A woman in her late twenties answered the door. Her preschool-aged son hung onto her skirt. "Hello?"

"Hi, I was passing through and heard you have a Golden. I just lost my Golden Retriever, Trixie, and was wondering if I could just look at your dog before I head back home to St. Louis. I miss my old girl so much and just need a Golden fix."

She was as unsuspicious as her neighbor.

Immediately, she agreed to show me Harley. And there, chained in the corner of the yard, was a handsome Golden Retriever.

Even though I was a stranger invading his territory, the dog didn't bark or growl. Like every other Golden I had ever met, Harley was ecstatic over the attention he was getting from a human. I knelt down in the dirt, put my arms around him and gave him a hug. "Oh my, he looks just like my sweet Trixie. He has the same eyes!"

The owner said, "He's a really good dog. We tried to bring him into the house but he kept chewing up stuff, so now he's an outside dog and he's happy." I heard another couple of kids still in the house, calling for her. "I'll be right back," she said, and headed across her large yard.

I looked around. The yard where Harley was chained had been dug up, either from boredom or from him trying to cool off during the horrendously hot days. There was a bowl of dirty water and a huge bucket of food; bugs were crawling around inside it. A spindly sapling and an enormous plastic barrel—on its side, with a doorway cut out—were the only shelter from the sun.

When the woman came back, my tears brimmed over because I knew how hungry this dog was for love and attention. And I figured he was on the verge of getting heatstroke. In just the few minutes I had been there I was already woozy from the heat, so I was certain this four-legged fellow was miserable. My mascara was running down my cheeks because I felt so sad. But that's not what I told the owner.

"Harley reminds me so much of Trixie, it makes me cry. He's the same shade of gold that she was, and he has the same long eyelashes. This is going to sound crazy, I know, but I was wondering if you'd agree to sell him. I miss my dog so much." I rooted around in my purse, got my wallet and pulled out the money I had brought. "Here, I've got $50. I know it's not much, but it's all I have."

"I don't think you want to buy him. He's got a hernia. We're gonna make an appointment for him as soon as we can scrape up the money." She had Harley lie down and roll over, and she showed me the tiny bulge near his belly. From our talk I found out that Harley needed surgery. He also was due for his shots, and the family couldn't afford heartworm medicine. This young family really couldn't afford this dog.

An hour and a half later, Harley and I walked across the street. As I loaded him into my car, I whispered, "Harley, you're going to have a great life." And from that point on, I never had to tell another untrue tale, and this sweet Golden Retriever never went without comfort and love.

Volunteering to save a dog's life… My only pay was the thump of a happy dog's tail, and some kisses from his long, droopy tongue. Was it worth it?

Definitely.

~Sioux Roslawski

Snake Lady

*In the end we will conserve only what we love. We will love
only what we understand. We will understand only what we are
taught.*
~Baba Dioum

Every eye in the room was fixed on the beautiful four-foot-long
snake slithering slowly through my hands. Adults shook their
heads in amazement. One excited youngster exclaimed, "This
is so cool!" Another added, "I want to do what you do when
I grow up!"

Most people envy my volunteer position as an educator for a
local wildlife rehabilitation group. They enjoy meeting our live education animals, and I love introducing the non-releasable feathered or
furry representatives of our state's indigenous species.

Although I work with songbirds, birds of prey and mammals as
well as reptiles, I am best known as the "Snake Lady." The title seems
ironic given my past feelings about the cold-blooded creatures. My
first close-up encounter with one did not go well.

In the spring of 1991, when I was seven months pregnant with
our daughter, I was bitten by a large, hungry snake in our suburban
garden. Thankfully, the snake was not venomous; an animal control
officer quickly relocated him to a new home. The baby was unharmed
and I was pronounced physically fine, but I developed a terrible fear
of snakes. Everyone, including me, assumed that I would dread them

for the rest of my days.

But Providence had other plans. Fifteen years and a move to the country later, I was to be educated by an injured snake named Schmiddy. My second serpentine encounter would transform me into a lifelong snake advocate, passionate about all snakes and proud to be called "Snake Lady."

On a freezing afternoon late in October of 2006, my husband discovered a snake sticking out from underneath the woodpile on our recently purchased farm. Dan could not understand why the young animal, barely eighteen inches from nose to tail, lay exposed to the elements. Its skin was so cold that the snake barely moved when Dan touched it. He scooped it up and headed toward the house to show his find to our ten-year-old son.

I was cooking dinner when Dan brought the black and yellow speckled stranger into the kitchen. My stomach turned over at the sight of the dark length lying across my husband's gloved hand. My hands grew clammy and I backed away. But the snake was very docile and both of our children were captivated by it so, despite my plaintive protests, Dan released the little reptile onto the throw rug.

We realized right away that something was very wrong. The upper third of the snake curved slightly to the right to form the distinctive S pattern of travel common to the species, but the remaining two-thirds of the skinny little body dragged behind straight as an arrow. Try as it might, the snake made little headway. Dan pointed out a sharp swollen knot along the top of its spinal cord.

The snake was obviously hurt. I guessed that its back must be broken. I was an experienced wildlife rehabber and educator; surely I could steel myself long enough to do something. The crippled creature made no attempt to strike at us or bite. It seemed to know we might be able to help.

And so we did. We took the snake to one of our volunteer veterinarians and he confirmed my diagnosis. The gentle reptile with the broken back became the first snake ever to be rehabilitated by a member of our wildlife group. Our son named it Schmiddy after a famous World War II machine gunner who was wounded at Guadalcanal and subsequently awarded several medals for extraordinary courage. The name stuck before we discovered that Schmiddy was a she.

We rehabbed Schmiddy for weeks. We fed her frozen mice that we thawed in a dedicated "mouse microwave," and we gave her shots of antibiotics. We swam her daily in a large plastic tub. We helped peel off her dead skin when she shed. We identified her as a speckled king snake and spent hours researching her specific subspecies and the broader suborder of *Serpentes*.

And all the time we were caring for Schmiddy, she was teaching us. I became so enamored of her plucky nature and the amazing things I learned about the benefits of snakes that I asked permission to include her in my education programs when she was healthy enough. I will never forget our first public appearance.

The two owls I brought to the library that day were well received as usual, and the frisky red fox squirrel was a hit. I saved Schmiddy for last, and no one had any idea that the covered container behind me contained a snake. Her appearance riveted and polarized the audience.

A collective gasp erupted from the crowd when I lifted Schmiddy out of her carrier. Many, like I had been, were deathly frightened of her. A few rose from their chairs and made a beeline for the back of the room. But as I held Schmiddy and told her story and how she had transformed my opinion of her kind, the faces before me softened. Education triumphed.

Snakes became a permanent part of my presentations, which included talks about safety around snakes, the identification of dangerous species, characteristics of snakes and the value of snakes. Schmiddy was a wonderful wildlife advocate. We traveled all over the state, opening minds and overcoming fears at schools and libraries, wildlife conferences, outdoor fairs, civic group meetings and private parties. Schmiddy even enjoyed an appearance on television.

I had hoped to work with her for many years to come, but it was not to be. Less than eighteen months after her teaching debut, Schmiddy developed spondylosis, a serious disease also found in people with spinal injuries, and we retired her. But I couldn't stop sharing what she had taught me. My reputation as the Snake Lady hung in the balance. Schmiddy had become the highlight of my programs.

I acquired a tri-colored captive-raised milk snake from a rehabber in another state. For my fiftieth birthday, my children bought me a hognose snake from a reputable breeder. My current presentations feature five snakes, including a beautiful speckled king snake that went through rehab after surviving multiple dog bites.

Schmiddy is still with me as well. She lives a quiet, comfortable life, secure in a big aquarium inside our home. Nearly a decade after I met her, the teaching continues. Thanks to the brave little snake with a broken back and a wildlife volunteer with a transformed heart, hundreds of people every year are introduced to snakes and taught to value them. Schmiddy taught this Snake Lady to understand, accept and appreciate her species. She taught me to love.

~Andi Lehman

95

Chicken Soup for the Soul

Tails of a Therapy Dog

Those who loved you and were helped by you will remember you when forget-me-nots have withered. Carve your name on hearts, not on marble.
~Charles H. Spurgeon

"Touching Lives, Warming Hearts." That's the motto of the pet therapy group we are privileged to volunteer with, and these words perfectly describe Chester, my lovable, goofy, fluffy, and tenderhearted Golden Retriever.

Countless tales spring to mind when I think of our many pet therapy visits throughout the years—the many people, young and old, who have touched our hearts so deeply. We have visited hospitals, retirement communities, memory loss homes, domestic violence shelters, classrooms and cancer survivor camps, just to name a few. Wherever a caring canine can bring joy and hope, that is where we go. And my heart is forever changed.

This particular story takes place on an ordinary day in an elementary school gymnasium filled with children and teachers. I remember walking into the auditorium with Chester by my side in his bright yellow vest, and feeling the excitement that rocked the room. I delighted hearing the loud whispers—"LOOK, IT'S A DOG!"—as I soaked in the view. A sea of children sat cross-legged on the floor in their classroom groups, circled like wagons, waiting with wiggles of anticipation to meet the star of the day, Chester!

Chester and I were invited by the principal to speak at a school assembly about pet therapy and what makes Chester so dog-gone special that he gets to visit cool places like schools and hospitals and airports! While Chester worked the crowd with his smiles, wags and doggie tricks, I told the students about my furry friend and pet therapy. The students loved hearing our stories, but no doubt about it, the highlight of our time together was the meet and greet with Chester. And as often happens, an ordinary day became extraordinary.

After the talk, Chester and I made our way to each circle of students. We strolled past every single child who wanted a chance to pet the fluffy Golden Retriever. My buddy pranced with a silly grin, tail wagging, ears flopping. He gave out endless love and received a gazillion pats, ear rubs and back scratches. He was in doggie heaven. So were the children.

After a very full morning, Chester and I were in our final assembly of the day with our last group of children. As we moved around the circle, Chester paused. Then he stopped. I gave a little tug on his leash, urging him to move forward. My buddy was not moving. His big old paws were firmly planted on the shiny gymnasium floor in front of a little girl with long brown hair and downcast eyes. Her curls partially covered her face, and her tiny hand gently rested on Chester's head.

"Looks like Chester doesn't want to move," I said, winking at the little girl. I have learned that if Chester speaks, I should pay attention. And so I paused. While waiting for these two brown-eyed sweethearts to have their moment, I noticed a woman standing near. Tears filled her eyes. She looked directly at me, then silently mouthed the words, "Her dog died yesterday."

Sigh.

I leaned in closer to the tenderhearted teacher. She pointed toward Chester, then whispered in my ear, "It's like he knows."

Tears leaked out. "He knows. I don't know how he knows, but he knows." I gently squeezed her hand.

After a bit of time, we continued to move around the circle so the rest of the class could reach out to my four-legged buddy. "Touching

Lives and Warming Hearts." It is Chester's specialty.

Because there is always time for one more hug, we strolled around the classroom circle one more time. As we approached Chester's friend again he stopped. This time he gave her a gentle slobbery kiss right on her little cheek. She smiled.

I knelt down, "Looks like Chester has found a friend," I said. "Would you like to give him a hug?"

She nodded, then gently wrapped her slender arms around Chester's fluffy tummy, nestling her head into the soft golden fur of his neck.

With tears, I waited.

~Diane Rima

96

Bed, Bath and Way Beyond

It is a happy talent to know how to play.
~Ralph Waldo Emerson

Volunteering wasn't my cup of tea. The thought of giving up my precious time in exchange for nothing didn't interest me. But then, at the ripe young age of fifty, I unexpectedly found myself unable to work as the result of a medical condition. Suddenly, I had way too much time on my hands.

The first year or so of my forced retirement was spent mostly sitting for hours alone feeling sorry for myself. The second year I spent my time cleaning out more closets, junk rooms and cubbyholes than I'd ever realized one home could have. There were times I was so bored with life that I actually contemplated knocking on my neighbors' doors to beg them to let me clean their forgotten spaces. The "postal lady" dreaded seeing me sitting on the porch when delivering the mail. I so longed for conversation I'd talk with her about anything that popped into my mind. The librarians at my local library called me by name because I'd spent so many hours bothering them.

By the time the third year rolled around I was still moping a bit, but with the tidiest garden on the street, the most organized pantry shelves, and the cleanest nooks and crannies on the block, I realized the thing I'd valued most in my life I'd been squandering.

One Sunday afternoon I saw an advertisement in the newspaper asking for community volunteers at the local Humane Society shelter.

I'd always loved animals, and having lost my own best friend and beloved Pit Bull a few months prior to my sudden illness, the idea of working with dogs that needed homes seemed a perfect fit. There was no time to waste. After all, if I procrastinated they'd surely find someone else to fill the open slots. I dashed off an e-mail to the shelter letting them know of my interest and before the day was up had a return e-mail telling me where and when to "report for duty."

After sitting through a two-hour orientation, my reluctance to volunteer was back in full force. Each volunteer was asked to complete a three-hour stint in "Bed, Bath and Beyond," a fancy title for scrubbing food bowls and litter pans and washing trash bins stuffed with dirty, smelly laundry. Who knew animals could dirty so many blankets in one day? But with all the determination I could muster I told myself to relax and enjoy the task at hand. After all, this was only the beginning of a long list of volunteer opportunities available at the shelter, a way of weeding out those not truly interested in giving their time. Once this task was complete I'd be promoted to bigger and better things, right?

With all the diligence and enthusiasm I'd become famous for at the shelter, I went right to work. There was never a dull moment and always a new animal that needed love and the reassurance that it would soon find its new home. There was the occasional shy, grown cat that just needed company while it waited for its new owner to arrive. There were dogs of all sizes and breeds—some excited, some scared, some wanting to play, others simply needing a bit of space while they adjusted to the new surroundings.

One blustery January morning I pulled open the shelter doors, punched the volunteer time clock and went to work. As I'd come to learn, no day is considered normal at the Humane Society, and this one was no different. I began by washing dishes and shoving a load of laundry into the washer—a rather mindless task I'd actually come to enjoy, especially after seeing firsthand what a benefit it was to the paid staff for a volunteer to do the "grunt work" so they could spend more time teaching the animals basic commands in preparation for their new owners.

With the laundry packed away and the dishes drying, I made my way through the shelter in search of a "newbie," a dog or cat just introduced to the shelter that needed a bit of extra tender love and care. I found an unexpected surprise. With her lipstick mouth, spotted floppy ears, and paws that seemed perfect for a dog four times her size, she was packed in a twelve-week-old package of energy and excitement, with hazel eyes that screamed, "You need me, you just haven't realized it yet!"

Just looking at her brought a long-forgotten smile to my face. Around and around the pen she ran, chasing her tail until she fell over from dizziness. She would grab her tail between her teeth and growl at it like it was an enemy she'd finally conquered. I laughed, and the sound of my own laughter startled me. It had been years since I'd laughed out loud.

I stood watching the puppy for what seemed like hours before I finally reached in and pulled her to my chest. She sniffed, wiggled her way up my shoulders to my face, and began licking me with her warm, wet tongue. After a while she calmed, laid her head on my chest and stared into my eyes. Then she closed her eyes tight and sighed as if to say, "I'm at peace now, you're here." She knew it before I did. We needed each other.

A fresh zeal for a changed life can often be found in the strangest places. Mine was found in the eyes of a pup I named Hazel, and I would have missed the opportunity altogether had I not been willing to give of the most precious thing in life—my time.

~Lisa Fowler

97

Walk On

The best things in life aren't things.
~Art Buchwald

drove down this street all the time on my way to and from the grocery store about a half-mile away, but this was the first time I had seen the big, bold, black letters on a white cardboard sign: VOLUNTEERS NEEDED.

I knew what was there: horse stables, a corral, and lots of open land with only a few trees for shade. It took up a huge corner of many acres right across from a big housing development. On my ride home, I caught sight of a girl riding high atop a chestnut-colored mare. The girl's hair was blowing in the breeze, the horse's canter gently bouncing her up and down in the saddle.

I love animals and have been privileged to share my life with many dogs and cats. I used to ride horses occasionally as a youngster, but I hadn't been around horses in years, ever since a horse rubbed me up against a tree. I guess he wanted to scratch his back or something, but it unnerved me when the handler had to come over and pull him away.

Swallowing my fear of horses, I turned left into the long, dusty driveway and drove slowly past a corral where a trainer worked with a beauty of a horse. She held the reins and led the horse around on a long rope, encouraging him to trot, then gallop, and to cool down after exercising.

The pungent smell of horses and hay filled my nostrils as I pulled up to the ramshackle building marked "Office."

"Hi," I said when I entered. "I'm inquiring about the volunteers needed."

"Come on in," a young woman said. "We need help with our therapeutic riding program."

"What does that mean?"

Darlene explained the value of a horse as a therapeutic tool to help disabled children and adults. "The natural motion of the horse moves the rider's pelvis in a way that is similar to walking. This motion assists in strengthening the rider's muscular and skeletal structure." She went on to explain that the horses provided emotional and psychological benefits, too. The horses' kind and gentle natures helped to build a bond with the riders, encouraging self-esteem and confidence.

"We need one person to lead and two people as side walkers for every horse and rider," Darlene explained. "Without volunteers, we do not ride."

The colorful brochure I picked up stated that individuals of all ages and most disabilities can be served by therapeutic riding, including those with autism, cerebral palsy, spinal bifida, muscular dystrophy, multiple sclerosis, spinal meningitis, Down syndrome, vision and hearing impairments, learning disabilities and mild mental retardation.

"So I wouldn't have to ride the horse?" That pleased me. Darlene led me out of the office and toward a small outdoor arena. "What would I be doing?"

"See that little girl on the chestnut mare? There's a leader at the front of the horse, and there are two people, one on each side, with their arms against the flank of the horse and their hands gently holding the little girl's legs. The side walker is there to assist if the rider slips, shifts in the saddle, if her foot comes out of the stirrup or she needs assistance of any kind."

"Would I have to be near the back of the horse?"

Darlene looked at me and grinned. "Afraid of what comes out back there?"

"No," I smiled back. "I just have a little fear of getting kicked." I didn't tell her about my run-in with the tree.

"Oh, our horses are extremely tame. We wouldn't put our clients on them if they weren't. We have the gentlest horses around."

"I think I'd like to be a side walker," I told Darlene when we returned to her office. After working out the details, I signed up to help.

I couldn't wait to start. The first day, I put on my oldest pair of blue jeans, tennis shoes and a lightweight cotton shirt. Darlene said the sun bears down all day and it gets hot out there, so I stuck a baseball hat on my head. After training, I was ready for my first side walking experience.

Riders come with various degrees of disability. Wednesdays were Angie days. She was a diminutive, dark-haired little girl around nine years old whose mother held her hand tightly as she squirmed and wiggled her way up the mounting ramp. She already had her helmet on. Darlene helped her mount the big rust-colored Quarter Horse, then adjusted the saddle straps and stirrups.

"Are you ready to ride, Angie?" Darlene asked.

"Yes, Miss Darlene."

"Then tell your horse to walk on."

"Walk on," Angie said. She had a sweet, confident smile on her face as her horse began to walk with me on one side and another side walker on the other. The horse leader led us in turns, stops and exercises for Angie, like picking up a colored cone atop a tall pole and putting it on another pole.

Angie's mother later told me, "I've never seen Angie sit still for so long. At first she was afraid of the horse and refused to even stroke him. But the instructors worked with her one step at a time and by the third lesson Angie not only petted the horse, but held her reins proudly as she sat and waited to ride. She's come a long way."

And so have I. Volunteering opened my heart up wide. And being around the gentle, sweet, giant horses didn't make me feel small anymore. It made me feel proud. Proud that I was doing something to help others.

~B.J. Taylor

Silly Me

Dogs are not our whole life, but they make our lives whole.
~Roger Caras

t started with a phone call from my son, Nate. "Mom, there's a dog here. She needs help. She's lost, hungry and afraid of people. Nobody can catch her. We tried, but she runs. I bet you can catch her. Please?" My teenage son's dramatic plea came from a visitor center where he volunteered.

"Not, now," I objected. I love dogs, but at that moment I did not want to take on another project.

"Can you please just take a look at her when you come pick me up?" He had confidence in my abilities.

I agreed, and soon I was looking at a scraggly, mud-covered mongrel that was resting in the shade of a hundred-year-old oak tree. Scratching from hordes of fleas, ticks and mange, the dog watched intently as people came and went from the visitor center. If a person approached her, she wagged her tail, then tucked it and ran. She was medium-sized, gold and white, with warm, pleading, caramel-colored eyes. She wanted to connect but she was afraid.

Many years of working with all kinds of distressed animals had hardened my heart. I thought of a thousand reasons I could not take a mangy dog home. I already had three dogs and when one of those finally trotted over the rainbow bridge, I wanted to get a dog that I could use as a therapy dog. I could see that this sad dog was not therapy dog material. Therapy dogs connect to people in ways that transcend human understanding. I turned and walked away.

I convinced Nate to wait a few days to see if the dog's owner would magically appear. Secretly, I was expecting the dog would disappear. She didn't.

A friend with a small animal rescue shelter took her for quarantine and treatment. I knew she was safe but the dog's eyes haunted me. That longing look kept returning to my mind, pleading for connection. After a couple of weeks, I succumbed and brought the dog home with me. She was quickly accepted by my "pack." Cleaned up and fed, she resembled a stocky gold and white Border Collie. I named her Leala.

A project she was. For six months, Leala avoided human contact. She was not at all aggressive, but she was terribly afraid to be touched by people. Then suddenly, one day, Nate engaged her in play. It did not take long before she actually wanted to be petted by all the house-humans.

A month or so later, at a routine checkup, the vet said, "This is a really good dog. You do not see many like this." His words opened my eyes to a new possibility.

Leala was kind to everyone, even the vet who stuck her with needles. Leala had quickly become the most well-behaved, sweetest dog I had ever owned. It was a stretch, but I wondered if she could be the therapy dog I had hoped for.

Within another month, Leala and I were in a therapy dog training class. She passed with flying colors. When we started making visits to nursing homes and mental hospitals, it was obvious Leala was one of those dogs that could relate to the internal pain so many people harbor. I do not know how it works but dogs can inspire hope in ways people cannot. I saw Leala do it.

On a visit to a children's group physical therapy session, a non-verbal ten-year-old girl suffering from a degenerative physiological condition had become depressed and refused to use her walker anymore. She insisted on being pushed in a wheelchair. When we first arrived, I avoided the girl as she indicated adamantly that she did not want Leala anywhere near her.

But the girl closely watched Leala as other children in the group took turns "walking the dog." I stood in the middle of the room with one long leash, while the kids held a second shorter leash and walked Leala in circles around me. Everyone, including Leala was having loads of fun.

Finally, the non-walking girl could not resist. She wanted a turn. She took hold of her walker, took the short leash, and away we went. She laughed and did not want to stop. Then she indicated she wanted to walk Leala without using her walker. Walking alone was a physical impossibility for this girl but a compassionate physical therapist walked behind the girl, supporting her under the arms.

Amazingly, the girl got even more adventurous. She indicated she wanted to leave the therapy room. So all four of us set off on a mini-adventure: the supporting therapist, the girl with the short leash, Leala and me with the long leash. We walked through the entire first floor of the hospital, through the lobby and down the halls. We all had a blast. When the girl left that day she was smiling. So was I.

I had my therapy dog. When I first looked into the warm caramel-colored eyes of that fearful, gold and white, flea-bitten dog resting under the tree, I did not dare to hope for an instant that she could be an outstanding therapy dog. Silly me.

~Jane Marie Allen Farmer

Canine Candy Striper

Until one has loved an animal a part of one's soul remains
unawakened.
~Anatole France

For weeks we listened to the news about the devastating damage wrought on New Orleans and the Louisiana coast by Hurricane Katrina. Being a former veterinarian, I was particularly sensitive to the horror stories I heard about the thousands of displaced pets. I felt compelled to do something, but what?

I remember awakening in the middle of the night with the clear message: "Go help the displaced pets." I was surprised by the message because I'd not been in practice as a veterinarian for over a decade and thought my small animal vet days were over. But as my mom was so fond of telling me, "Once a vet, always a vet."

The next morning I searched the Internet and found that the Humane Society of the United States had a special need for volunteers who could travel to Gonzales, Louisiana within the next seventy-two hours. Seeing this, I rearranged my schedule to answer the call.

On Wednesday morning, September 21st, as I had breakfast with my family, we planned how to make my trip safe and of the most service possible. My thirteen-year-old daughter Amber, who I believe received a double dose of the "pet loving gene," volunteered to call local animal hospitals and grooming parlors to ask if they would donate supplies for me to take. By that afternoon the van was filled, not only with gas, but also with donated pet food and medical supplies.

My destination was the Lamar Dixon Exposition Center in Gonzales, Louisiana, where over 1,200 displaced pets were housed. The warning on the instructions stated: "You must realize the Gonzales facility is extremely chaotic. You must be able to work independently as well as follow direction of the incident command and lead veterinary staff. Housing is up to you and involves camping. You will need to make your own travel arrangements and assume all related travel costs."

I wondered what I was getting myself into. I had over fifteen hours to ponder that question as I drove south listening to increasingly alarming warnings on the radio about another tropical storm approaching Louisiana—Hurricane Rita. I confess, by Wednesday evening I had serious doubts about this mission of mercy as I watched the Weather Channel from my hotel room in Atlanta. I almost turned back for home—home to the love and safety of my family. Then I remembered the van full of supplies entrusted to my care by the other veterinarians and groomers. There was no way I was going home before I delivered them.

Shortly after arriving in Gonzales in the late afternoon on Thursday, I connected with Dr. Eric Davis, director of Rural Area Veterinary Services (RAVS), who had organized a team of veterinarians, techs and other volunteers to transport about one hundred and fifty dogs, plus about two dozen geese, ducks and chickens, to the farm at the Dixon Correctional Institute north of Baton Rouge. They believed the animals would be safer from the approaching hurricane, and there they could be cared for by the inmates under Dr. Davis's supervision.

With the donated pet and medical supplies in my van, I felt compelled to be sure these generous donations were well utilized. I was guided to offer them to Dr. Davis and his team, of which I was now a part. We loaded the poultry in a couple of vans and the dogs in two large semi-trucks, and our team of about twenty volunteers traveled to the farm of Dixon Correctional Institute, arriving in the early morning hours. We worked until about four a.m. checking the animals in, making sure they were properly identified and comfortable in sections of the barn that the inmates we were working with referred to as cellblocks.

Everyone on the team worked diligently to bring order out of the chaos that we'd experienced at Dixon. For the next four days we made sure all the animals' records were updated and accurate. Several of the veterinarians and techs began examining the pets and caring for those who needed medical attention. We ate prison food for our meals and were thankful to receive it. Most of the predominantly female team slept in the barn or the nearby farmhouse on palettes on the floor, six to eight per room. Although I had brought a tent, the weather was hardly conducive to outdoor camping, so I ended up borrowing a dog pillow from the donated pile of supplies to soften the back seat of my van, where I slept each night, including on the windy, turbulent night that Hurricane Rita blew through our area.

I awoke the next morning stiff but thankful to be alive and noticed that the barn that had become the center of my universe was still standing and had suffered only superficial damage to its metal roof.

During those four days and nights of helping establish a safe haven for the pets, I fell in love with all one hundred fifty of them. Among other roles, I appointed myself as their "canine candy striper." I found a supply of donated pet toys, chew toys and dog biscuits that had been generously donated by people around the country. While everyone else was busy with the many other tasks of caring for dislocated pets, I made sure they each had something to play with and chew on, as well as giving them a little extra love and attention.

I left the farm late in the afternoon on Sunday for the long trek home, thinking my job was done, but somewhere between Louisiana and the mountains of North Carolina, I realized this little project of mine was far from over. I realized that many of these loving animals would never be reunited with their original families. What would happen to them? What an injustice it would be for so many people to save these courageous animals only to later have them euthanized. While they were receiving excellent care at the prison that was only a temporary solution. So, upon reaching home, I connected with the Animal Compassion Network, the largest no-kill, non-profit animal rescue organization located in Western North Carolina. I learned that through the hard work of other volunteers and foster homes they had found loving, permanent homes for more than 2,500 cats and dogs since 1999. I also learned they were receiving shipments of displaced pets from the Gulf States, no doubt some of which came from the D.C.I. Farm.

I guess my mom was right. "Once a vet, always a vet," and may I never lose my love and compassion for our four-legged friends. It really has made for a most interesting life of purpose.

~W. Bradford Swift

A Little Magic

A little magic can take you a long way.
~Roald Dahl

Magic was a four-year-old German Shepherd about to be euthanized at the animal shelter along with hundreds of other dogs, at least that is how I remember it. I was editing a news promo for WNBC/New York. The reporter announced that the dogs and cats would be put down if no one came by the end of the day. My friend Rosie and I left work and rushed to the pound to save whoever we could. She got a cat and I asked the shelter worker for the biggest dog they had. His name was Magic.

I was single, self-absorbed, and without responsibilities. I went to rock concerts, hung out with friends at bars, and worked hard. Just a twenty-something who didn't realize I was missing family and community. I had tried volunteering once but the guy on the phone said he needed people to stuff and lick envelopes. That didn't turn me on. In hindsight, it was a blessing. My gluten allergy would have made me a *Seinfeld* episode. You know the one, where Susan, George's fiancée, dies from licking envelopes?

So I brought Magic home. When I stepped out of the elevator, my neighbor smiled and said, "You did a mitzvah!"

"A what?"

"A mitzvah! You did a good deed without asking for anything in return. It's a good thing."

There wasn't a lot of trust at first. Magic would take the food out of his bowl, bring it in front of me and eat it one nibble at a time. My co-workers were pretty sure I was crazy and that this would be a huge mistake. But slowly Magic and I got to know each other. We became best friends. For the first time, my apartment felt like a home. We walked together through Central Park every morning and night.

My friends invited me to parties, but I just wanted to be home with Magic. Our lives were happy. For the first time, I was content. Unfortunately, Magic didn't like being left alone during my working hours. To remedy the issue, I tried doggie day care, a dog therapist and running to tire him out. In the end, I realized he was lonely.

Enter Whiskey. She was a pit bull/boxer mix, scarred from the dog fighting streets where guns and hate were rampant. Her name was Kissy, but that wasn't working for me. So I renamed her Whiskey. Magic and Whiskey fell in love and our home was complete. At least I thought so.

The neighbor below did not agree. He worked nights and had a loft bed. The pitter-patter of their feet and playing irked him. And, it turned out, my landlord did not allow dogs. Paying $1,600 for a studio apartment on the Upper West Side with duct tape holding the plumbing together suddenly lost its appeal. I didn't realize it but my "babies" and I had grown out of our home—and essentially New York City.

Since the age of seventeen I had dreamed of heading out west. Land to hike, spacious homes and thoughts of friendly people filled my head. I was discontented with my job, my lack of social life and the constant noise of the city. I made plans to leave.

I took a trip to Arizona and fell in love. It was perfect. I was at peace. Deadheads, hippies and Allman Brothers music playing at the outdoor bar on a sunny day in Flagstaff made me complete. So Magic, Whiskey and I moved away.

My friend helped me drive across the country, and I found a place near a cousin of mine. It was a three-bedroom house for a few hundred dollars a month in Bullhead City, Arizona. The sunsets blew me away. I couldn't understand why everyone wasn't stopping on the side of the road as the sun went down, releasing an array of colors that painted the sky pink, orange, blue, purple, yellow and red.

I began working at a domestic violence shelter. I wanted to help others. It lasted for a while, but it wasn't enough. I started to travel more, taking odd jobs around the country. Magic and Whiskey came with me everywhere. A friend from Arizona was heading back to Kansas. The Midwest sounded interesting.

A small town in western Kansas became my home. Small towns always need volunteers. And someone who had no obligations besides work was an easy target. I helped at everything—the county fair, the alumni lunch, a local church…. It was social, community-oriented work. And I loved it! It was gratifying. I came home tired yet satisfied. I helped people enjoy themselves. Funny enough, I enjoyed it more than if I had been a guest.

A couple of years later I volunteered for Relay for Life in my area and met my husband. A few more years after that I volunteered at a substance abuse treatment center where I met a woman who later became pregnant and wanted me to adopt her child (a story for another time).

Volunteering has brought me dogs, a wonderful husband and an amazing daughter. And it all started with a little Magic!

~Michele Boy

Bella

The world would be a nicer place if everyone had the ability to love as unconditionally as a dog.

~M.K. Clinton

The pit bull lay near a weather-beaten doghouse in a fenced-in front yard. I shortened my dogs' retractable leashes as we came closer, just in case, but the thick-boned, red-nosed old girl was friendly and watched us with wide golden-brown eyes. Rising, she approached the fence, pressing the dusty tip of her nose between the fence posts in an attempt to greet us.

Conan, my Dachshund mix, ignored the friendly overtures, but Lisa, a pint-sized Aussie mix, stopped to exchange sniffs and the two touched noses. I looked around. The yard was devoid of creature comforts, except for a faded blanket on the doghouse floor and a grimy, half-filled water bowl near the side gate. Piles of poop dotted the bare ground.

"You poor dog," I said. The dog understood my feelings, if not my words, and when I reached down to her nose level, she licked my hand.

The next time I saw her, school was out and kids were playing nearby. She watched them expectantly, but no one acknowledged her. Another day, en route to the post office, I saw people exiting her owner's house, and although she barked and whined for attention, she was ignored.

Maybe her person works late, I thought. Surely she's not out here 24/7? Troubled, I slipped her treats through the fence before returning my dogs to the warmth of our home and the bed they shared with my husband and me.

One stormy night I felt compelled to check on her. She gazed at me, sleepily, in the beam from my flashlight. I understood then—she was out there all the time.

***

It was 1988: the year I became conscious of animal mistreatment, stopped eating or wearing them, and pledged to defend their rights. I couldn't just pretend I didn't see this neglected dog right in my own neighborhood. But what could I do about it?

In response to my complaint, the local humane society sent an officer to check on her. "She's fed and sheltered," I was told. "The owner promised to clean up the yard. Sorry, that's all we can do." Frustrated, I continued to visit the dog, offering treats, a few minutes of attention and a deep desire to do more.

One afternoon, a white-haired woman stood beside the enclosure, caressing the dog through the fence posts. "You're the lady who gives treats to my Bella," she said, smiling. "I watch you from my window."

Joan was eighty-five and lived alone in her son's house. She used to live with her husband on a huge fenced-in property with a whole pack of dogs. Joan's face crinkled with pleasure remembering. "Bella was a house dog, then. They all were. We spoiled them. They sat on our furniture; slept on our bed."

When her husband died, the big place overwhelmed her. Her son sold it and moved her here. Twelve-year-old Bella, the last of the dogs, was moved to the doghouse. Her son believed dogs belonged outside. I sighed, imagining Bella's pain—a pack animal, cast from her pack.

Joan was arthritic and couldn't get around easily. Her kids and grandkids didn't come by that often. She jumped at my offer to walk Bella three afternoons a week and to clean her pen. "You must be Bella's guardian angel," she said, hugging me.

Bella cried out when I visited—so overjoyed that her squat, brick-like body leaped up and down. Old as she was she was strong as an ox. Walking her and my dogs required a friend or family member to hold Conan and Lisa while I entered the enclosure and gave Bella treats. While she gobbled them, I scooped her poop into a garbage can and poured her fresh water.

By then Bella was whining with excitement, wanting to go. I snapped a leash onto her collar, opened the gate and, dragging me behind her, she rushed from that yard. She and Lisa touched noses, Conan tolerated her, and we all walked side by side. For the next two hours, Bella sniffed and explored her surroundings. She was happy. She had a pack.

Her whole body seemed to shrink when our walk concluded and, reluctantly, she reentered the yard. "Sorry girl, I need to go now," I said, while she entreated me with her eyes. Sadly, I locked her in again and walked away with her pack.

I followed this routine for nearly two years. I brought Bella food, a clean water bowl and soft bedding for her house. On days when no one came with me, I walked my dogs first and then walked her alone. I offered to adopt her, but Joan cried and wouldn't part with her.

My friends thought I was crazy to spend my time that way. "You can't help every needy animal in the world," they said.

"I know I can't help them all," I said, "but I can help this one."

***

One night I dreamed of running with Bella through a cool, shady forest. She was unleashed and raced ahead of me through the trees and then circled back. She licked my hand like she did when we first met. Joy emanated from her. I'd swear she was smiling.

I knew she'd died when I woke the next morning. Joan was crying when she told me that afternoon. But I didn't cry—instead, I was thankful I'd taken the time to make a small difference in her life.

For me, the dream confirmed the path I had chosen. One by one, I thought, we change the world for the better, whenever we can, because we can.

Bella knew that too. That's why she came to say goodbye.

~Lynn Sunday

Meet Our Contributors

Sonia M. Agron has been a volunteer docent for the 9/11 Tribute Center for seven years. She shares her personal experience of 9/11/01 with visitors who come from all over the country. She speaks to visitors to honor all those who were taken from us on 9/11, delivering messages of honor, hope, courage, peace and resilience.

T.A. Barbella holds a bachelor's degree in art and a master's degree in special education. Originally from the East Coast, she resides in San Jose, CA, where she enjoys teaching art part-time and volunteering her services with various organizations. She is a published author and a professional illustrator.

Sara Dobie Bauer is a Pushcart Prize–nominated writer and prison volunteer in Phoenix, AZ, with an honors degree in creative writing from Ohio University. She is an official book nerd at SheKnows.com and author of the novel *Life without Harry*. Read more about Sara at saradobie.wordpress.com.

The author of *Shared Challenges*, **Penny Black** lives in the North of England. She received her B.A. with honours through the Open University and, after working for many years in government jobs, now works for the country's free National Health Service. *Shared Challenges* describes a time in her life that was full of learning and great change.

Jennifer Bly is a freelance writer and blogger at *The Deliberate Mom*. Mother of two girls and wife to one amazing husband, she spends her days homeschooling and living life fully. Jennifer regularly writes about parenting, homeschooling, blogging and her Christian faith. Her writing has been featured on *The Huffington Post*.

Since childhood, curiosity and wanderlust have inspired **Linda J. Bottjer** to create. Notebooks filled with sketches and stories document her life's journey. Her words have appeared with CBS News and *The New York Times* newspaper group, and her first book was published in 2014 through History Press. Children's historical fiction is her passion.

Andrea Bowen is a middle school Language Arts teacher in Oregon. She enjoys dabbling in recreational writing and would like to thank her husband and children for providing inspiration. Andrea would also like to dedicate her story to her best friend Holly who was a tremendous support to her during her husband's deployment.

Michele Boy received her Bachelor of Arts degree in Communications at Queens College, NY. She is a transplanted New Yorker living in western Kansas where she helps her husband on their farm and raises their daughter. She writes a blog for *Kansas Agland*. E-mail her at Micheleaboy@gmail.com.

Jennie Bradstreet is a freelance writer and homemaker. Married to Erik for twenty-two years, they have two adult children — Audra and Parker — and this past year completed their family by adopting their son Isaiah. This family has had its share of craziness over the years, giving Jennie a plethora of stories to share.

John P. Buentello has published short stories, essays, poetry and nonfiction. He is the author of the novel *Reproduction Rights* and the short story collections *Binary Tales* and *Night Rose of the Mountain*. E-mail him at jakkhakk@yahoo.com.

Leslie Calderoni has just finished her first young adult novel. She has four children and more than a few rescue animals. She loves to cook, read, and nap whenever possible. She enjoys writing in various coffee shops on the central coast of California.

Debby Carroll is a former teacher, educational publisher, and author. Her latest work is a memoir, *Tales From The Family Crypt*, a compelling story of extreme family dysfunction told with humor and insight to help others with difficult siblings. Wife, mother, grandmother, and runner are her most important titles.

Belinda Cohen is a freelance writer who has published over 100 articles and short stories, either in print or online. Her previous short stories can be found in *Not Your Mother's Book: On Working Stiffs* and *Not Your Mother's Book: On Sex*.

Phyllis Coletta has led a joyful, adventurous life that includes careers in litigation, teaching, and healthcare. She has worked on ski mountains, as a wilderness guide, as an EMT, and as a Zen Buddhist chaplain. She is a speaker, coach, and writer living in Ocean City, NJ. Learn more at www.phylliscoletta.com.

James Colmenares received his B.S. degree in Finance and Economics from the University of California at Berkeley. He is a catalyst for technologies that make our world a better place. He lives in New York with his son Marco Philip and his muse Katie.

Tracy Crump enjoys storytelling (the good kind) and has published fourteen stories in the *Chicken Soup for the Soul* series. She encourages others through her Write Life Workshops and webinars and edits a popular writers newsletter, *The Write Life*. But her most important job is Grandma to little Nellie. Visit Tracy at WriteLifeWorkshops.com.

Judy Davidson received her Bachelors of Science degree in Education from Temple University and received her certification as a professional fundraiser from Wharton. She credits her husband and daughter for reawakening the writer that resides in her. She is happy to share her stories because she has known wonderful people on her life's journey.

MaryLou Driedger lives in Winnipeg, Manitoba. She is a newspaper columnist, blogger and freelance writer currently working on an education curriculum project and the manuscript for a children's book about art. She loves to write stories for her grandson.

Paul Driscoll is a Board Member of Wigan and Leigh Housing in the north of England. He holds a master's degree in Theology from Oxford University. He is the proud and busy father of six children. Paul writes both fiction and nonfiction pieces across a wide range of subjects, from cult TV to theology and social issues.

Terri Elders, LCSW, served as a Peace Corps volunteer four times, and as an Americorps VISTA, all after the age of fifty. Her stories appear in over a hundred anthologies, including multiple *Chicken Soup for the Soul* books.

Jane Allen Farmer is employed teaching people how to understand and enjoy the wonderful natural and cultural resources of our country. In her free time, she makes visits with her two therapy dogs, plays with her two non-therapy dogs and three cats, and enjoys riding her horses. She also paints and draws.

John Farnam supports the Morgridge Family Foundation through his public relations firm. In this role he works to advance the mission of the organization through discovery of innovative approaches to education and aligning resources for the organization behind a common goal. John is a graduate of the University of Wyoming.

Jean Ferratier writes to inspire and honor others who face life challenges. She is a retired teacher who promotes self-development through her Clarity of Now Coaching Practice. Jean is the author of *Reading Symbolic Signs: How to Connect the Dots of Your Spiritual Life.* Visit her website at synchronousmoments.wordpress.com.

Malinda Dunlap Fillingim is a recent widow who is volunteering at Jubilee Partners in Comer, GA.

June Rogers Flahie is an editor and writer for a variety of Canadian news, travel, health and women's publications. She loves playing the ukulele, dancing the samba and writing poetry.

Lisa Fowler lives in the Blue Ridge Mountains of Western North Carolina with her goofy American Bulldog, Hazel, and her loyal Pit Bull, Abby. Her writing interests are concentrated on middle-grade novels and early chapter books. When not penning stories, Lisa enjoys playing trumpet, reading, and flower gardening.

Office grunt by day, mad word-slinger by night, **A. K. Francis** lives in Tulsa with her husband, their assorted children, and three fuzzy roommates of the canine and feline persuasions. When not tending her weedy garden, mothering, working, or PTSA presidenting, she tells her tales via keyboard and moonlight.

Sally Friedman is a graduate of the University of Pennsylvania. Her personal essays have appeared in *The New York Times*, *Family Circle*, *Ladies' Home Journal* and *The Huffington Post*. Her family provides ample material for musings about how we live our lives. E-mail her at pinegander@aol.com.

James A. Gemmell is a married father of two grown children. Most summers he can be found walking one of the Caminos de Santiago in Spain or France. His other hobbies are writing, playing guitar, drawing and painting, and collecting art.

Christine Cosse Gray received her Bachelor of Arts degree in English from the State University of New York at Buffalo in 1976. She has only recently decided to try to write for publication. She lives in Berthoud, CO with her son and three dogs.

Robin Hakanson-Grunder is a freelance journalist, speaker and photographer, but most of her time is spent answering to the name of "Mom." Robin and her husband live in the Midwest with their blended family of seven children, two dogs and one cat. It's kind of like *The Brady Bunch*, except with more kids, more animals and no maid.

Christian Harch served twenty years in the U.S. Navy Reserves, including three years of active duty. He is a member of his town's Veterans Commission and a member of the American Legion.

Christian is retired and enjoys surf fishing with his grandchildren. He also enjoys metal sculpting. He has been happily married for fifty-one years.

Stephen Hayes is a Northwest humorist and creator of *Chubby Chatterbox*, a blog focused on humor, culture and travel. Hayes is an artist, traveler and world-class screw-up. His writing is an unabashedly sentimental exploration of growing up in the 1950s, 1960s and beyond. His work can be found at chubbychatterbox.com.

Paul Heitzenrater lives with his partner John and their three puppies in Denver, CO. He is a therapist at National Jewish Health in the Rehabilitation Department. Paul and John have a garden and they donate their produce to a food pantry. They like to travel, ski, hike, bike and entertain their family and friends.

Maggie Hofstaedter is a freelance writer who tries to find inspiration in everyday life and express it with her writing. She works from her home in Lansdale, PA, where she lives with her husband Dan, their kids Molly and Zach, and their dog Casey.

Kathryn M. Hearst received her Master of Education degree from Saint Joseph's College. She is a Navy mom and full-time writer living near Orlando, FL. Kathryn enjoys reading and movies and spending time with family, including her three rescue dogs.

Julie Hornok's stories have appeared in several publications and websites. This is her third story in the *Chicken Soup for the Soul* series. When she is not busy driving her three kids all around the DFW Metroplex, she loves to support families living with autism. Contact her at www.juliehornok.com.

Jeanie Jacobson is on the leadership team of Wordsowers Christian Writers in Omaha, NE. She's published in six *Chicken Soup for the Soul* books, and is writing a Christian-slanted young adult fantasy series. Jeanie loves visiting family and friends, reading, hiking, praise dancing, and gardening. Connect with her at jeaniejacobson.com.

Kelly Kittel is a fish biologist turned author who lives in Rhode Island. She is still married to Andy and they have five living children. She has been published in magazines and anthologies and her first book, *Breathe: A Memoir of Motherhood, Grief, and Family Conflict* was published in May 2014. Learn more at www.kellykittel.com.

Alice Klies has contributed to two other *Chicken Soup for the Soul* books. She is published in eight other anthology books, as well as *Angels on Earth* and *The Wordsmith's Journal*. Alice is currently writing a memoir. She is president of Northern Arizona Word Weavers. E-mail her at alice.klies@gmail.com.

Cathi LaMarche is a novelist, essayist, and poet. Her work has appeared in over two-dozen anthologies. In addition to owning Top College Essays, a college essay coaching service, she teaches composition and literature. She resides in Missouri with her husband, two children, and two rescue dogs.

Dr. JC Lau was a philosophy professor before becoming a writer. Her publications range from academic journal articles to video game news.She is a staff writer for "GeekGirlCon" and likes blogging, cooking and roller derby. An Australian transplant, JC lives in Seattle, WA with her husband and foster ferrets, Ben and Jerry.

Jody Lebel's short stories have sold to *Woman's World*, *Pages of Stories*, *Cosmo UK*, and dozens of others. Her romantic/suspense novel, *Playing Dead*, was released by The Wild Rose Press in 2012 to excellent reviews. Jody lives in South Florida with her two cats.

Austin Lees is an active fourth grader. He enjoys soccer, street hockey, snowboarding, and volunteering. He is active in his church and loves Jesus. He lives with his mom, dad, and two dogs, Cooper and Winston.

Andi Lehman has volunteered in support of wild and domestic animals since 1988, serving two wildlife groups and the Germantown Animal Control Commission as past chairman. She lives in Mississippi with her husband, mother and two children, plus myriad beloved critters. Andi holds a B.A., with honors, from the University of Memphis.

Jacob Lief is Co-Founder and CEO of Ubuntu Education Fund, a non-profit organization that takes vulnerable children in Port Elizabeth, South Africa from cradle to career. Jacob's book, *I Am Because You Are*, was published in May 2015. He splits his time between Brooklyn, NY, where he lives with his wife and two sons, and South Africa.

Linda Lohman retired after forty years in the accounting profession to write slice-of-life short stories. Knowing that truth is always better than fiction, she has over 150 *Chicken Soup for the Soul* books in her collection. She loves Chicken Soup — the books and her mom's soup! E-mail her at lindaalohman@yahoo.com.

Corrie Lopez has been a teacher for over twenty years. She and her husband, Mark, work alongside her parents in their quest for affordable Christian education for local students. Besides teaching, she loves leading music at her church and spending time with her beautiful children, Mercy and Creed.

Linda Lowen is a radio producer/co-host, writing instructor, parenting magazine columnist and freelance writer. She's won regional and national awards for her online, broadcast and print work covering women's issues, politics, health, wellness and motherhood. Her two daughters keep her young — her husband keeps her solvent.

Susan Lugli is a Christian speaker and author. Her stories have been published in many *Chicken Soup for the Soul* books. She is an advocate for burn survivors and speaks on their behalf. E-mail her at suenrusty@aol.com.

Kathie Mitchell earned a B.S. degree from Liberty University and has been writing since she was a child. She and her husband have two married children and four grandsons. She plays cornet in several community bands and enjoys gardening, backpacking, writing, and spending time with her grandsons.

Originally editor of an in-house magazine, **Marsha Warren Mittman** recently returned to writing. Many of her poems and short stories have been published in anthologies, as well as a chapbook for use in meditation programs. A second chapbook, *Patriarchal Chronicles*, was just completed. She is the recipient of six writing awards.

Scott Newport is married and has three children. He started to write when his son, Evan, was born. Scott's passion is to make sense out of Evan's short life through helping other families with sick kids. He is working with C.S. Mott Children's Hospital to start a program incorporating woodworking and writing as outlets for families in the ICUs.

Dee Dee Parker draws on her uniquely Southern experience as a minister's wife in her career as an author and speaker. Dee Dee's children's book, *Josie Jo's Got to Know*, was written to fund research of breast cancer in younger women. Married to Jim, they live in the beautiful Appalachian Mountains of North Carolina.

Stuart M. Perkins enjoys relating observations of everyday life and sharing recollections of growing up in a large Southern family. He believes that layers of ordinary reality can be peeled back to reveal humorous or poignant themes. Stuart blogs his observations at storyshucker.wordpress.com.

Yvonne Pesquera is a freelance writer for magazines and newspapers. She writes feature articles about art, history, and the type of travel most people call "roughing it."

Linda Peters has volunteered at the local community kitchen and the NICU of Children's Hospital. She lives in North Georgia with her indulgent husband, a son, two dogs and a wayward cat. She also has a daughter and four grandchildren who live nearby.

Elizabeth Peterson currently lives in rural Kentucky, waiting patiently for her husband to finish his graduate degree. She has three young children and loves to paint, write, and rack up incredible fines at her local library. She blogs annually and hopes to write more when her kids go to college.

Connie Pombo is a freelance writer, speaker, author of two books and a regular contributor to the *Chicken Soup for the Soul* series. When she's not writing or speaking, she enjoys traveling and volunteering for various organizations around the world. For more information visit: www.conniepombo.com.

Claudia Porter has her B.A. degree in Literature and Creative Writing from the University of Arizona, with postgraduate work in Music. She is the Founder/U.S. Director of Aggie's Baby Home for abandoned babies in Uganda. She teaches music, is a motivational speaker, singer and pastor. Married, she has three children and a grandson.

Kori Reed is Vice President, Cause and Foundation, at ConAgra Foods. She is responsible for integrating the company's cause of fighting child hunger across the company, from philanthropy and employee engagement to product donations and cause-branding platforms. Kori and her husband Mike are the parents of four active teenage children. They reside in Omaha, NE.

Linda Rettstatt is an award-winning author of more than twenty-five women's fiction and contemporary romance novels. Her first published writing appeared in her hometown newspaper in the form of theater reviews and the occasional human-interest story. A native of Pennsylvania, she now resides in NW Mississippi.

Diane Rima lives on the Central Coast of California with her husband and Chester, their lovable Golden Retriever. She is a wife, mom, Gigi, and teacher. Diane enjoys her family, the sea, writing, working with children, and bringing joy and tail wags to young and old through pet therapy.

Lenore Rogers is a co-founder and the Board President of the all-volunteer non-profit Amy's Treat. She works as a regional sales manager for a New England food distribution company. Also a writer, Lenore enjoys traveling, most outdoor activities, and just about anyone and anything that will make her laugh.

Alicia Rosen possesses an MFA degree in Fiction from The New School. Her stories have appeared in numerous journals and magazines published in North America. She is a voracious reader, and a sketcher of family focused cartoons. She lives in Brooklyn, NY with her husband, her dog Nosh, and hundreds of books.

Sioux Roslawski is a wife, mother, grammy, teacher and dog rescuer for Love a Golden. In her spare time she blogs, reads voraciously, toils sporadically on a novel and freelances. Read her blog at siouxspage.blogspot.com.

Beth Ford Roth is a broadcast and digital journalist whose work has appeared in outlets like NPR, BBC, CNN, *Mental Floss*, and *xoJane*. She lives in California with her husband, three dogs, and one very old cat. Beth is working on her first historical true crime book. E-mail her at beth@fordroth.net.

Carolyn Roy-Bornstein is the author of *Crash: A Mother, A Son, and the Journey from Grief to Gratitude* (Globe Pequot Press) and co-author of *Chicken Soup for the Soul: Recovering from Traumatic Brain Injuries*. Her essays have appeared in the *The Boston Globe*, *JAMA*, and *The Writer*. Read more at www.carolroybornstein.com.

Stephen Rusiniak is a former police detective who specialized in juvenile/family matters. Today he shares his thoughts through his writing, including stories in several *Chicken Soup for the Soul* books. Contact him via Facebook, on Twitter @StephenRusiniak or by e-mail at StephenRusiniak@yahoo.com.

Jeremy Dean Russell almost died in a car accident eighteen years ago. Ironically, the accident set his life in a new direction that ended up saving his life. He found his destiny was to honor veterans by carving a 100-ton sculpture of an eagle inside a 13,000-foot mountain.

KoAnn Rutter received her master's degree in Education and taught for the Elmwood School District for thirty-five years. She has two children and two grandchildren. She and her husband divide their retirement time with their family, traveling to Florida in winter, and to their vacation property in Michigan. E-mail her at koannrutter@yahoo.com.

Daria Schaffnit is a writer and the founder of Dragonfly Joy Spiritual Coaching. She lives in Michigan with her wife, Jeannene. When she's not working, she loves to play in the kitchen, noodle around with art, hang with the Wild Mango Queens, indulge in mermaid practice, or dive into a great book.

Jane Self is a freelance writer and copywriter living in Durham, NC. She retired as Features Editor from *The Tuscaloosa News* in 2007 after eight years and was previously Assistant Features Editor for the *Macon Telegraph* for twelve years. E-mail her at jane@janeself.com.

Tanya Shearer lives in Alabama with her husband, Clay. Their family includes two wonderful grown children, and their spouses, and granddaughter Zoey Clayre. Tanya enjoys writing children's stories and devotions. This is her third story published in the *Chicken Soup for the Soul* series. E-mail her at tshearer24@yahoo.com.

Deborah Shouse is a writer, speaker, editor, and creativity catalyst. Deborah's book, *Love in the Land of Dementia: Finding Hope in the Caregiver's Journey*, raised more than $80,000 for Alzheimer's causes. Visit her blog at DementiaJourney.org.

Cassie Silva has her social work degree and works with youth and children near Vancouver, British Columbia. She has been volunteering with Make-A-Wish British Columbia and Yukon since December 2008. She was previously published in *Chicken Soup for the Soul: The Cancer Book* (2009). E-mail her at cassiesilva@ymail.com.

Dominique Smith currently resides in Fort Worth, TX. In addition to his volunteer work with refugees, Smith also helps a local food pantry. Smith is involved with many local non-profits and uses his experience with homelessness to help others.

Toni Somers lives in Springfield, MO with her husband of sixty years and two Miniature Schnauzers. Somers' poetry, fiction, and memoir have won local and national awards and been published in *Today's Woman* magazine, *Chicken Soup for the Soul* books, and in four anthologies. E-mail her at txlaughinggull@gmail.com.

Sumer Sorensen-Bain is the mother of two amazing children and raises them with her partner in Westminster, CO. These beautiful kids have taught her so much about life, love, and how to enjoy each and every moment. Kylan and Nikia are her "Difference Makers."

James Strickland moved to NYC after graduating from the University of Texas at Austin with degrees in sociology and psychology. James worked as a case manager in the homeless shelter system until 2004 and has volunteered at God's Love We Deliver since 1987. James also participates in his church and spends time with his Yorkie, Zeke.

L.A. Strucke is a writer and songwriter from New Jersey. A graduate of Rowan University, she is a frequent contributor to the *Chicken Soup for the Soul* series. Her four children have inspired many of her stories. She loves playing the piano and spending time with Hermione and Jadzia. Read more at www.lastrucke.com.

Sharon Struth enjoys a mid-life career change writing women's romantic fiction. Her books about life, love and a little bit more include the *A Blue Moon Lake Romance* series (Kensington Publishing) and *The Hourglass* (Etopia Press). She's honored to share this story with Chicken Soup for the Soul readers. Learn more about Sharon at www.sharonstruth.com.

Thomas Sullivan is the author of the humor essay collection *So Much Time, So Little Change*. He also writes for the website Humoroutcasts.com. Thomas lives in Seattle, WA. Learn more at www.thomassullivanhumor.com.

Lynn Sunday is an artist, writer, and animal advocate who lives near San Francisco with her husband and senior rescue dog. Six of her stories appear in five other *Chicken Soup for the Soul* books, and numerous other publications. E-mail her at Sunday11@aol.com.

W. Bradford Swift has written several true-life stories for the *Chicken Soup for the Soul* series. He and his wife co-founded Life On Purpose Institute in 1996 (www.lifeonpurpose.com). He also writes speculative fiction under the pen name of Orrin Jason Bradford. Learn more at www.wbradfordswift.com.

Mary Vigliante Szydlowski has published six novels, one novella, and three children's books under various pseudonyms. A fourth children's book is due out soon. Her articles, essays, short stories, poetry, and kids' stories appear in anthologies, magazines, newspapers, and on the Internet. She lives in Albany, NY.

B.J. Taylor admires the challenged children who conquer their fears and ride. She is an award-winning author whose work has appeared in *Guideposts*, many *Chicken Soup for the Soul* books, and numerous magazines and newspapers. You can reach B.J. at www.bjtaylor.com and check out her dog blog at www.bjtaylorblog.wordpress.com.

Edward Tooley is a Social Studies teacher at Heritage Christian School in Northridge, CA. He is also a freelance writer who has a passion for writing stories that motivate and encourage the soul. He is currently writing a children's book entitled *Rounding Third and Headed for Home*. E-mail him at tooleyhouse@yahoo.com.

Joanna Montagna Torreano is a retired teacher who enjoys writing and taking long walks with her husband Paul and their dog Sky. She's a behind-the-scenes volunteer for her son Jason's non-profit organization, Inkululeko. She also enjoys volunteering for Literacy Volunteers and Camp Hope. Learn more at www.niagarahospice.org.

Lynne Turner received a Journalism degree from Ryerson University in Toronto and spent the next nearly forty years as a reporter, editor and manager at the *Mount Forest Confederate* newspaper in Ontario. She enjoys writing, reading, walking and spending time with her family. Her mother is an inspiration to all who know her.

Ann Van Hine started her own small business and met her future husband Bruce all on the very same day. Ann has recently retired and now divides her time between writing, speaking and volunteering at the 9/11 Tribute Center and at her local church. She has two daughters and one grandson. She enjoys traveling and reading.

Janice VanHorne-Lane lives with her husband and two daughters in Ohio. She enjoys reading, writing and crafting and works as a church secretary. When not spending time with her family or working, she volunteers for many local charities and societies. Her other works include local histories.

Jen Ward is an intuitive gifted healer and innovator of cutting-edge practices to empower individuals to be their own healers. She works passionately to mainstream modalities of healing that would otherwise seem foreign to the average person in search of assistance beyond conventional means. Learn more at www.jenuinehealing.com.

K. Michael Ware is a retired Air Force and commercial pilot. Born in West Virginia, he has a BSEE from WVU and an MPA from Troy State. Besides volunteering, he loves to write, play golf, and spend time with family — especially chasing grandchildren. He is a published author of short stories, devotionals and prayers.

Nicole Webster has been interested in writing since the age of eight. She has self-published a children's book with her sister, titled *Sleepingcinderpunzlewhite*, available on blurb.com. Her other interests include reading, scrapbooking and cooking. She currently resides in Utah with her husband and four children.

Kathy Whirity is a syndicated newspaper columnist who shares her sentimental musings on family life. She is the author of *Life is a Kaleidoscope*, a compilation of her most popular columns. Kathy is also a regular contributor to the *Chicken Soup for the Soul* series. E-mail her at kathywhirity@yahoo.com.

Kate White is a thirty-one-year-old author who lives just outside Detroit, MI with her spouse and their son, Jace. She has previously been published in *Chicken Soup for the Soul: The Power of Forgiveness* and *Chicken Soup for the Soul: From Lemons to Lemonade,* as well as in *The Floating Bridge Review* and *The Linor Project.*

Amanda Yancey recently graduated from Portland State University with a B.S. degree in Psychology. She co-founded and runs *The Be Ok Blog* at www.thebeokblog.com. You can find her fun travel vlogs on YouTube. She'd like to further her education and is seeking a career in neuroscience. Amanda also loves volunteering!

Meet Amy Newmark

Amy Newmark was a writer, speaker, Wall Street analyst and business executive in the worlds of finance and telecommunications for thirty years. Today she is publisher, editor-in-chief and coauthor of the *Chicken Soup for the Soul* book series. By curating and editing inspirational true stories from ordinary people who have had extraordinary experiences, Amy has kept the twenty-two-year-old Chicken Soup for the Soul brand fresh and relevant, and still part of the social zeitgeist.

Amy graduated *magna cum laude* from Harvard University where she majored in Portuguese and minored in French. She wrote her thesis about popular, spoken-word poetry in Brazil, which involved traveling throughout Brazil and meeting with poets and writers to collect their stories. She is delighted to have come full circle in her writing career — from collecting poetry "from the people" in Brazil as a twenty-year-old to, three decades later, collecting stories and poems "from the people" for Chicken Soup for the Soul.

Amy has a national syndicated newspaper column and is a frequent radio and TV guest, passing along the real-life lessons and useful tips she has picked up from reading and editing thousands of Chicken Soup for the Soul stories.

She and her husband are the proud parents of four grown children. Follow her on Twitter @amynewmark and @chickensoupsoul.

Meet Carrie Morgridge

Carrie Morgridge is the author of: *Every Gift Matters – How Your Passion Can Change the World* and currently serves as the Morgridge Family Foundation's vice president. Over the past several years, Carrie and her husband John have defined the philanthropic focus of their foundation on transformative gifts in education, conservation, the arts and health and wellness.

The foundation has been instrumental in supporting major capital projects at the Denver Museum of Nature and Science, National Jewish Health, University of Central Florida, University of Denver, Mile High United Way, The Nature Conservancy and Second Harvest Food Bank of Orlando, Florida. Not only does the foundation work on large projects, Carrie and her husband spend numerous hours on 185 different projects each and every year.

Carrie founded Student Support Foundation, a youth philanthropy club, to cultivate high school and college philanthropists to educate and teach them the importance of giving, through hands-on learning. Through these clubs, the students actually taught the foundation the importance of smaller gifts.

With their hands-on philosophy of giving, Carrie and John noticed a huge gap in teacher training when they started investing in technology in the classroom almost a decade ago. This gap led the foundation to create an event that is called Share Fair Nation. This national event has trained thousands of teachers on how to integrate technology in the classroom. STEMosphere®, the public side to Share Fair Nation, allows students, teachers and families to experience hands-on "brains-on" learning and fun. STEMosphere allows the students to learn side by side with the teachers who attend the event. Thus far, the Share Fair Nation event has provided hundreds of hours of free high-quality teacher professional development, and is expanding to a digital platform in the coming year.

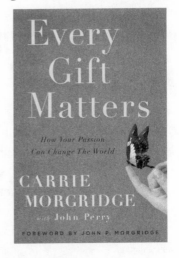

In 2010, Carrie received the Frances Wisebart Jacobs – Mile High United Way Woman of the Year Award. She currently serves on the Board of Trustees at the University of Denver, the Denver Museum of Nature & Science, and the New Jersey Center for Teaching and Learning, and on the Colorado Mountain College Board of Overseers. Carrie serves in an advisory capacity for many nonprofits and speaks nationally to education advocacy and technology-focused forums.

Carrie and her husband divide their time between Colorado and Florida. Their children John and Michelle are both recent college graduates and enjoy living and working in Denver. Their beloved dog Nina is an enthusiastic hiker, swimmer, boater and ball chaser. Carrie graduated *summa cum laude* from the International Academy of Design and Technology. She is an avid outdoorsman and has finished nine Ironman competitions and several marathons, and in her spare time loves to play tennis.

Share with Us

We all have had Chicken Soup for the Soul moments in our lives. If you would like to share your story or poem with millions of people around the world, go to chickensoup.com and click on "Submit Your Story." You may be able to help another reader, and become a published author at the same time. Some of our past contributors have launched writing and speaking careers from the publication of their stories in our books!

We only accept story submissions via our website. They are no longer accepted via mail or fax.

To contact us regarding other matters, please send us an e-mail through webmaster@chickensoupforthesoul.com, or fax or write us at:

Chicken Soup for the Soul
P.O. Box 700
Cos Cob, CT 06807-0700
Fax: 203-861-7194

One more note from your friends at Chicken Soup for the Soul: Occasionally, we receive an unsolicited book manuscript from one of our readers, and we would like to respectfully inform you that we do not accept unsolicited manuscripts and we must discard the ones that appear.

Sharing Happiness, Inspiration, and Wellness

Real people sharing real stories, every day, all over the world. In 2007, *USA Today* named *Chicken Soup for the Soul* one of the five most memorable books in the last quarter-century. With over 100 million books sold to date in the U.S. and Canada alone, more than 200 titles in print, and translations into more than forty languages, "chicken soup for the soul" is one of the world's best-known phrases.

Today, twenty-two years after we first began sharing happiness, inspiration and wellness through our books, we continue to delight our readers with new titles, but have also evolved beyond the book-store, with super premium pet food, a line of high quality food to bring people together for healthy meals, and a variety of licensed products and digital offerings, all inspired by stories. Chicken Soup for the Soul has recently expanded into visual storytelling through movies and television. Chicken Soup for the Soul is "changing the world one story at a time®." Thanks for reading!

Chicken Soup for the Soul

For moments that become stories™

www.chickensoup.com